MASTERING THE ART OF
NEGOTIATION

SEVEN GUIDES FOR CREATING YOUR JOURNEY

Geurt Jan de Heus

B/SPUBLISHERS

BIS Publishers
Building Het Sieraad
Postjesweg 1
1057 DT Amsterdam
The Netherlands
T +31 (0)20 515 02 30
bis@bispublishers.com
www.bispublishers.com

ISBN 978 90 6369 431 9

Design by Buro BRAND
Den Haag, The Netherlands
www.burobrand.nl

Illustrations by Geurt Jan de Heus

For Jacob, Merel and David

You are negotiating every day. The challenge isn't to get as much for yourself as you can at the other's expense. It's in the art of searching together for possibilities that serve as many interests as possible. For you, the other party, and the wider circle. Maybe looking for a win-win-win. But always with a clear head, a warm heart and standing firm. Will you always manage that? No, but it's definitely worth looking at. A long time ago, I was given a book called *Getting to Yes*. I still use the insights it gave me every day, and I am now passing them on in a different form. I hope that it will be useful for all of you in the course of your lives. Have a good journey – I'm sure you will!

Dad

CONTENTS

PREFACE

I'm writing this in 2015-2016. Turbulent times. Dramatic events in Syria, attacks in Turkey, Paris, Brussels, Nice... is anywhere immune? Then a financial crisis, the refugee crisis, Brexit. It seems as if we've collectively lost our way and that it is becoming increasingly difficult to show leadership, cooperate and find constructive solutions to problems. Many leaders are calling for more solidarity, dialogue, respect, looking out for each other, tolerance, less egotism and more sustainable solutions. These themes and appeals are nothing new. Calls to treat each other with respect and to collaborate. Are these calls falling on deaf ears? Do we actually want to achieve a dialogue, respecting the other party?

The desire to win seems to be the cause of many conflicts. Often it obstructs a constructive dialogue and in a broader context. It seems as if the will to win is ruining the world. At least, if you want to win at the other's expense when you could equally well work together. It puts great pressure on relationships so that cooperation becomes tougher, trust simply disappears and conflicts can arise. Wanting to serve your own interests at the expense of the other seems to be a reflex for many people. The winner takes all. I've got absolutely nothing against competition and you're perfectly entitled to want to be cleverer and smarter than 'them'. There is nothing wrong with wanting to win, but tackling things together becomes very awkward if the relationship is constantly under pressure. In most cases it's better to embrace the other than to exclude them as there is generally much more that unites us than separates us. It is a rapidly changing world in which organisations are becoming less hierarchical, networks are developing and we need and want to work together: it seems as if we are embracing new business models and ways of cooperating, but our behaviour is still locked into the old model. Focusing on 'me and I' is often blocking thinking about 'we and us'.

WHAT ARE YOU AIMING FOR?

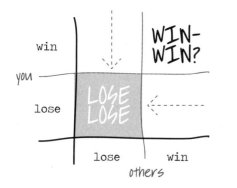

Particularly if you put yourself first and want to win, whatever the cost, you can get into a complex situation and can end up in a deadlock or conflict. You may have thought the deal was on the cards, but you ended up empty-handed.

Achieving robust solutions together is a major challenge, making negotiation much more than just closing deals and making financial agreements. The negotiation dynamics involve a wide range of subjects, skills and attitudes. As far as I'm concerned, such dynamics are present wherever you are influencing each other and want to make progress. You negotiate every day and in my opinion you can't start learning young enough!

I've been a trainer, coach and consultant for nearly twenty years now, involved in negotiation issues in business contexts. It's fascinating and sometimes very complex.

During this period, I came across many people with challenges and questions that they were not able to answer themselves. Over the years, I saw the questions change from run-of-the-mill negotiation challenges to issues of cooperation, managing complexity and providing leadership in decision-making processes.

Tips and advice from work colleagues had helped a bit in practice. Books about the subject were not widely read – other than *Getting to Yes*, about which I'll be saying more later – and when people did read them, they didn't find them very practical. It also struck me that people often knew what they should be doing, but did not actually do it. Or that they didn't understand why they lost the nerve to negotiate when the tension and pressure increased. Or perhaps even more fundamentally, I saw a lot of people who were not aware of the fact that they were negotiating all the time. The workshops opened up a new world to them. Regularly I heard someone say, "If I'd known this before, it would have helped me a lot." Visualising concepts made the penny drop. "Oh, now I can see it. And I get the relationship between the various steps."

I was asked more and more often if the insights and visuals were also available in book form and whether I might not want to write a book myself. I hesitated for a long time. Writing a book about a topic that so much has already been written about: is there any added value in that?

I decided eventually to embark on this adventure because I very much wanted to make a contribution to improving the way in which people negotiate with each other. I've chosen to bundle together the art and skills of negotiation in a very broad sense. Communication, cooperation, showing leadership, managing decision-making processes, cultural elements and creativity are not areas that should be focused on in isolation: in my opinion, they all come together in the dynamic of the negotiation. I hope that this book will add something to the sum total of what was already known, giving you insights that will help you cooperate better and take better decisions, even when the situation is complex. Helping you lead projects where you can be satisfied with the relationships and the outcome. Helping you reach constructive, long-lasting solutions with others, prevent conflicts and understand how you can resolve them if they do arise. I want to take you step by step towards mastery, based on practical foundations.

I am standing on the shoulders of many. There have been many sources of inspiration for me. I myself have trodden a path where I have been (and still am) inspired by various people: spiritual figures, philo-sophers, psychologists, anthropologists, legal minds, artists, customers, course participants, students and family. I would like to mention William Ury in particular. He and Roger Fisher were responsible for the first edition of *Getting to Yes*. This is an approach I came across during a management training course when I was working in the pharmaceutical industry. It has become the basis of our way of looking at negotiation issues, a foundation that many people have used as inspiration to build on. So have we. I keep saying "we" very deliberately, because John Routs – my business partner who is sadly no longer with us – played a major role. In this book, I've added a few nuances and put a couple of extra storeys on top of the building.

When I was first confronted with the *Getting to Yes* approach, a new world opened up before my eyes. Frits Philips Jr., John Routs, Joep Laeven, Hans Loots and many others around them introduced this way of thinking to the Netherlands. I am delighted that I found out about it and that I have been able to stack other insights up on top of it. For years now I stand shoulder to shoulder with my beloved Pien, my love and my friend. She gave me plenty of room for this voyage of discov-ery. Our children Jacob, Merel and David have given me great pleasure, holding up a mirror for many learning moments. A wonderful experience! My parents were there when I started out on my own path and they are still there with me now, albeit now less steady and more fragile. It makes you aware of your roots, what you have received, what you are taking with you and what you want to pass on.

Hugo, my business partner and friend: without you, this book would never have happened. Thank you for your loyal friend-ship. Cornelis, thank you for thinking so many things through with me. Rudolph and Bionda, you jumped in at the deep end with me and I'm delighted that Harry put me in contact with you. Thank you for that. Willemien and Hester, you understood my pictures and made them better. Frank and Koert, you helped me along the way with your incisive observations. Marjolijn, you made the text much better and Mike and Clare, translating is also an art and more! Customers and course participants: thank you for the trust you have shown and all the memorable encounters. My job and writing this book have let me meet a lot of excep-tional people. I feel privileged.

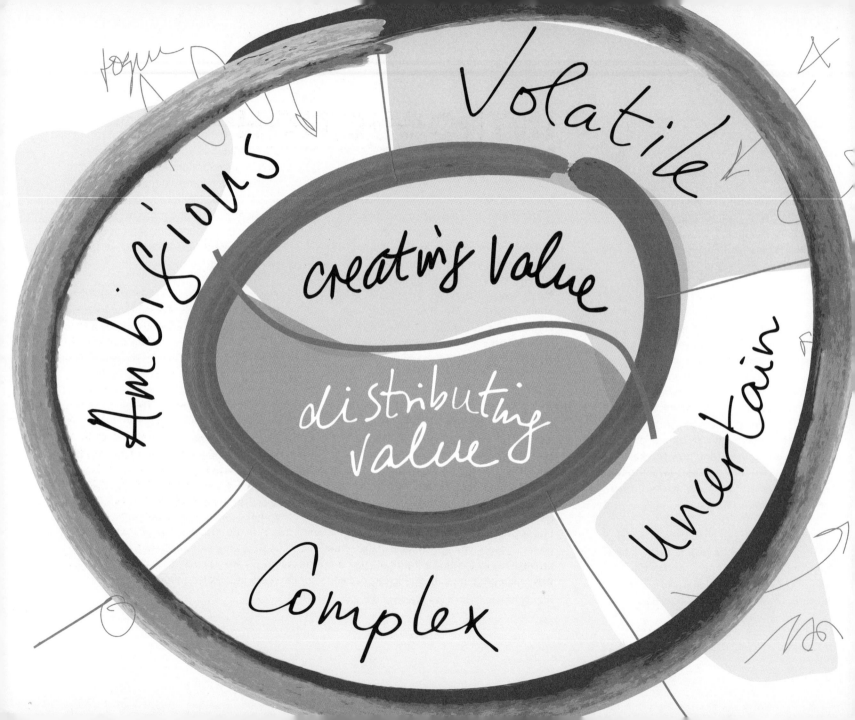

1 INTRODUCTION

NEGOTIATION MATTERS NOW MORE THAN EVER

We negotiate in a VUCA world and the heat is on
The one constant factor is that the world is changing rapidly. Many people perceive uncertainty and increasing complexity. Things are no longer unambiguous and there is often more than one possible solution. All roads may indeed lead to Rome, but which route should we take? It seems as if our surroundings are changing fast, but our behaviour isn't keeping pace. You see this in companies, organisations and networks or cooperative partnerships. Our actions have to be more business-like: faster, sooner, and with more added value. Projects are becoming larger and more complex, with larger vested interests and often with more risks as a result. Major projects often overrun, cost more money and yield deliverables of poorer quality than expected. Relationships are under pressure during the process, trust fades and irritations increase. We are often not trying to prevent conflicts by constructive dialogues, but are looking for conflicts so we have to settle, or see each other in court. In complex projects, the number of lawyers is dramatically increasing, the contracts grow thicker, and it looks like we have forgotten how to deal with a complex dialogue at the negotiation table. Everyone's trying to outsmart the next person, all playing the same little games. We start out on the road looking for constructive cooperation, but all too often find that it's a turbulent path. We are under pressure and that in turn puts pressure on the other party. If you don't know how to cope with this, you will become more uncertain. Will you bluster away and then disguise that uncertainty by starting a fight? Will you drop the issue? Or are you able to find a constructive way of keeping the dialogue going, serving your interests and making progress?

INTERNAL AND EXTERNAL NETWORKS

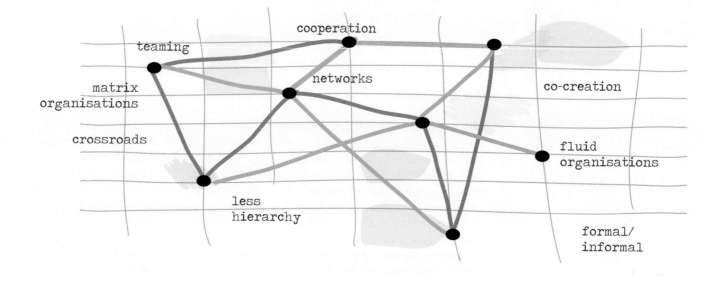

Cooperation is becoming more important and a different, personal, style of leadership is needed

In all kinds of areas, you can observe a shift towards 'sharing' and 'togetherness' and a call for 'transparency'. Sharing a vegetable garden, a car or tools. Generating energy together. Companies too are looking for new ways of working together and providing leadership. Hybrid cooperative ventures are appearing and there is an ongoing quest for new business models. Companies that are unable to find them will have a difficult time. We want to share knowledge to allow faster innovation and we are developing new revenue models for that. But if we want to cooperate more often, with multiple parties, how do we then distribute the value that is on the table? Should that be decided by whoever holds the purse strings? Is the customer *always* right? Is it the law of the jungle? The one who shouts loudest?

You will see that society and organisations are becoming 'flatter' and less hierarchical. Statements such as "I'm the boss and you do what I tell you" are a thing of the past. The keywords that you will find in leadership literature are about values, service, participation, credibility, trust, bonding, togetherness, transparency, coaching and the longer term. These are also keywords for negotiation. To show leadership, you have to be able to negotiate, and negotiating requires you to be capable of demonstrating personal leadership skills. You want to show soft power, providing leadership and at the same time getting people to go along with you.

When William Ury was recently interviewed by the *Wall Street Journal*, he was asked what had changed since his book was published in 1981. The American author's reply was, roughly, "I recently asked a group of business executives: take the ten most important decisions you made in the last year. They said that nine to ten were acts of negotiation. It has become the pre-eminent process for making decisions. Because the basic form of organisation has shifted to flatter organisation, the form of decision-making has shifted from vertical to horizontal."

In younger generations in particular, there is a growing realisation that entrepreneurship can tie multiple interests together.

Adding value, looking beyond your own immediate surroundings, contributing to society: it's no longer exclusively about money. There are many more interests that can play a role, and you can't go it alone (and shouldn't want to). Impact investment, social enterprises, new enterprise forms: a different way of looking at serving interests, cooperation and consequently a different vision on how the costs and benefits should be shared out. Working together to achieve win-win-win solutions.

It seems more and more difficult to hold a constructive dialogue
A robust exchange of words soon turns into a battle, often resulting in a deadlock or conflict. If you haven't got the gift of the gab or if you feel uncomfortable, you soon back down and think, "Whatever". Everyone can think of examples in their immediate surroundings of discussions that went off the rails and may well have deteriorated into tensions and conflict. At home, with their parents or children, or amongst themselves. Opinions are slapped down on the table, without progress being made. Arguments between neighbours about rights of way, the height of a hedge or a tree that is blocking the light. Overtime for TV judges.

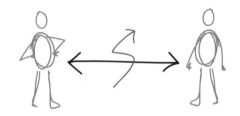

PRESSURE ON RELATIONSHIPS

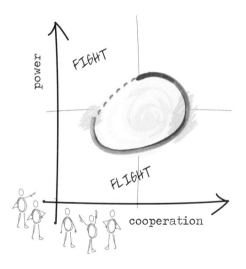

FIGHT OR FLIGHT?

Discussions in which entrenched positions are adopted are a familiar feature in business (both public and private) and politics. Debates, consultations and what are allegedly dialogues soon have us standing on opposite sides. Politicians who cry havoc but then won't release the dogs of war. Society and the business environment seem to have hardened. I haven't researched this – I did look for answers, but haven't found any – but that's the impression I get. We quickly make up our minds, and are even quicker to take offence or get annoyed, or we switch off. It's no longer all about the facts, but instead about managing perceptions. I get the impression that there are more and more people who give vent to all kinds of opinions, and others who back down and avoid confrontation. The middle road seems to be taken less and less often, genuine dialogues are rarer and people are often spoiling for a fight. Do people think this serves their own interests, or is it an expression of impotence, anger and irritation? Indeed, it seems as if we only know two strategies: fight or flight.

We often find it difficult to start up a good dialogue – taking time to think about the reply, not responding for a moment and looking to see what the best solution is. The trick is to resolve a difference of opinion or a conflict using words, and keep the dialogue moving constructively.

A constructive way of negotiating is needed now more than ever
How can you create a dialogue in a VUCA environment when you are under pressure? When organisations become flatter, how can you make good decisions together? How can you reach long-term solutions in collaborative relationships that are continually changing? Are you able to hold a discussion, even when the pressure increases, in which you handle the differences, the disparate opinions, ideas and philosophies, without triggering a fight-or-flight mode? Can you get along with other people who have different positions, interests and alternatives, or with people whose behaviour is different and who come from other cultures? Do you therefore know the right steps to take, at the right moment and with the right people? These are all negotiation challenges.

NEGOTIATION IS A JOURNEY

You set off on a journey. You've come from somewhere, you've got your personal stuff with you in a rucksack, and you're going somewhere. There are times when that luggage prevents you from walking easily, making you uncomfortable. With hindsight, you perhaps realise that taking all that baggage with you wasn't so smart. Sometimes you travel alone, at other times you may gather a group around you, and other occasions will see you as a member of a group. You will come across new people on your journey. You like some of them more than others. Perhaps your expectations of the journey are very different from theirs. There may possibly be different ideas about the final destination, the route or the mode of transport. So how do you reach a decision then? Does one person impose their opinion on the rest, or do you reach a solution together? There will be setbacks along the way, of course. Sometimes the wind will be at your back and at other times in your face. You may find a route blocked, or have to tackle a steep climb. You need a plan, a route, a map, a compass, sturdy shoes, food and water. The rucksack can't be too heavy, or else it will become a major burden. You don't want too much food and drink either: just enough. And you know that you need to eat and drink even if you're not hungry or thirsty yet. Otherwise it may be too late, particularly when major efforts are demanded. And yes, you can get in your own way. Aren't there times when you yourself are the biggest obstacle on your own path?

Travelling together. I'd like to accompany you on that journey and I hope that I can help you get on the right path and stay on it, with a clear head, a warm heart and while remaining resolute and flexible – the 'strong legs and nimble feet' in the draw-

ing. First of all, I'd like to give you a grounding in the basics; you'll only get the extra baggage later on when things get tougher and more complex.

Before you read any further
I've used the masculine form 'he' when referring to individuals. I've also tried to avoid constantly referring to discussions, planning meetings, consultations and so forth. There is always a negotiation dynamic in these various conversations and gatherings, so for the sake of readability, I've simply referred to them all as 'negotiation'. I have chosen not to pres-

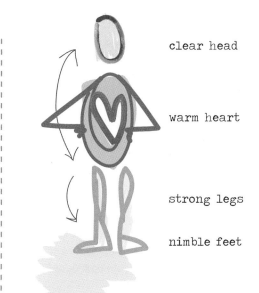

clear head

warm heart

strong legs

nimble feet

7 guides for creating

your journey in a VUCA world

ent too many case studies. Sure, cases are interesting – but I'm assuming that if you've bought this book, you're interested in the subject matter and you have your own practical situations in your mind's eye. If you go through the book step by step, you will be able to test your own cases against what you are reading. This means that it is above all an inspirational book, a manual for your daily negotiation activities when you face situations in which multiple interests and numerous actors and parties are involved and you perceive an increasing level of complexity. I am trying to lead you step by step through an approach that will let you see for yourself what you could do differently in your own practice, and what you could devote more (or less) attention to.

Over the years, I have accumulated all kinds of perceptions and insights, although I no longer know exactly where they all came from. I've already said that I have above all been dipping into the well of knowledge provided by *Getting to Yes*. It is a way of looking and acting that I feel a strong affinity with, a basis that – as far as I'm concerned – can't be highlighted enough. At the same time, I do use other sources too. If people think that they have

not received the credit that they deserve for that, I'll be happy to hear from them. I have made every effort to be careful in listing my sources, where they aren't already in the public domain.

CONNECTING THE DOTS

At the end of 2014, I was in New York for six weeks as part of a sabbatical. I wanted to be there for a while so that I could really get a grip on the book. To think up a structure that could link together the broad spectrum of negotiation topics. It was a fascinating period. I sometimes felt rather lonely and forlorn, but I was not alone. The edgy nature of the city, the beauty of its imperfection, the energy, the water, the boat trips on the East River, the views, the subway, the people you can watch or meet by chance. Each with their own story, and every one of them on a journey.

I observed, learned, looked back, connected a number of insights together... and came up with the structure of the book
The map of New York alone – the street grid, the subway system, the subway map, Vignelli's design for it, MoMA. The view at

the end of the day from the Wythe Hotel patio, from Williamsburg and looking out over the East River and the city. The boat trips from Staten Island to Manhattan. They gave me insights and ideas on how you can bring structure and an overview into an apparently unfathomable situation. We're all on a journey – but how do you know if you're on the right path if you don't know where you're going?

My visit to Tim Keller's Redeemer Church was highly inspirational. A lively and bustling community. Music first, then a good sermon that was actually about something and that you could put to direct use. Beautiful songs that plucked at the heartstrings. A church community firmly embedded in society, with a mission and a vision and a plan. Searching for connections and added value in people's daily lives. Being inclusive rather than exclusive. During an interview with Malcolm Gladwell about his views on New York's community, I heard about the 'soft power' approach to tackling crime in Brooklyn. Fascinating. Hard and soft, clear while providing space, inspirational and persistent. I spent a week there with my daughter Merel too. Walking along the High Line with a coffee – what more could you want? I was confirmed in my belief

CONNECTING SOME DOTS

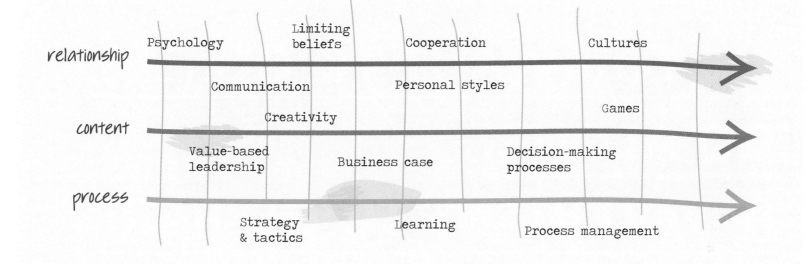

of how valuable it is to treat others with respect, to have an open mind and to walk the path together.

I went to Harvard again for a negotiation workshop. Straight from the horse's mouth, as it were. I spoke with William Ury about the Abraham Path, a trail that has been developed from southern Turkey through Israel to the Sinai Desert from Abraham's place of birth to his desert grave. Abraham was known for his hospitality instead of hostility and is a father for Christians, Muslims and Jews – a connecting figure. Ury is one of the founding fathers of this exceptional initiative. You are unfortunately no longer able to walk the trail through countries such as Syria anymore, but there's still plenty of it left. Doing the walk you will meet and talk to a lot of people. This will probably let you reframe your perception of the complex problems in the region. At the same time you will be helping local development. You have to eat, drink, sleep and be guided, so you are helping the development of local small-scale entrepreneurship. The path is a

"IF YOU WANT TO GO FAST,
GO ALONE.
IF YOU WANT TO GO FAR,
GO TOGETHER"

AFRICAN PROVERB

physical metaphor for negotiation. Going on a journey, shoulder to shoulder rather than opposite each other towards a common goal.

I took part in an international family business congress, where I experienced once again the significant added value of thinking like a steward. Stewardship – a forgotten word, even if it is described in the Bible. Now it is also being used by family shareholders in family businesses, to indicate that they do not so much own the company or assets themselves as manage it so that it can be passed on to the next generation. This involves some important long-term thinking: attention is paid to the short-term interests that always play a role in the business operations, while at the same time keeping an eye on the continuity and the longer timeframe. That approach and set of values certainly colours your thoughts and actions! Durability and sustainability with an underlying intrinsic motive. I saw families who had sold their companies and earned money by doing so, but had lost their sense of identity at the same time. It just shows you that money doesn't necessarily make you happy. What a difference there is between the longer-term focus of family companies and the short-term

orientation so common in companies listed on the stock exchange!
In that context, I came across a familiar quote that many of you will know: "If you want to go fast, go alone; if you want to go far, go together." To me, this inspirational African proverb summarises the whole idea of constructive negotiation. Try to go together and focus on the short and longer term.

I thought back to my role as the eldest in a family of five children. How that moulds you and how it fills your rucksack with memories, both cherished and less so. Or to my medical training and my interest in people and the systems in which they function. I've never lost my fascination for the psychological and psychiatric aspects. I thought back to my career in the private sector. To the good bosses and the poor ones, to when it clicked and when it didn't. To major projects that went squirly, or others that went fantastically. To my switch twenty years ago to the all-encompassing field of 'negotiation'. To the many people I have had on courses, both in groups and one on one. To the challenges that they faced and the patterns I began to see. The shape and substance of the book that I wanted to write started to develop. Linking

together experience, research, everyday practice, new insights, didactics and layout. A journey with lots of fellow-travellers, a map, various images. Negotiation as an art and a skill. The various elements became connected.

FREQUENTLY ASKED QUESTIONS AND STRUCTURE OF THE BOOK

I've kept a list of the questions that course participants have asked me most often over the years. They're quite diverse in nature, and there's an immediate sense of recognition when they turn up. They often involve a number of issues all at the same time rather than one single question. It then often becomes complex and course students see it as a black hole: a complicated tangle that is awkward to unravel. What should I do now, how do I handle this, and when and where should I actually begin? A few examples of frequently asked questions and comments (see next page).

FREQUENTLY ASKED QUESTIONS

I'm not aware of when a discussion is a negotiation, or of when there's a transition to the dynamic of a negotiation. How can I even recognise a negotiation?

I mean, aren't negotiations only about money? I'm not responsible for that, so I don't negotiate. Or do I?

I wasn't aware that I was in a negotiation and had already given away something of value. How can I prevent that in the future?

With twenty-twenty hindsight, I thought this could have been done differently. I only realised it too late. Can I avoid that?

I've noticed that we look at the real situation from very different perspectives during our discussions. How do you handle that?

How can you build up trust and what do you do if the trust between people has gone?

I noticed that I don't trust the other side, because I'm not getting enough (or incorrect) information. How should I cope with that?

We have an important partnership, but I get put under a lot of pressure and I'm not treated with respect. How should I cope with that?

How open can I be and when does that become naive? Can you be open without becoming vulnerable? How do I deal with people who are not open?

My client and I ended up with major problems because we both had very different ideas of the final result. How could I have tackled it differently?

I often find the discussions complex. If there are tensions between the various parties, I have a tendency to back away. How should I tackle this?

How can you reach good agreements if there are tensions between people?

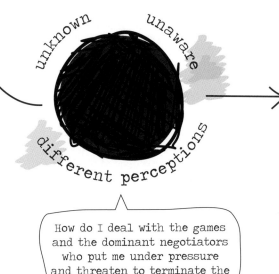

NEGOTIATING

unknown unaware

different perceptions

How do I deal with the games and the dominant negotiators who put me under pressure and threaten to terminate the relationship?

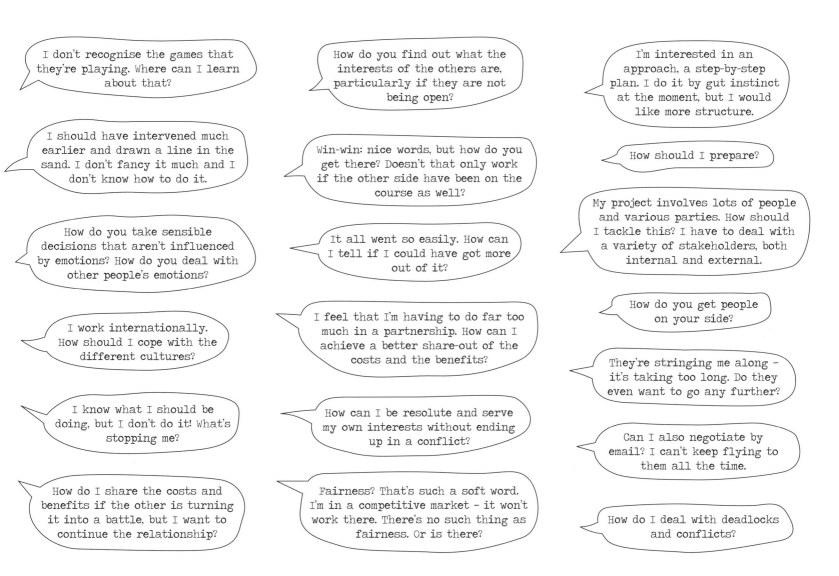

I hope that reading this book will let you answer your questions for yourself. That you will be capable of finding answers to your problems for yourself in an increasingly VUCA environment and able to help others along the way. To be able to achieve that, I've chosen a setup in which you can accumulate knowledge and insights, step by step. I will be going one step further each time, hoping to use a number of basic elements to help you along the road to mastery. If you would like to learn to negotiate or want to improve your skills, there are lots of aspects that you can take a moment to consider. I've chosen to highlight aspects that I have observed are able to help you further in practice and I have arranged these aspects in a logical flow.

STRUCTURE OF THE BOOK

Before we start our journey

I'm going to start with seven dilemmas that always raise their heads to some extent in the dynamic of a negotiation. Are you aware of the dynamics? How comfortable are you with this? Once we've run through that, I would like to introduce you to my way of looking at the art of negotiating. What exactly is negotiating? How can you approach the complex dynamics involved, and how can you get a clear picture and create insights? Can you unravel the complexity and impose a rationale or sequential order on it?

The journey:
A mindset and seven guides for your actions

You will get to know a number of values that can typify your attitude and your approach – or to put it another way, the foundations underpinning everything you do. You will also learn all about seven guides that can add substance to the wheeling and dealing. You can use them when preparing for your journey, just as

a real-life guide might tell you what to pack. As well as helping you get a picture beforehand of the route you want to take (again like guides in the real world), they are also useful during the actual process, and you can use them after the event in the evaluation and when looking at the lessons learned.

Everything comes together at the negotiating table

The best process is obtained when the guides come together in a particular way in a logical, step-by-step plan that can steer your approach, letting you take control of things. That's how you go about it when your journey gets a bit more complicated, when there are more people travelling with you and the route has become more challenging. You will get to know the structural and procedural steps for helping you find an efficient and effective approach that also lets you manage decision-making processes. The process sometimes takes shape in just a single conversation or meeting, or it may need to progress through a number of stages.

Next level up: mastering the art

Once you have understood the basics and are able to apply them, there are several more aspects I'd like to show you in order to add more depth and breadth. I'll restrict this to a few items that I see as being about the ability to speed up and improve the process itself and about being able to cope with the increasing complexity in terms of the relationships and the substance. I would like to give you some extras to take with you on the journey, to help give you a clear view and to keep you sturdy and agile, with a warm heart and strong legs and nimble feet, able to stay on the right path when the going gets tough.

Expanding your circle of influence

I'm going to give you some points of leverage so you are able to intervene in the process if you think it should be moving more quickly, more effectively or in another direction. You'll learn how to look at things from the outside in, as an observer. And I'll have a few things to say about a 'time out' as a way of taking a step back from the process. I'll also introduce you to a number of ways of making a deal more attractive

and more of a win-win situation, focusing on creativity in particular. I will end by telling you how you can keep learning from negotiation processes and how you can deliberately speed up that learning process in your role as leader or person responsible for a project.

A clearer view and more agile

The way you influence each other affects the negotiation process. You will get additional insights into each other's communication pitfalls and limitations, so that you can 'read' the other person better and see why people regularly end up talking at cross purposes, why you tend to irritate one another, or why discussions can stagnate. I will introduce a way of staying connected with the other person in communicative processes, so that you can make progress together. I'll also take a look at specific biases (distortions and misrepresentations of the facts) that play a part when information is exchanged and interpreted, which will let you develop a keener eye for the factual content. I'll also take a moment to reflect on cultural differences, which can be important when you

get involved in negotiations. The insights acquired start coming together when things get more tense: I'll give you an idea of the games that people commonly play, so that you'll be able to cope with them.

The journey's over: Time for the next adventure

Have you picked up some good insights for getting a grip on VUCA and developing VUCA skills? Are you capable of dealing with the increasing complexity? We can take a look back together and I will make some suggestions to help you assess where you are and what aspects you would like to develop further.

Preparation and checklist

I'll take a moment to look at some points that need attention during your preparation and I've given a checklist that you can use.

Inspiration and literature

I've included a list of books, articles, blogs, websites and videos to feed you with inspiration in the field of negotiation. This is also where I've listed my sources.

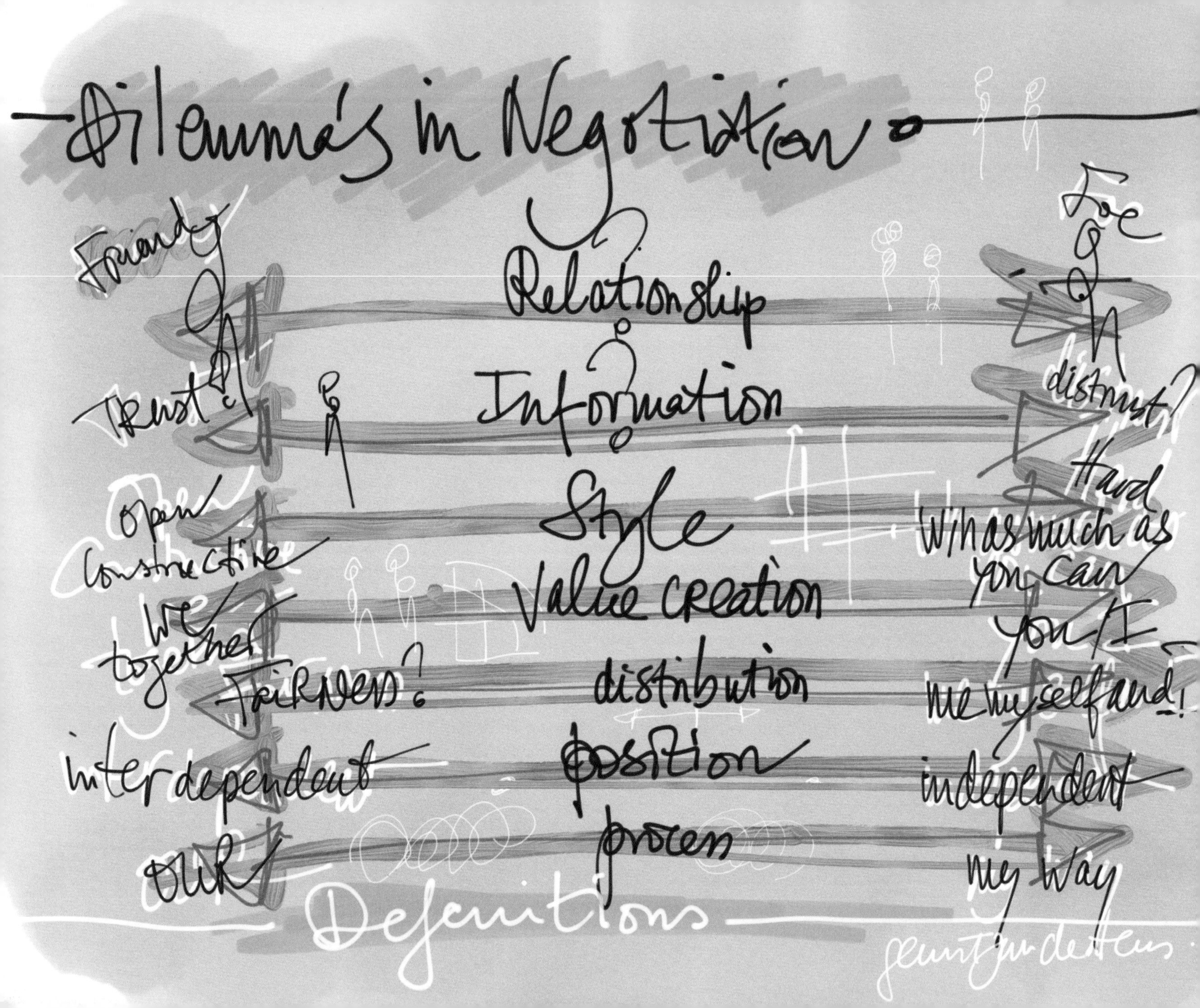

Dilemmas in Negotiation

Friendly — Foe

Trust? — distrust?

Open — Hard
Constructive — What as much as you can
We together — you / I

Fairness? — me myself and!

interdependent — independent

OUR — my way

Relationship
Information
Style
Value creation
distribution
position
process

Definitions

BEFORE WE START OUR JOURNEY

Before we start our journey, it's a good idea to agree a couple of things. There are a number of dilemmas that keep reappearing in all kinds of negotiation situations. If you are aware of that and start to see that you are negotiating every day, you may be able to enhance your learning process and take some small steps towards mastery. I'll also discuss what I mean by 'negotiation' and I would like to ask you how you want to approach negotiation situations. Are you in it just for yourself, do you want to get as much as you can as quickly as possible, or is there an alternative route? I'll take a moment to look at how you can get an overview of the increasing complexity that you come across, letting you get a grip on how to investigate your preferred personal style, in a quick scan. With this in your baggage, you'll be better able to cope with the rest of our journey of discovery.

DILEMMAS THAT ALWAYS RAISE THEIR HEAD

If you watch how people interact with each other during negotiations, the same dilemmas seem to be playing a role all the time, to a greater or lesser extent. These dilemmas are common to all times and all cultures. If you recognise what is happening and can deal with it, you'll be able to remain relaxed and increase your agility. I'm stating the dilemmas here as extremes, because you may at times feel as if you are being bounced back and forth between these extreme positions. These dilemmas will be perceived both by you and by 'them'.

How do you perceive yourself and each other, and how do you react to each other?

1. Do you see each other as friends or enemies?

This dilemma is about communication and the dynamics of relationships between people. Einstein once said, "If you see those around you as your enemies, you'll be hostile to each other." If you look at the other party through a more amicable filter, you are generally more likely to treat them constructively. You often do not know the people you have business (and other) relationships with, and you wonder how you should interact. Cultural differences can also play a role in this, which can make it particularly complicated. Should you stay aloof and keep a bit of a distance, or should you try to create a good under-standing quickly? This issue comes up in teams and with your colleagues, managers and clients.

How do you handle information and trust?

2. Do you trust the information that is being exchanged or not?

An extension of the first dilemma is whether or not you trust each other. What information are you basing your deci-sion on? Do you look at things through rose-tinted spectacles, seeing everyone

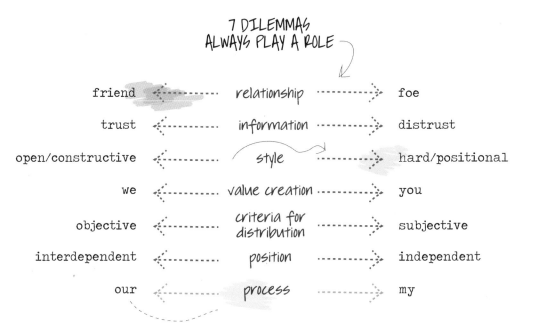

as trustworthy until proved otherwise, or do you assume nobody can be trusted? A tricky dilemma. The following statement is one that you've undoubtedly heard from an external party at some point. "This is how we tackled it last time too, and it won't work." Or what about "You're much more expensive than the competition." And "I've still got to discuss it internally, but you can take it from me that it'll be fine." Or

internally – colleagues who tell you that the deadline will be no problem, that you'll get the report on time, that the project's pro-gressing nicely. Both internal and external negotiations put you in situations where you're wondering whether the information is correct or whether someone's playing games. And if you have your doubts, you soon start feeling the dilemma personally: do you still trust them?

What's your game plan?

3. An entrenched position, or open and constructive?

What attitude do you adopt in a negotiation? That's the way it is: like it or lump it? Or do you go in with an open mind, see what's happening and then decide how to proceed? Are you open about your interests, or do you keep your cards close to your chest for your own protection? An awkward dilemma: what attitude to adopt, what position to take. This turns up in all kinds of decision-making processes. Opinions are stated as if written on tablets of stone. People stick to their guns and positions harden to create deadlocks. Who makes the first move then? And what does it say about your credibility if you then have to make a U-turn?

How do you find solutions?

4. Together or alone?

It's often said that whoever makes the initial proposal is in a strong position. But is that really the case? The first proposal is often the starting point in the negotiation and it does give you some influence. The question is whether a proposal is a starting point for a healthy dialogue, or in fact the beginning of another common pattern: you offer a proposal, it gets shot down, you have to tweak it a bit, it's still not enough, you reach a limit and then it's like it or lump it. Or are people ready to look at it together and see what's best for both sides? Is there a will to investigate jointly how to maximise the added value? A dialogue tells you more and the solution may be better. How do you handle this dilemma? People may be reticent and often don't want to talk about it with the other side. Sometimes they're not allowed to talk to you, because a process has been agreed that excludes dialogue between the parties. In any event, the reflex to get 'them' to do the work by coming up with a proposal seems to be powerful. And vice versa. The other party is thinking that any proposal they can get on the table will become the basis. It's one way of keeping each other busy...

Distribution issues are often a source of tension. How should things be shared out?

5. Fairness as a principle – or is there no such thing?

Who gets what and who takes what? How can we share out the costs and the benefits? Distribution issues almost automatically create tensions, particularly if you are up against people who want as big a slice of the pie as possible while shifting the consequences to you. In partnerships too, you see that pressure is applied in order to get as much out of the negotiation as possible. Many people see negotiation primarily as a question of sharing out the pie, in which they mainly just want to win, often at the other's expense. As a result, this dilemma can feel extremely uncomfortable. Should distribution be based on who shouts loudest, or according to power or strength or emotions? Or do you look to see what's fair in the situation?

Who has the power?

6. Are you dependent on the situation or independent of it?

What is the balance of power? What position are you in with respect to the other side? Who has the power and how much do you and the other party want to make a deal? Is this because you want a deal, or because you need a deal? Are they more powerful simply because of their size? You may automatically feel small and vulnerable, even if your position is actually strong. In any event, positions are adopted and the degree of independence (or otherwise) colours your negotiations. Where are the boundaries? How far should you go and will you let it happen?

Who takes the lead, when and how?

7. Do you take responsibility for the process, or do you leave that to them?
You don't want to look too manipulative, but you do want your own interests to be served. You may have expected that they would lead the meeting, but that isn't happening. Or not properly at any rate, and you can see that your interests are not being taken into account. Nobody knows where they are at. Can you intervene? Do you have the authority? When and how do you add structure to what you are doing? (Particularly in the case of multi-level and multi-party negotiations.) How do you turn it into a process, and what steps should you take? And what do you do if the process is stagnating?

These dilemmas can be felt even more acutely when the terrain becomes more complex: if the interests become more significant, if more parties are involved and when people are negotiating on behalf of others. (After all, they've got their own interests too.) The seven guides will give you some answers showing how to deal with these dilemmas (see pages 46-72).

ARE YOU AWARE OF THE DYNAMIC OF THE NEGOTIATION?

The dilemmas I've just listed play a part in all sorts of negotiation situations. The question is whether you are aware of it and whether you are aware of the dynamics of the negotiation. The common perception of the word 'negotiate' does not exactly foster that awareness. I've always found it a cumbersome word because it so often has a negative connotation. The term makes many people think of the empty promises and offers of market stallholders. If I ask people who are taking part in a training course about the people they negotiate with, there are plenty who say they don't do it at all. That's something for others – salesmen, account managers, the boss, the department head or the project manager. I hear it regularly: "I don't negotiate because I don't have a commercial job." You are apparently often unaware of the fact that you're negotiating all day long.

Of course negotiation can be about closing deals and making financial agreements, but there is so much more. If I ask for examples of good negotiators at a workshop, the picture soon changes. Then I get remarks about children. "My four-year-old son just keeps on until he gets what he wants. The kid knows exactly which buttons to press." Before adding with a wink, "Just like his mother!" Or "My baby girl isn't even twelve months yet, and she's at it already. She sure lets you know when she's hungry. She cries until she's picked up. She's got her mum wrapped round her little finger already." Negotiation then suddenly seems a lot closer to home. Even so, there's still that same perception of negotiation as getting what you want and hammering on until you get it.

In addition to these perceptions of what negotiation means, there is often an idea that you have to be a born negotiator. You can spot them right away, the people who are always asking for discounts. Either it's in your DNA or it isn't. If you think that negotiation is only about money, you won't see that you're actually negotiating all the time.

There may be a blind spot...

- if expectations have already been raised, information has already been shared and value has already been 'given away'.
- if things you have promised start to lead

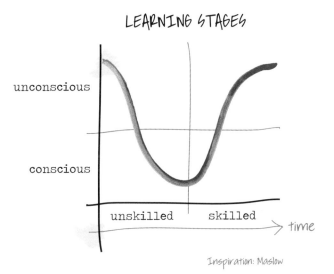

LEARNING STAGES

unconscious

conscious

unskilled   skilled

→ time

Inspiration: Maslow

dilemmas. In the end, I hope that you will become 'unconsciously skilled', but that won't always be achievable. Unconsciously skilled means that it takes no effort and goes naturally, that it's part of you and it feels right. That is possible to achieve at the communication level, but because negotiation involves so much more than that, you will always have to be fully aware and totally alert as things progress.

lives of their own and you only discover how awkward that is after the event.
- if the other party has already adopted a position and thereby already set the ground rules.
- if you have done a lot for the other party and realise after the event that the balance between give and take is lopsided.
- if you don't notice that the other party has gone beyond your limit ages ago.
- if you aren't aware that your own style may have led to the stand-off.

You see afterwards that you could have responded earlier or differently. If you'd been more aware of the dynamics of the negotiation, maybe you would have handled those situations differently. To improve your awareness, I'd like to share my picture of the dynamics of a negotiation with you, and then add some other opinions. Then we'll be starting from the same baseline for the subsequent steps and (after introducing a couple of concepts) we can look at how we can handle the

EVERYTHING IS NEGOTIATION: MY VISION, A DEFINITION AND A FEW CONCEPTS

EVERYTHING IS NEGOTIATION

I take a broad view of negotiation. I use it to mean any conversation between people who want to get from point A to point B, where there's anything at stake. Where it's important for them and where each can exert influence on the other.

We experience this dynamic in conversations where expectations should be discussed, but are often left unclear.

Where emotions can run high, and interests are shared. Or not.

Where information may be kept back, or cards put on the table.

Where aspects have to be weighed up against one another and choices have to be made.

Where we say things we don't mean, where we realise afterwards what we had wanted to say but didn't when the tension rose. Where we were overwhelmed by emotions and said the wrong things and regretted it for years. Where we sometimes had a feeling that there was no way out, put others under pressure or were pressured ourselves. Where we thought we'd won, but turned out to have drawn the short straw. Where we weren't aware of the boundaries and didn't dare say no.

Where we wanted to intervene, but didn't. Where we noticed that the discussion or meeting was heading in completely the wrong direction, but nobody intervened. Where we couldn't find a good solution, where willpower got in our way.

Where we didn't trust it, but continued anyway.

We see this dynamic in operation when trying to win new business, with initial discussions feeling the way, presentation of a proposal and closing the deal. When putting together a team, in working groups, during kick-off meetings, project meetings, discussions about changes to the work scope or evaluation meetings.

Where people are going to be collaborating or are already collaborating. Where one person is leading another, or decisions have to be made and you wonder if it isn't going too quickly and whether the right information is available.

Where you want to select other parties, make coalitions and create partnerships.

Where you're developing innovations, launching a start-up or arranging funding.

Where you're taking a company over or downsizing one.

Anytime, any place, anywhere: you're negotiating all the time.

Everything is negotiation.

WE NEGOTIATE ALL THE TIME...

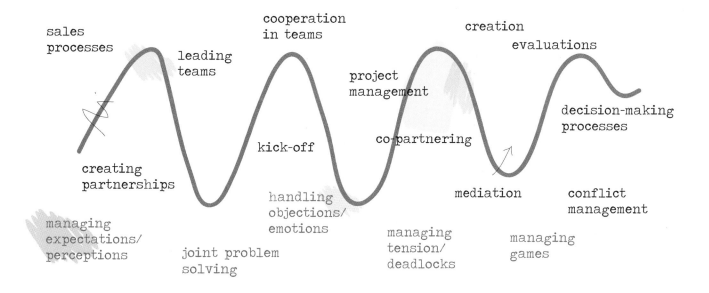

sales processes

cooperation in teams

creation

evaluations

leading teams

project management

decision-making processes

kick-off

co-partnering

creating partnerships

mediation

conflict management

managing expectations/ perceptions

handling objections/ emotions

joint problem solving

managing tension/ deadlocks

managing games

So there you have it. As far as I'm concerned, wherever there's anything at stake and wherever the two sides can influence each other and you want progress, then you're negotiating. We negotiate all the time. Of course there are many different perceptions of 'exactly what negotiation is' and there's no absolute truth. However, your idea of what negotiation is *does* determine your view on what you want to learn and develop further.

PERCEPTIONS OF NEGOTIATION

WORLD ECONOMIC
FORUM 2020

1 Complex problem solving
2 Critical thinking
3 Creativity
4 People management
5 Coordinating with others
6 Emotional intelligence
7 Judgement and decision-making
8 Service orientation
9 Negotiation
10 Cognitive flexiblity

NEGOTIATION DYNAMICS

If you look at the report that was recently published by the World Economic Forum – by no means a lightweight – then you will see that 'negotiation' has dropped to number nine on the list of expected core competences in 2020. As far as I'm concerned, you need a lot of the competences listed in order to be able to negotiate. I will pay attention to many of these.

I like the definition given by Carsten de Dreu, a professor of social and organisational psychology. Freely translated: "Negotiation is about creating and distributing value, in which the profits and losses (costs and benefits) always play a part. You also have to cope with the shorter and longer term issues and it may or may not be certain that the benefits will be obtained and exactly what the costs could be." If you put this interpretation in a VUCA context, you immediately see the additional challenge that many people experience. Increased complexity and uncertainty exacerbate the tensions between people, as the different perceptions and expectations associated with the issues (e.g. of sharing) come into play.

If you go back to the questions that play a part for many people when it comes to 'negotiation' and try to categorise them, you'll see that three aspects play a role in the dynamic of the negotiation.

Relational aspects: personal and psychological aspects and their interaction in communication
- You yourself are an element in each and every one of your negotiations, but are you really aware that a negotiation is going on? Are you aware of your own style, your strengths and your pitfalls or weaknesses, and the effect they have on others? To what extent does your own personal baggage colour the way you interact, and how much does this help or hinder the result?
- How do people influence one another? What is said, and what is left unsaid

or implicit? How does the actual reality get distorted by assumptions and rose-tinted (or otherwise distorting) spectacles? How do people forge a bond and how can that bond sometimes rupture again unexpectedly? How can you 'read' people and build trust? How can cultural differences play a role in negotiations?
- What part does language play in creating and maintaining the connection with the other party? Sometimes you see

that there is a bond, but using the wrong words can snap it and create a distance, potentially resulting in deadlocks and conflicts. What games are being played – can you recognise them and cope with them?

Substantive aspects
- How can you add content and substance to your case? What negotiation challenges are you facing?
- What interests are involved, what solu-

tions have been thought up, and how should we share the costs and benefits?
- Are there any alternatives?

Process-related aspects
- How can you manage a process and how do you deal with resistance and delays?
- What moves should you make? Sometimes you're playing simultaneous chess, several boards at once. Is there structure and a sequence?
- How are you going to tackle strategic and tactical questions and how do you reach the right decisions and get a good agreement or deal?

In every negotiation challenge that you face, you may be able to reduce the complexity shown earlier on page 20 as a black blob to challenges relating to the relationships, the content and the process. That will give you a better overview. A master negotiator is inside all the circles, where the relationships, the content and the process can all be managed at the same time. This three-way split will be the foundation for our further journey. In many of the visuals, I will use red to highlight the relational aspects, blue for the substantive content and green for the process-related side.

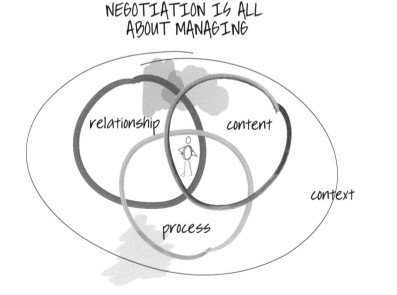

NEGOTIATION IS ALL ABOUT MANAGING

relationship content

process

context

NEGOTIATION IN A VUCA WORLD

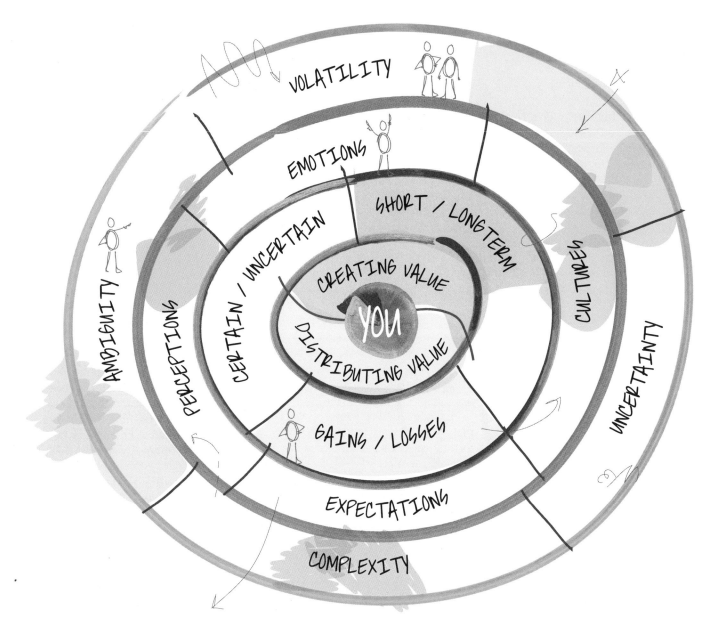

INTERESTS ALWAYS PLAY A CENTRAL ROLE

Interests play a key role in negotiation jargon. What do we understand by that? Personal and business interests are always involved. Personal interests are also referred to as motivators or core interests, what it's essentially all about and the reason why you're doing it. A couple of examples:

Personal interests
Aspects such as ambition, image, status, performance, wanting more and career-building can all be intrinsic motivators. Personal interests can also be of a different nature, such as personal financial gain, keeping your job or personal development.

Business interests
These are the interests that are often related to your task or your responsibility: generating revenue, increasing volume, optimising profit, strengthening cooperation, accelerating innovation, solving problems, raising customer satisfaction and keeping the relationship going. There is a hierarchy of interests and some are worth more than others.

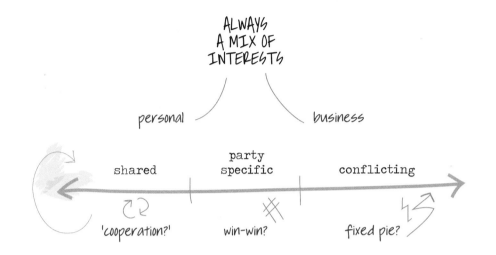

There are three categories of interests that you can approach differently and that will play a role in a negotiation situation to a greater or lesser extent:

Shared interests
Also referred to as 'joint interests' or 'common interests', these are interests that both parties value similarly. You may for instance want to deliver an assignment together on time, reduce the costs and continue the relationship. There will be a large number of shared interests in genuine partnerships. The parties feel the usefulness and the necessity of resolving a conflict and both attach equal value to this. You can also expect numerous 'shared interests' to play a part in private contexts as well. People often talk about commonality without actually fitting the actions to the words.

Party-specific interests
These are interests that are important and weigh heavily for one party, but do not harm or affect the other. They can be personal or business interests. One party may place a high value on developing its image further, whereas the other may not care either way. A procurement officer may

find it important to reduce his costs, but this may be at your expense if you have to lower your rates as a result. Nevertheless, it may also be possible to look for ways of cutting his costs without it affecting your own margin. Party-specific interests often seem to be in conflict, but they don't have to be. Some people turn everything into an issue of how to share out the pie: "I need to reduce my costs, so you've got to lower your price or rates." Or "I've got to stick within my budget and you're going to help me do that." It's a question of how you look at it. You can serve both interests. Party-specific interests can be interlinked, resulting in win-win solutions.

Conflicting interests

These are distribution issues by definition. More for one means less for the other. Distributing the consequences is often perceived to be 'awkward' and that is why it often causes conflict and tension. It boils down to who gets what, who does what and who takes what. How will we allocate the extra returns, the losses, the extra costs, time, capacity and so forth? What is it allowed to cost? Will the distribution be determined by who makes the most fuss, who is powerful, the positions, random chance or by gut instinct?

WHAT'S YOUR ANGLE?

What beliefs underpin the way you look at negotiation challenges? What is your mindset? This question involves some of the dilemmas I mentioned earlier. I've given you my way of looking at the dynamic of a negotiation, but how are you going to play the game, with what underlying beliefs? Do you want to win above all else, no matter how?

Or are you going to create room for a joint process, and do you want to see first whether you can make the pie bigger so that you've all got more when it's time to share it out?
Your beliefs colour the way you see things, your thoughts and the way you act. Both consciously and unconsciously, they colour your preparation, tactics and strategy, as well as your perception of the results achieved. I would like to run a few well-known negotiation principles past you, or 'paradigms' as they are known. The way that you cope with tense situations and conflicts may bring it all together, and a 'quick scan' will give you an impression of your preferred style. See if that tells you anything.

"I AM NOT ABOUT CARING. I AM ABOUT WINNING"

Harvey Spectre
Netflix, Suits

WHAT ARE YOU AIMING FOR?

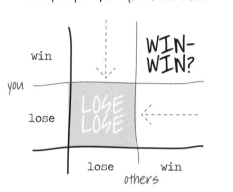

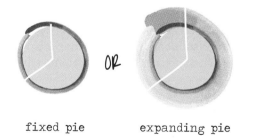

fixed pie   OR   expanding pie

One of the negotiation paradigms you hear a lot about is 'win as much as you can', a caricature of one set of principles. You're in it to win it – possibly at any cost. Negotiation is then primarily a question of distributing the gains, and you want as much as possible. The pie is a fixed size and it's all about sharing it out.

You do not value the importance of the relationship that much. If both parties take the approach that it's "all about me, I want more than you", then your worlds will soon collide and there will be a stand-off.

The question is of course whether adopting this position serves your own interests. Is maximising your short-term profit (thereby hurting the other) in your own interests if you want to keep doing business in the longer term? Or can the pie be expanded so that more remains for the various parties? And if the pie can't be made bigger, do you then want to take a constructive look at solutions that are desirable and achievable for both, or are you primarily looking out for yourself? People regularly seem to choose – consciously or otherwise – between the relationship on one hand and a good deal on the other. They pay no attention to the

relationship and focus on getting a good deal. You're in it to win it. Winning is also respected. It is often expected of you, and winning plays a key role in some cultures. It is also understandable and logical that we appreciate winners, because we look up to people who achieve their objectives and are successful. The question is whether it is at the expense of the other party or simply at any cost. 'Winner takes all' does not seem to be a tenable position at the moment.

'Win as much as you can' or working together constructively? Me or us?
Some people will say that the answer to this question depends on the situation. There's something to be said for that. Purchasers have developed a nice framework for that. I've tweaked it a little (see next page), but it boils down to the same thing: if you don't place much value on someone's products and/or services and you have plenty of offers of comparable alternatives, then you are not dependent on them and it's legitimate to be tough in the negotiating and get a lot out of it. That sounds fair to me too. The question is how far you go, as the party making the purchase, or how far you let it go, as the supplier. There's nothing wrong with

POSITIONAL DYNAMICS

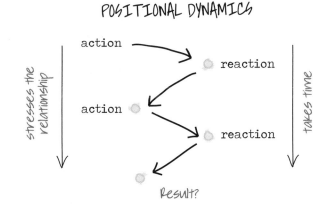

CONSTRUCTIVE DIALOGUE?

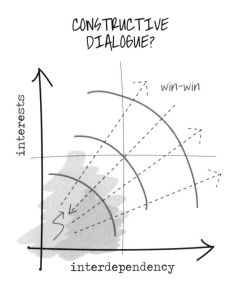

a razor-sharp negotiation. The question is therefore where the boundaries lie, in terms of both the content and the relationship.

In practice there are all sorts of interesting examples of partnerships in which the parties value each other and are also genuinely important to each other and mutually dependent. A cooperation in which the 'switching costs' can be high. Nevertheless, you see that all kinds of games are played that create tensions and conflicts, despite the fact that you need each other badly. You are actually up in

the top right quadrant of the diagram, but get treated as if you're unimportant and there's no interdependency. All kinds of deadlocks arise and the process becomes dysfunctional. People then often look back at it disbelievingly: how did we manage to get into that situation? Why didn't anybody intervene? Why did we make it so difficult for each other? But we are apparently unaware of what's going on during the process itself, and we just keep on struggling.

If you approach the negotiation from the 'win as much as you can' angle, you often see a positional dynamic arise, in which one side adopts a position and the other responds by adopting a position of their own. Arguments fly back and forth to support the positions, creating a dynamic of attack and defence. A classic action/reaction pattern. This costs time and puts pressure on the relationship and on the result. People then often say that it's part and parcel of the game – perfectly normal. The net result is a process that everyone can see is counterproductive, but which is condoned by the actors involved. Major projects overrun in terms of time and money, things eventually escalate and reach the board room, the wrinkles are ironed out and then we get back to business. Our inability to deal with such situations costs us a lot. My preference is above all to start by seeing if you can cooperate constructively to bake that pie and perhaps even expand it. That makes more for both of you. This may not always be feasible or even desirable, but I'm talking about a basic attitude here, fundamental for your actions.

When the going gets tough is when your basic attitude is often most visible. Your primary response pattern then comes to the fore. See if that gets you anywhere.

NEGOTIATING AND DEALING WITH CONFLICTS: WHAT'S YOUR PREFERRED STYLE?

People often mention a questionnaire by Thomas Kilmann in this context. A comparable questionnaire is the Dutch Test for Conflict Handling (the 'DUTCH' as they themselves call it, given here in English), which is based on work by Van de Vliert and later validated by De Dreu and others. With the help of the following questionnaire, you can get a first impression of your preferred style for dealing with conflict situations, where there are incompatibilities that seem impossible to bridge and where pressure is being applied. Is it every man for himself, or cooperation? Do you avoid things and back away (A), accommodate and make concessions to your own detriment (B), want to cooperate and solve the issue (C), or dive into the fray and enjoy the competition (D) ?

The central position is also sometimes called the 'compromise' position, though I'd rather call it the position of a negotiator who is aware of what is happening and capable of a flexible, agile response to the situation. Negotiators who are prepared to take responsibility for their actions.

I have filled in the answers of a random course participant as an example. Go through the questions and then add up your score for the five preferred styles, as instructed at the bottom left of the list. What's your preferred style for dealing with conflicts? Think back to the previous section. What's your angle?

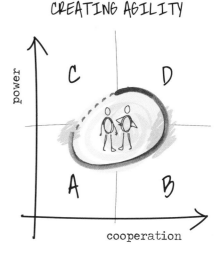

CREATING AGILITY

power — cooperation

C   D

A   B

EXAMPLE SCORE		NEVER	RARELY	SOMETIMES	REGULARLY	(ALMOST) ALWAYS
1	I give in to the other side's wishes.	1	**2**	3	4	5
2	I study the issue until I find a solution that both of us are genuinely satisfied with.	1	2	3	4	**5**
3	I try to find a compromise.	1	2	**3**	4	5
4	I avoid a confrontation about our differences.	1	2	**3**	4	5
5	I impose my own standpoint.	1	2	**3**	4	5
6	I accept the other party is right.	1	2	**3**	4	5
7	I stand up for my own objectives and interests and those of other people.	1	2	3	**4**	5
8	I emphasise that we need to find a middle way.	1	**2**	3	4	5
9	I circumvent differences of opinion where possible.	1	2	3	4	5
10	I try to make a profit.	1	2	3	**4**	5
11	I try to meet them half way.	1	**2**	3	4	5
12	I investigate ideas from both sides to come up with the optimum solution for both of us.	1	2	3	**4**	5
13	I insist that we both water down our demands a little.	1	2	**3**	4	5
14	I try to make the differences look less stark.	1	**2**	3	4	5

	EXAMPLE SCORE	NEVER	RARELY	SOMETIMES	REGULARLY	(ALMOST) ALWAYS
15	I fight for a good result for myself.	1	**2**	3	4	5
16	I adjust my position to suit their interests and objectives.	1	2	**3**	4	5
17	I work on a solution that serves both my interests and theirs as well as possible.	1	2	**3**	4	5
18	I aim for a compromise where possible.	1	2	**3**	4	5
19	I try to avoid a confrontation with them.	1	2	**3**	4	5
20	I do everything I can to make sure I win.	1	2	3	4	5
	Acceding: add up the scores for questions 1, 6, 11 and 16	10				
	Solving: add up the scores for questions 2, 7, 12 and 17	17	Preference for this style			
	Compromising: add up the scores for questions 3, 8, 13 and 18	10				
	Avoiding: add up the scores for questions 4, 9, 14 and 19	12				
	Competing: add up the scores for questions 5, 10, 15 and 20	12				

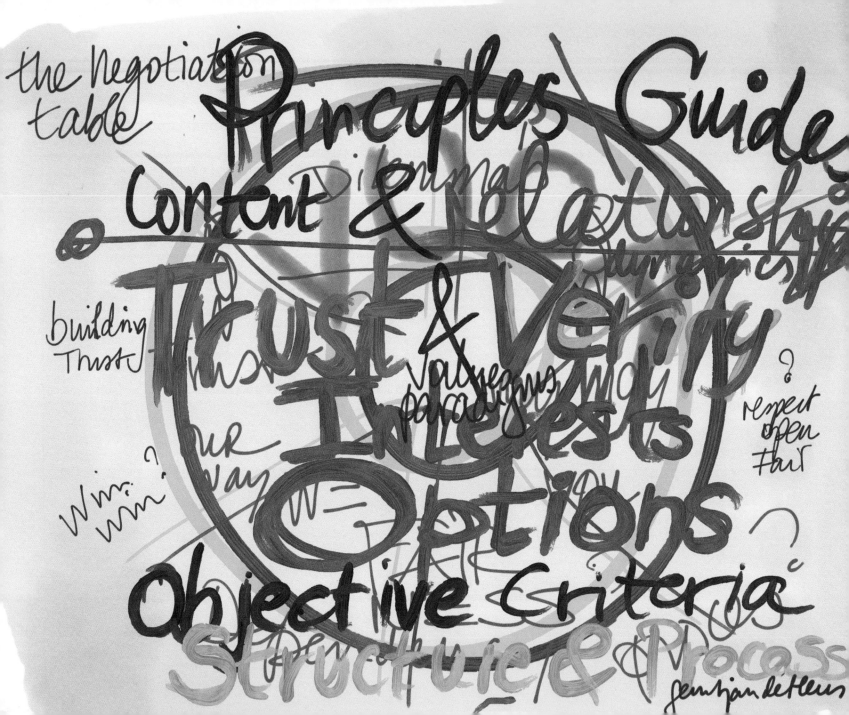

THE JOURNEY: VALUES AND GUIDES FOR YOUR THOUGHTS AND ACTIONS

In order to be able to tackle the negotiation properly, I'd like to start by taking a moment to look at a number of values that can help you find an effective method. What set of values do you want to be the baseline for approaching the other party and how will you then deal with the seven dilemmas that always play a part in negotiation challenges? The seven guides can be seen as answers to that question of how to deal with the seven dilemmas. I will be discussing the seven guides as a leitmotif for your actions and I will then offer a number of insights and angles for more in-depth exploration. We'll take it step by step.

OPENNESS, RESPECT AND FAIRNESS

Is it every man for himself, or cooperation? Do you primarily look at negotiation as questions of distribution, or can the pie be expanded first? As discussed earlier, that mindset can colour the wheeling and dealing to quite an extent, determining how you act. In addition, you can

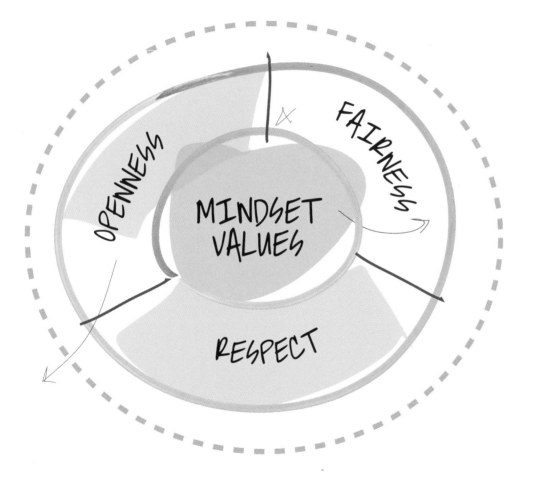

TOUCHING BASE

OPENNESS

FAIRNESS

MINDSET VALUES

RESPECT

also think about how you intend to treat each other. I believe that you can create better relationships and agreements if your attitude to the other party is based on openness, respect and fairness. As far as I'm concerned, these are the core values that underpin everything.

Openness

An open, inviting attitude yields good connections and solutions more quickly. If neither side knows what matters to the other and the requisite information doesn't come to the surface, then it's not easy to find good solutions and agreements. If you aren't open about your interests, they aren't going to be part of the solution. That cuts both ways. At the same time, you do not want to be naive. There are limits to openness and you don't want to lay all your cards on the table. Everyone is entitled to have their own hidden agendas. You won't want to share everything because that could make you vulnerable, allowing the other to use or misuse the situation. There are times when you have not 'earned the right' to ask for an open dialogue and then you will have to create trust step by step. In some cultures it can take a long time before any kind of trust and openness coalesces. There's a saying in Dutch that trust comes in on foot and flees on horseback. Everything you've built up can be lost in an instant, so it requires care and attention.

If you aren't open, can you really expect it from the other party? Conversely, if you go in with your guard lowered and a constructive attitude, it may encourage openness from the other side. The question you have to answer is how you want to handle the issue of being open and creating openness. Where's your limit and how will you tackle any lack of openness? Creating a secure situation in which people feel encouraged to be open about their interests and opinions is an art. You will undoubtedly notice that people become open with you when you invest in the relationship, paying attention to them and genuinely showing interest. You can long for openness, but you can't force it.

Respect

I assume that you want to be respectful to the other party. You don't have to agree with them, you may have differences of opinion, you can disagree passionately so much that conflict situations arise. The art is to remain respectful in your dealings with each other. Take the situation as it is. Accepting that the other side may think dif-ferently, that games may be played, some-times right on the edge of what is accept-able or even beyond. Yet at the same time, there are boundaries. Yours and theirs. If you are respectful and act that way, you can expect the same in return. That raises a question that will be answered later: what to do if you aren't treated with respect.

Fairness

Some people say there's no such thing as fairness. That you ought not to be fair or reasonable when your own interests are at stake. That's not how I think. To me, it's the fundamental of the musical key that your actions are expressed in. That you aren't aiming to get as much as you can as fast as you can at the expense of the other party. Certainly not when it gets down to sharing out the pie. Again, if you start from fair principles and try to find a solution, then you can expect the same in return. Will that always happen? Of course not. It is a starting point for your actions, and others may see things otherwise. That is precisely the challenge for the negotiator: getting people to see things your way, in this specific case.

You hope it will be reciprocated, a two-way street. If you are open and take a reasonable attitude, you hope to get the same in return. If you treat the other respectfully, you hope they will behave the same way. Fortunately, that is generally true and you do often reap what you sow, but it's not a foregone conclusion. Maybe you shouldn't anticipate it. Tensions can run high, games may be played and you might be confronted with a different basic attitude. I do not want to create the impression that you should make yourself vulnerable – naively showing your hand – so that they can serve their own interests at the expense of yours. The challenge is to be agile and flexible, starting from that basic premise, in order to cope with others whose approach differs. Being firm when necessary, being open at the right moments and remaining respectful even when there's a conflict.

In that context, there's another thing I'd like to share with you. The psychologist Amy Cuddy, a professor at Harvard University, has done research into first impressions. It transpires that people very quickly assess two questions when they meet you: whether they can trust you and whether they respect you. It is often assumed that what you need most of all is to show that you have knowledge and expertise.

However, you actually get weighed up on a very different kind of scale. I think that approaching people with openness, respect and fairness sets the tone nicely.

SEVEN GUIDES

So how are you going to deal with the dilemmas mentioned earlier, which you will encounter in all kinds of negotiation situations? A set of values such as that described above provides the foundations; the guides give you answers. Taken individually, they can always be applied anywhere: they affect your preparation, your negotiations and your plan for evaluation and improvement. They all come together at the negotiating table and you will discover a natural sequence. I will begin by discussing the guides in a general sense and then I will give a few practical examples to illustrate them, after which the tactical and strategic components will appear. First, I'm going to discuss two communication guides, because they are continually in play no matter what you are doing. The extent to which you then want to express the guides explicitly or more implicitly depends for instance on the context – cultural or otherwise – in which you are

working. There will be more about that later (see page 159).

RELATIONSHIP AND CONTENT

Suppose you are sitting in a meeting that is not going well and you notice a degree of reticence among some of those present. What is going on? What do you do? You're in the kick-off meeting for a large project. You can see that there are differing perceptions about the project that is

to be delivered. There hasn't been enough discussion about this, but you're uncomfortable bringing this up yourself. You think that it would be better to get started on the project first. You're talking to one another and you aren't on the same wavelength. It's as if you keep talking at cross purposes. You notice that someone is irritated and that unreasonable comments are being made that are aimed at you. You feel overwhelmed; you clam up and don't know what you should be doing. You notice that people seem to be taking the wrong deci-

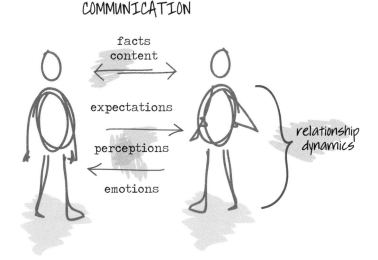

COMMUNICATION

facts content

expectations

perceptions

emotions

relationship dynamics

sions in a key meeting, based on emotions. You're in a meeting and being pressured to do more than you actually think is fair. This is the umpteenth attempt to get you off balance.

Communication involves things that are unclear, assumptions, implicit expectations and emotions. These can all make things awkward for you. In order to help you deal with this, I would first like to tell you more about communication in general. Communication between people operates at a variety of levels, as shown in the figure.

- You are always exchanging substantive, factual information, in what you say. And at the same time, you have...
- Expectations, of each other or of the situations, that are implicitly assumed, or explicitly stated.
- You have a picture of each other and of the situation. In other words, the visions, perceptions and impressions. How you see each other, and...
- You have feelings and emotions about each other or about the situation. You may be satisfied or pleased, you may feel you have been listed to and accepted. Or you may be cross, irritated or disappointed.

The relationship level can also be seen as an undercurrent. The dynamics of the relationship are how you interact and influence each other. You have impressions and expectations of each other and of the situation, and there are always emotions. The undercurrent always affects the layers above. If that undercurrent is positive in nature, the substantive discussions will be easy. You want to pay attention to the relationship in order to create and maintain trust and a good understanding. However, the positive relationship can also muddy the waters in terms of the content, so that you see things less clearly.

If there is an undercurrent of tension, it is more difficult – or even impossible sometimes – to have a proper discussion about the content. Emotions or certain perceptions of the situation may block you or the other party from being able to listen properly and make that connection. If the expectations people have of one another are not clearly expressed, there may be a lot of hiss and crackle on the line and people start talking at cross purposes. This can inhibit the progress of the discussion. It is possible that people may be playing games and using emotions to get even. You feel pressured and may perhaps give way to the emotional pressure even though

you do not feel that it is fair. Aspects of the content and the relationship are constantly getting intertwined. Sometimes that happens spontaneously and sometimes tension is built up deliberately in the relationship in order to squeeze more out of the negotiation.

Guide 1 helps you deal more consciously with the undercurrent and the surface layers. It is more than just a communication guide and it can be applied throughout the process. It has been stated for you on the next page.

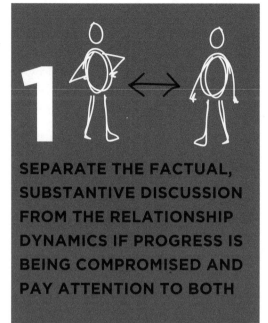

1

SEPARATE THE FACTUAL, SUBSTANTIVE DISCUSSION FROM THE RELATIONSHIP DYNAMICS IF PROGRESS IS BEING COMPROMISED AND PAY ATTENTION TO BOTH

This guide has several dimensions and you can apply it in various ways.

- Take time during your preparations – even if only for a moment – to make sure you are aware of your emotions about the discussions you are going to be having. This is particularly important if you notice that your emotions are getting in the way and stopping you from thinking and acting calmly and clearly. Prepare mentally for the negotiation. This doesn't have to take long; it's primarily about awareness at a meta-level. What are you experiencing and feeling? What are the underlying reasons for your emotions? What are you worried about? Are you unnecessarily painting yourself into a corner? Go through your case and do a reality check, for example by talking it through with others. This mental preparation alone may be enough to make you calmer.
- Put yourself in the other party's shoes and feel it their way. Look at yourself from their position and think what perceptions and expectations they have of you and of the situation. Consider what is being perceived and expected – in both directions – and see whether that could obstruct the negotiation and whether you

want to pay attention to it explicitly.
- During a discussion, always pay attention first to the relational side of things before getting down to the content. Invest in the relationship and work on a good understanding: respectful and attentive.
- Think whether you want to state your emotions explicitly and talk about them because they can be a hindrance to you and are blocking progress. There's an Italian expression saying you should "put the fish on the table", so that everyone can see it and won't wonder what the funny smell is, but mentioning emotions is sometimes undesirable or inappropriate, or the quality of the relationship may not be good enough to permit that. You should then above all look at what is causing the emotions and discuss *that* if possible. If you see notice that the expectations you have of each other are unclear, you can discuss them. You ought also to discuss any perceptions (particularly negative ones) that are inhibiting progress and trust before you go any further.
- Putting you under pressure by creating unrealistic expectations is sometimes part of the game — airing negative images and applying emotional pressure. This is covered in more depth in

MANAGE YOURSELF

MANAGE INTERACTION

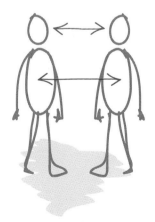

'If games are being played' (page 163). Here too, it is important to separate the relationship dynamics from the content, to stop the wrong substantive decisions being taken based on the games being played. Refer to Guides 2 and 5 for this too.

Guide 1 will be with you throughout your journey. Keep checking the undercurrent and the surface currents, taking responsibility when the two get entangled, either deliberately or otherwise.

Examples
A customer is annoyed and says in an irritated voice, "I can't see this collaboration working any more. We should draw a line under it." You can feel the emotion, which is literally creating a problem for the content. You would like to discuss the emotion first and then start on the actual substantive discussions. One possible response could be, "Fred, I can see that you're pretty irritated about it. Tell me…" It may be legitimate to speak about the emotions at that point. "Fred, that worries me. I can see that you're unhappy with the way things are going. What's bothering you?" You are then giving him an opportunity to 'put the fish on the table'. Once the emotions have

been expressed and due attention paid to them, the other party will feel that they have been listened to and will be ready to discuss substantive matters. The bark will often turn out to be worse than the bite. You need to understand that emotion first, pay attention to it and only then move on to a solution in terms of the content.

If you notice that there are perceptions that are getting in the way of progress, you may want to pay attention to that first: "Wilma, I get the impression that we aren't looking at this situation in the same way. Should we consider that for a moment before we continue?" Or "I can see that we've got different ideas about the desired end result. Let's take a look at that before we go any further." If you notice that the expectations are different and you're talking at cross purposes, you may want to do something about it: "Barney, I can tell that we've each got different ideas about what to expect from our collaboration. I think it'd be smart if we each made clear what our expectations are first, and then we can look at the best way to continue." If you feel that it's not a good idea to continue, it's important to say so: "Fred, I'm noticing that I'm not really happy with this. We agreed earlier that there'd be a partic-

"WITHOUT DATA YOU ARE JUST ANOTHER PERSON WITH AN OPINION"

W. EDWARDS DEMING

ular way of tackling it, but that's gone now and it is really important to me. I suggest that we take a moment to look at that."

Should you always separate the content from the relationship? And what if it's in your own best interest to mix them? I mean, can't you make use of that as well? The rule of thumb is actually that you ought to pause for thought as soon as you notice that your interests are not being served and progress is being inhibited. That's when you want to uncouple the substantive content explicitly from the relationship dynamics. You mix them together in order to strengthen the relationship. If you have a good relationship with each other, the content items will also go more smoothly. Perhaps too smoothly.

You can exert pressure on people by responding emotionally, for instance. By not expressing expectations clearly, thereby allowing grey areas to grow that you may be able to make use of later. You can drag up all kinds of old grievances to beat the other about the head with. You can play the game deliberately, taking a dominant and leading position in a discussion so that you can get as much out of it as possible. If you have people opposite who are susceptible to such manoeuvres,

you may gain a lot. If you encounter people who are also prepared to play the game, though, it can become a battle and it's open to question who will win or who will blink first.

In my opinion there are moral limits to such games and, no matter what your role, you can therefore ask whether playing the game hard and tough genuinely serves your interests (including in the longer term). You may be able to force the other party to say yes to a deal that isn't good for them. In the short term, you get what you want. But how does that work in the medium or longer term? What are 'they' going to do in order to make the deal better for themselves? Are you running risks by tackling it this way? You may have won a Pyrrhic victory – a case of "penny wise, pound foolish". You may even think that it's their problem because you've got it nicely covered contractually. But will that attitude help you? And suppose that it ends up as a legal battle: will that be in your interests? Is there no middle course?

As far as I'm concerned, the values mentioned earlier – respect, openness and fairness – can be touchstones for your actions. Sometimes you are negotiating from a position of strength and you can

demand a great deal. How far do you go? It's a fine line, which is why negotiation is needed. You're on a journey that can sometimes get disrupted or you may notice that it isn't plain sailing and you want to do something about it. You can keep going, but it is better to stop now and again for reflection. Sometimes you may be forced to stop. Then you have to act and you need to apply Guide 1. Another time you may be the one who brings things to a halt, when you want to intervene.

If you follow Guide 1, looking and listening, you will see things differently and become more aware of the quality of the communication. It helps you strengthen the bonding and make your actions more effective.

TRUST AND VERIFICATION

"Fine – we'll arrange that."
"I understand that the proposal has been agreed."
"Your quotation is way more expensive that your competitor's."
"We tackled it that way last time as well, so it'll work."
"I think we should work with partner A because they've got the best track record for this job."

"That's covered by the scope, so we're not going to pay separately for it."
"No problem, you'll get that report on Monday."
"Of course it'll get sorted." Sound familiar?

You regularly hear completely abstract information that makes you wonder what they're actually saying, or trying to say. Or you wonder whether the information obtained is correct. Or you get incomplete information, intentionally or otherwise. Perhaps you notice that incorrect assumptions are being used and that decisions are being based on distorted information. Maybe there are loose ends remaining after a discussion and no clear agreements have been made.
You often have to communicate with people you don't know yet, or don't know well, and with whom you have not yet built up a relationship. You often don't know whether you can trust each other yet, and any information that turns out to be incomplete or distorted can keep raising doubts about that trust. In short, the second dilemma always plays a role to a certain extent in negotiations. In order to respond to that appropriately, Guide 2 is important at all times.

2

SEPARATE THE PERSONAL TRUST FROM THE SUBJECT MATTER, DEMAND AND PROVIDE VERIFICATION AND BUILD UP THE TRUST

This applies in all sorts of situations, whether they involve discussions with team members or other colleagues, with suppliers or with customers. Irrespective of whether or not you have a good relationship and trust each other, making things verifiable ensures clarity and lets you make good decisions.

Providing and demanding verification gets things into focus and helps create trust. Verification has become an underlying principle in all kinds of project management processes. System engineering and SOPs (standard operating procedures) are all based on the importance of having the right – verifiable – information. In practice, people may allow grey areas to form because they think it's in their own interest. Agreements are deliberately kept vague so that they retain the option of saying later that this wasn't what had been agreed. Managing expectations is also important in this context. In some industries it might then for example be about defining a 'scope'. You will be running all kinds of risks if you do not make clear – and verifiable – agreements about what you are and are not doing, exactly what may be expected from you and what the concrete ideas are about the intended solution

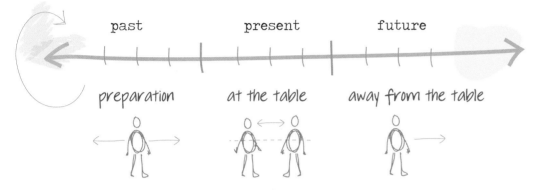

VERIFICATION ALL THE WAY

past   present   future

preparation   at the table   away from the table

or end result. And if it is too early to say anything about the solution or end result, you need to make clear agreements about how to deal with that. Make a verifiable point of the fact that some aspect isn't verifiable yet.

If agreements are not clear, it gets awkward to come back to them later on. Discussions about additional work can then become very tricky, for instance. "You were supposed to be doing this too: it was in the scope, so I'm not paying for it." You could query that statement in order to make

things verifiable. Questions such as when it was agreed, with whom, and where it was recorded can help you clarify the situation.

Keeping communicating effectively with each other and making clear agreements about the future also helps you prevent issues of trust occurring. This doesn't mean that you should always lay your cards on the table. That can be naive. Everyone is entitled to have a hidden agenda. Some information is yours alone and not intended for the others. The question is what information you need in order to be

able to take a step forward and whether the information is correct when you do get it. Verifiable information plays a part in:

- your **preparation**: what factual data do you need? What is missing? Is the information that has been exchanged so far correct? What information as a minimum do you want everyone to share and interpret in the same way, so that they are all starting from the same baseline? This is sometimes a negotiation in its own right.
- the **negotiation**: listen closely to the information that is being exchanged. Is the information correct? Does it line up with earlier data? Is it consistent? Is anything missing? Does it match your picture of that information? Is new information suddenly being presented?
- the **future**: have clear agreements been made about the next steps to take? Has the information been properly recorded? Who, what, how, where, when?

A few examples of how to deal with abstruse and vague information

Although they're expressed in rather black-and-white terms here to make the point, I've given a few examples of how to use Guide 2 in your response (R) when abstruse and vague information (I) is provided:

I: "Fine – we'll arrange that."

R: "Good to hear! May I ask exactly what you're going to do and who you're going to agree it with internally?"

The familiar comparison of apples and oranges:

I: "You're more expensive than your competitor."

R: "Could be. I suspect it depends on exactly what you're comparing. Shall we share our information, go through it point by point, and evaluate it together?"

I: "That's what we agreed with your colleague."

R: "Fair enough. I'd be intrigued to know what was agreed. Who did you agree it with, and where can I find the details?"

I: "Project X hasn't been going very well lately. You'll have to sort this out."

R: "I'm sorry to hear that. Let's we take a look at exactly what's not going well and find out why. Then we can look at how we can resolve the issue."

I: "Don't worry, that report will come on time."

R: "I very much hope so – I know you're very busy. How are you going to manage this?" Or "Perhaps we could have a look at it together? It's very important for me, after all."

If you're looking for verification, you may get a reaction along the lines of:

I: "What, don't you trust me?"

R: "You know, it's not a question of trusting or not trusting. I think it's crucial that we have the same picture of the information, so that the next steps can be taken."

That lets you uncouple the trust issue from the subject matter.

You can build trust by paying deliberate attention to the items David Maister mentions in his Trust equation. The formula speaks for itself: if you can create and improve your credibility, you're improving trust. Doing what you promise and showing why you're doing what you do will all help the reliability aspect. If you pay attention to the relationship and can connect to the people and the problem, you create intimacy. And last but not least: don't focus too much on yourself. Focus on the other party! *To build* is a verb: overall, you are building trust. You can consciously do something about it and build it up.

Don't forget that you can also ask about it: "What should we do to build further trust in our approach?"

"What would make you convinced about our track record?" "How could we help you take the next step with us?"

"I can see you still have your doubts. What would be needed to create confidence and let us continue together?" In short, pay attention to whatever the other party needs for keeping or improving trust. You can investigate that, and build up their confidence as you do so.

$$TRUST = \frac{CREDIBILITY \times RELIABILITY \times INTIMACY}{SELF\text{-}ORIENTATION}$$

In summary

- Verification is a guide, a basic attitude throughout the process.
- If you make things verifiable yourself, you can ask the other side to do the same.
- Say that it is important for the process. Earn the right to continue. "If we're to find a good solution, it's crucial that we also have the same picture of the facts, which is why I'm asking you..."
- You want to have the right information and the same information if you're to go any further. In the first instance, negotiations are often about what information you're going to be using and what baseline assumptions will be made. This also lets you find out what data you're missing, whether both sides see the information in the same way, and whether or not they're playing games.
- Invest in building up trust. It's something you can work on consciously by making yourself verifiable.

A SUMMARY OF GUIDES 1 AND 2: A GOOD NEGOTIATOR HAS A CLEAR PICTURE OF THE CONTENT AND AND EYE ON THE RELATIONSHIP DYNAMICS

INTERESTS AND POSITIONS

When do you take up a position? Do you first search for the common ground, or would it be preferable to draw a line in the sand first? Discussions often involve exchanges of standpoints or positions. To put it another way, opinions are quickly given or statements are made: "I don't want to pay."
"We aren't going to do that."
"That's not how it works here."
"I think that we shouldn't go ahead." Or perhaps, "I think that this is exactly what we ought to do." People often adopt a position because they think it's in their own best interests.

Action and reaction

When someone adopts a position or standpoint, they are communicating a decision. "I want X." You can either agree or disagree, but it's binary: no wiggle room. If you are faced with someone who is adopting a position, it may not yet be clear what the other party thinks is important. A position can be seen as an expression of their underlying views or their underlying interests. People have a strong tendency to state what they do or don't want or think. One side takes up a position, and the other responds with a counter-position. Before you know it, you end up with 'positional discussions'. One side slaps an opinion down onto the table, and the other responds with something different. This often leads to a pattern of actions and reactions. Attack and defence. You want to outsmart the other, trumping them with better arguments. It turns into a battle of words before you know it. Which side can convince the other they're right? That puts the relationship under severe pressure, wastes time and is often counter-productive. An exchange of positions and standpoints does not automatically serve the participants' interests.

To deal with the third dilemma, you can use Guide 3 as an approach to that kind of discussion.

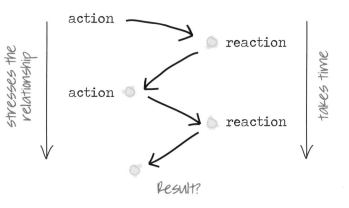

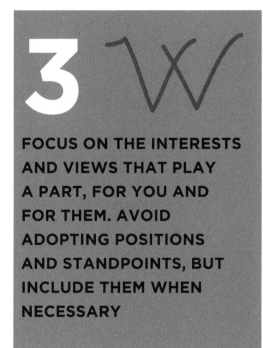

3

FOCUS ON THE INTERESTS AND VIEWS THAT PLAY A PART, FOR YOU AND FOR THEM. AVOID ADOPTING POSITIONS AND STANDPOINTS, BUT INCLUDE THEM WHEN NECESSARY

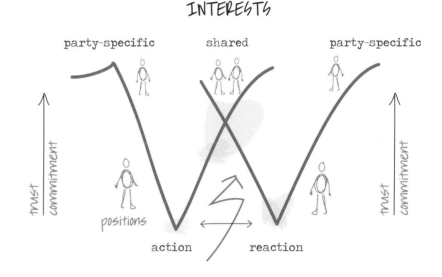

Focus on each other's interests and views – how they see things – but adopt strict standpoints as little as possible. Interests, preconditions and objectives are all extensions of each other.

You want to talk about the interests because that creates the scope for possible solutions later and because that helps you understand each other, thereby strengthening the relationship. It creates a connection, a bond. Focus first on the oth-er's interests; then your own interests will get a turn. And you'll benefit too. In general people enjoy talking about what's important to them. So ask about it. A negotiator who can ask good questions, can listen, can find mutual interests, knows when to probe deeper and when to shut up, will be regarded as trustworthy. Stephen Covey put it like this: "Seek first to understand, then to be understood." A lower price, a certain solution or an opinion that is expressed are not 'interests'. By searching for the underlying interests and views, you develop an understanding of the context, a conception of the other party's interests and you create room for manoeuvre.

I'm not trying to say that you should never adopt a position. If something is highly important to you, it may be a non-negotiable position. Not up for discussion – a no-go zone. It may be extremely important for you that you do at least get a fair share of the pie, not dropping the rate below X or being able to implement a certain element in the solution yourself. Be aware of what matters to you, what is important and what is and is not negotiable. If you want to adopt a position, it may help you if you state the background to that position (your interests). You should then indicate why something is not open to discussion as far as you are concerned, while at the same time saying where you do see scope for solutions. "Doing more in terms of X is not feasible for us at the moment *[the position]* since we are limited due to... *[the interests]*. If we could find a solution for that issue, then we would be able to move towards you more in terms of Y *[creating room for other options]*." You need the interests on the table and then you can find proper solutions. Please refer to the process for more on how this is applied (page 81).

MY OPTIONS AND THEIRS

Are you going to work alone or together to create solutions? A tricky dilemma. You often see a pattern arise in which one side makes a suggestion, the other shoots it down, modifications are suggested, counter-proposals are put on the table, and so forth. The pattern thus created then repeats itself. "Make a proposal." "Surprise us–I'd like to hear your solutions." You're undoubtedly familiar with such remarks. That pattern is regularly and deliberately used as an element in the negotiation tactics. You will also see the same 'positional' way of talking about solutions in discussions between colleagues. "This is how I see it..." "What I reckon is..." "This is how we ought to be doing it..." These statements merely trigger reactions opposing them. You should aim to prevent this dynamic; it's smarter to use the Guide 4 as a response to the dilemma.

4 ▭ ◯ △

THINK UP VARIOUS OPTIONS FIRST, TOGETHER, AND THEN DECIDE TOGETHER WHICH OPTIONS SERVE THE INTERESTS BEST

Basing your thoughts and actions on Guide 4 is the quickest possible way to get into a joint process. You would like to look at the options together and explore possibilities that can serve both parties' interests, because two heads are better than one, working together creates a bond, and you are able to utilise each other's creativity to find a better answer. Together, you can bake the pie and make it bigger. First, you want to explore as many options, implementations or potential solutions as possible, and only then make the choices. Diverge first and then converge. The consequences of the solutions (who does what, who gets what, etc.) are distribution issues that can be tackled using the Guide 5.

In practice, deals are often less than optimal. The added value that could have been created together is not achieved. People have looked too quickly for the obvious solutions and what they came up with is far from pretty and not broad enough. The 'value zone' has not been explored.

Don't be satisfied with that. If a discussion is threatening to get bogged down, you can investigate ways of coming up with ideas to get things moving again. It may be the case that not enough interests have been

made explicit for you to work with. So take a step back to look at the interests again and check that you didn't miss anything. Looking for as many solutions as possible that can serve as many interests as possible is a challenge. It demands a deliberate approach, which can cost time. See it as an investment.

Many people are increasingly working in fluid groups and with different partners, in project teams, for co-creation and in partnerships. Collaboration is often remote too. It is often not possible to have a face-to-face dialogue about exploring the options, yet at the same time that exploration of the options may progress more efficiently and more effectively if you can see and meet one another. This is an intriguing challenge: when are you happy with a process that goes by e-mail, when do you accept a process using Skype or a video conference and when do you opt for face-to-face contact? My suggestion would be that loads of information can be exchanged without live contact. If you do need input from each other and that exchange is important, organise contacts via Skype or video conferencing, and face to face if that is achievable.
Naturally, there are also situations in which

expanding pie

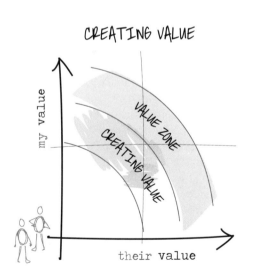

CREATING VALUE

WIN-WIN COMMUNICATION:

"The single biggest problem in communication is the illusion that it has taken place."

GEORGE BERNARD SHAW

face-to-face contact is not permitted, such as tendering procedures. That's a *fait accompli* that can't be influenced; I'm referring here to contact moments when you do have a choice.

SHARING AND FAIRNESS

Every option you select and everything that you do for or with another has consequences in terms of time, money, quality, activities, revenues, losses, and so forth. So how do you share out the gains and the losses? Guide 5 helps you deal with these distribution issues. Sharing things

out can be a tricky process and it's also often where the game-playing takes off. Is the share-out based on power, strength, emotions or random chance? It is a major challenge to define conditions that are fair in your eyes too, given the effort and the potential solutions. You want to serve your own interests and be duly rewarded for your contribution and your added value.

A negotiator in a dominant position often turns negotiations into a distribution issue as quickly as possible. "I want X and I'm ready to pay Y." I recently heard a nice anecdote from Brian Mandell, a Harvard professor. It was about Rambo and Bambi

going out for a meal together, an anecdote that juxtaposes a positional negotiator with an evasive and lenient opponent. I quote freely, "Imagine the following situation, which turns up a lot in practice: Rambo and Bambi go out for a meal together. Rambo eats his own food, followed by everything on Bambi's plate, and then gives the bill to Bambi." They take the benefits, including yours, and leave you with the consequences. It's something you should want to avoid in real life. To retain your focus when the share-out is being determined and to improve the chance that you'll be able to avoid positional games, it's useful to have the Guide 5 at your fingertips at all times.

FAIR DISTRIBUTION?

subjective criteria?

power emotions games

objective criteria?

WHEN SHARING OUT THE CONSEQUENCES USE OBJECTIVE CRITERIA TO SUPPORT YOUR VIEW OF FAIRNESS IN THE DECISION MAKING

Subjective criteria are often employed. "I think X is enough." "I don't want to give more than Y." Or "I want Z." However, you want a fair distribution of the gains and losses. Criteria that can't be circumvented, that go beyond a subjective battle of wills, and that both sides can say yes to: objective criteria, such as what is normally done, a deal is a deal, standards, being in line with the market, distribution criteria that were used in the past, or a third party if necessary in the event of disputes. Criteria that provide good justification for your case and that are acceptable for the other party. Also think about the arguments that they might come up with to undermine your approach. It's better to prepare for the discussions that are going to be held on that point. Objective criteria can vary widely in nature. If you add a lot of value in a cooperative effort, it isn't reasonable for them to wring you dry. A certain amount of reciprocity can be expected when you are cooperating. If that isn't there, it isn't reasonable. The other party may see it differently, but you then therefore have a negotiation about what you should be able to expect, where the limits are and what is or is not fair. That discussion often doesn't happen in practice. Lady Justice embodies the philosophy of the Guide 5: blindfolded (unable to see the person's appearance, to maintain her objectivity) and with scales (so that every aspect is weighed fairly), she takes her decision (sharing out by cutting with the sword), using the book of laws (legislation and jurisprudence as objective criteria) as her guide.

Examples of objective criteria in language

Human interactions mean that we have a lot that needs sharing out, and these accumulated experiences have become criteria of fairness over the course of time, as worded in numerous expressions:

Cut or choose. The greatest good of the greatest number. Promises are promises. Everything has its price. First come, first served. There's no so thing as a free lunch. You'll never score if you don't shoot. Tit for tat. What's sauce for the goose is sauce for the gander. From each according to his ability, to each according to his needs. Share the good times and the bad. You can't make an omelette without breaking eggs. The polluter pays. Avoid having to tackle issues twice. You can't have your cake and eat it. The best seats in the house aren't the cheapest.

raise your voice Don't ra

Don't raise your voice

ur voice Don't raise yo

Don't raise your

IMPROVE
YOUR ARGUMENT

Harvey Spectre [Netflix: Suits]

These ideas and expressions can help you add clout to what you are saying when getting down to brass tacks and justifying what you think is fair.

Examples of distribution issues

You want to go on a holiday with your partner. Do you choose South America, or should it be Asia? This kind of discussion can quickly acquire a dynamic involving positions. A dynamic of sharing things out. Who decides and what's the decision based on? The one who keeps harping on? Or do you go back to the interests and look at it together, based on aspects that the two of you think are important, to decide what the best option is? And if you can't agree, how do you come to a decision? Heads or tails? Or do you let your partner choose this time and you'll choose next year? Tit for tat? Or does one push it through and the other caves in? These can be sensitive discussions that need a carefully considered dialogue. Before you know it, you can have problems not only with the matter at hand but also with the relationship.

You may notice in a project that one side is doing more than the other, and it won't feel right. When something doesn't feel quite kosher, it's often a sign that it's unfair; your challenge is to put that into words. If you want to hold a clear-the-air discussion about it, you should look for a criterion that will help underpin what you are saying. You can look at the distribution issue as a function of someone's role or responsibility ("Given John's responsibilities in Project X, it seems fair to me that he should also do Task Y"), or based on the knowledge that someone has about the situation. Or would the limited amount of time that someone has available be a fair way of justifying it? If one person doesn't have time and another does, it still doesn't mean that you have to accept that one does everything and the other does nothing.

Someone doesn't want to pay more than X and so they say, "I think X is enough." They are applying a subjective norm to the amount being paid. You want to know what that's based on and what the background is to that statement. It's possible that there will be a perfectly good reason behind it. If someone can get the same product or service elsewhere much more cheaply, then "I think X is enough" carries a very different message than if it's just a random remark. There can however also be a difference between a fair price – determined on 'fair' grounds – and the price someone is willing (or able) to pay. If the budget is insufficient, you may perhaps be able to find a different solution, though it does not necessarily have to be found by lowering a price or rate.

"We've incurred losses as a result and you ought to be paying!" The question is what exactly happened and who is responsible. Depending on the degree of responsibility, there may also need to be a formula for apportioning the costs. After all, if one party is fully responsible for the losses it isn't unreasonable to have them cover one hundred per cent of the costs. If the situation turns out to be not that simple and a question of the kettle calling the pot black, it may be a perfectly reasonable solution to split the costs fifty-fifty. In practice someone may attempt to place as much of the blame or burden on you as possible, but that is then part of the game. The question is whether you are capable of addressing the unfair aspects and justifying what would be more fair. All kinds of emotions may play a role, putting further pressure on the way things are shared. In that case, you should apply Guide 1 and deal with the emotions before you get onto the distribution issue.

Two companies are going to merge and they are looking for a new location. How do we decide what the best place would be for the new office? "Given our position, I think it's fair that the head office should be close to where we come from!" The other side will probably think differently. What criteria do you use for the apportionment? The one that makes the most noise, a power play, by threatening to quit? Or should we search together for a criterion that both sides are able to accept? And that search is of course a negotiation in itself. Various criteria could be considered: the numbers of employees, differences in commuting times for the staff to one location or the other, or the most suitable location for customers. If you can't reach a solution, you can get somebody else to decide. That too is an objective criterion. Heads or tails is another way, but a working group made up of equal numbers of people from each of the two companies could also consider other possible solutions. It is then very important that the parties commit to accepting the outcome beforehand, otherwise there's no point beginning negotiations in the first place.

Differences of opinion have a dynamic of opposition: you think X, they think Y. These positions can harden and you have a stand-off before you know it. Then you need to go back to the information that is needed for making a good decision, weighing up the interests and the possibilities. If you can't resolve it together, then discuss who or what can help you reach a solution nonetheless.

MY BATNA AND THEIRS

"Otherwise we'll do it ourselves." "If you don't like that, we'll go ahead with your competitor." "There are dozens just like you." Parties often want to give the other party the impression that one side is more dependent on the other or vice versa (see the sixth dilemma). It goes further than that: the fact may even be explicitly used – or misused – in all kinds of negotiations. Looking for each other's limits. If they know that *you* are dependent on *them*, then they might misuse their position. Conversely, if you make it crystal clear to them that you don't need them, then your position is stronger. Your position in a negotiation is partly determined by how dependent you are on the other party. This applies both ways. If you don't have an alternative but they do, then you're the one whose negotiating position is weaker. This disparity in power can sway the negotiations, which is something you have to be aware of. Guide 6, which is described on the next page, lets you cope with this appropriately.

6

DEAL?
___
BATNA

KNOW YOUR BATNA – AND DEVELOP ONE IF NECESSARY – AND BE AWARE OF THEIRS

BATNA stands for the 'best alternative to a negotiated agreement'. What should you do if you can't come to an agreement? And what will they do? During the preparations, your BATNA determines whether you want to negotiate or not. Sometimes the alternative may be so good that you go for it anyway. After all, you're negotiating because you think you need to and it helps serve your interests. If that's not the case, you're better off spending your time on something else. A BATNA is a Plan B. You may only have a so-so BATNA, which exacerbates the need to negotiate well. If you don't have a BATNA, the question is whether you can develop one. Do watch out for the investment that is involved, though. Deciding whether to develop a BATNA means weighing up whether the costs in time, effort and money are worthwhile.

Examples of BATNAs
Doing nothing for now, doing it yourself instead of getting them to do it, a competitor's proposal, taking legal steps or looking for another client with whom you could attain the same turnover and profit. Looking for another job, another partner, a new member of the project team. "If Jerry doesn't want to be in my team now, who

else could help me?" Escalation to a higher level, bringing in an independent third party when you're at an impasse. In an interview with the *Wall Street Journal*, William Ury said roughly: "Every negotiation takes place within the shadow of your alternative. Your BATNA is probably the major determinant of leverage or power. And yet what I find is we just focus on getting the agreement and we become so dependent on it that we'd give up anything to get it. So a BATNA gives you a sense of freedom – knowing you can just walk away."

Thinking about your BATNA gives you a clear picture of the position you can adopt with respect to the other party during the negotiation. The two sides' BATNAs determine whether you have a position or not. If you go into salary negotiations with a job offer in your pocket and you know that your current employer will have major problems if you quit, then this alters your position. The fact that one party is much bigger than the other does not automatically mean that they have the power. A small party may be vital to a large and powerful one because it possesses something that the large one lacks.

"NEXT TIME YOU WALK AWAY FROM THE TABLE, BE PREPARED TO WALK AWAY FROM THE TABLE"

HARVEY SPECTRE [NETFLIX: SUITS]

Estimate the other's BATNA: what are they going to do if you don't work things out? You then often see that you are better placed than you thought, making you feel less dependent and less uncertain. Awareness of your position and having a BATNA can give you a feeling of freedom and independence. You often see that they are more dependent on you than they are pretending, as you will see by putting yourself in their shoes and looking at their BATNA. Suppose that you don't get an agreement: what are the consequences? Who has the problem? Will the work stop? Can't people get any further? Will time be lost? Are there extra costs? Will they lose ground in the market? Might they lose face? BATNAs are often used as threats, such as (temporarily) stopping the work, or implying that legal steps may be taken, although that may not be realistic and certainly not be desirable. Are you then capable of moving them away from that position? It may just be an expression of emotions that you need to pay attention to (back to Guide 1).

There is another context in which it may also be well worth while to consider the BATNAs: if the playing field is more complex and you could work with several parties and would like to determine which

are best for you, then it's a good idea to list your interests and weigh them up against the various BATNAs. That gives you a verifiable overview of your possible alternatives and helps you choose between the parties.

STRUCTURE AND PROCESS

In practice, I rarely see people giving much consideration to the setup for meetings (structure), or thinking strategically about which steps will help you get a good result (process). If you can build a structure into your discussions, you'll get a better overview and have a greater impact. If you know what steps you want to take in the discussion and when, you will operate more efficiently and more effectively. That will put you in a better position to serve your own interests. Many negotiations involve taking steps both internally in your own organisation and externally. That can be at multiple levels and often involves multiple parties.

I find it intriguing why you see so little attention being paid to this side of negotiations in organisations and partnerships, from senior management down to the lower ranks. I followed this up explicitly for

a while. In key discussions where multiple parties had roles, I asked the principal figure a few questions. What do you want to have achieved by the end of this? How are you going to get there? Which parties have a part to play and what steps are you going to take to make sure your own interests are suitably served?

Many of them found these difficult questions to answer. They were aspects that often hadn't been considered thoroughly enough. Despite the major interests at stake, such discussions often run on autopilot. Key meetings are convened without much preparation. And if attention is paid at all to the preparations, I mostly see that the focus is on the subject matter. Discussions seem often to be regarded as exchanges of information and not as a negotiation challenge in which you want to promote your interests, manage the relationships and create progress. If you don't know where you want to get to, will any old path take you there? As I see it, Guide 7 can help you increase the influence you have on the process.

PREPARE FOR THE PROCESS

look ahead

think back

organise your journey

7 BRING THE GUIDES TOGETHER AND FEEL RESPONSIBLE FOR THE STRUCTURE AND THE PROCESS

If there are items that are important for you, and you want to progress (from A to B) despite increasing complexity, you'll get nowhere without structured discussions and a carefully considered approach to the process. Sometimes you will explicitly have been given the responsibility for leading a discussion or chairing a meeting. And even if that's not your role, you may still feel partly responsible for a process – if you know how it's going to proceed – because you want to act in your own best interests. You can then intervene if you think it's not going the way you want.

I mentioned it before. I see the negotiation process as a journey that you may already have embarked upon. At any rate, you'll always have a number of travelling companions. You've come from somewhere, you may already have had various adventures together, and you've got a destination. You will have to pause regularly for a moment to check everyone's still with you, that you're still on the right track and that you're going to make it to your objective. All kinds of things can happen *en route*: traps, potholes, crossroads, wind in your face, rain or sun. Differences in ideas, tensions in the relationships, new fellow travellers, additional information, perhaps even a dead end…

STRUCTURE & PROCESS

MULTIPLE LOOPS

SINGLE LOOP

B

A

interests

complexity

1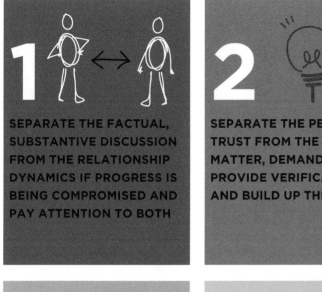

SEPARATE THE FACTUAL, SUBSTANTIVE DISCUSSION FROM THE RELATIONSHIP DYNAMICS IF PROGRESS IS BEING COMPROMISED AND PAY ATTENTION TO BOTH

2

SEPARATE THE PERSONAL TRUST FROM THE SUBJECT MATTER, DEMAND AND PROVIDE VERIFICATION AND BUILD UP THE TRUST

3 W

FOCUS ON THE INTERESTS AND VIEWS THAT PLAY A PART, FOR YOU AND FOR THEM. AVOID ADOPTING POSITIONS AND STANDPOINTS, BUT INCLUDE THEM WHEN NECESSARY

4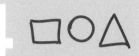

THINK UP VARIOUS OPTIONS FIRST, TOGETHER, AND THEN DECIDE TOGETHER WHICH OPTIONS SERVE THE INTERESTS BEST

5

WHEN SHARING OUT THE BENEFITS AND BURDENS, KEEP IT FAIR AND USE OBJECTIVE CRITERIA TO SUPPORT YOUR VIEW OF FAIRNESS IN THE DECISION-MAKING

6

DEAL? / BATNA

KNOW YOUR BATNA – AND DEVELOP ONE IF NECESSARY – AND BE AWARE OF THEIRS

7

BRING THE GUIDES TOGETHER AND FEEL RESPONSIBLE FOR THE STRUCTURE AND THE PROCESS

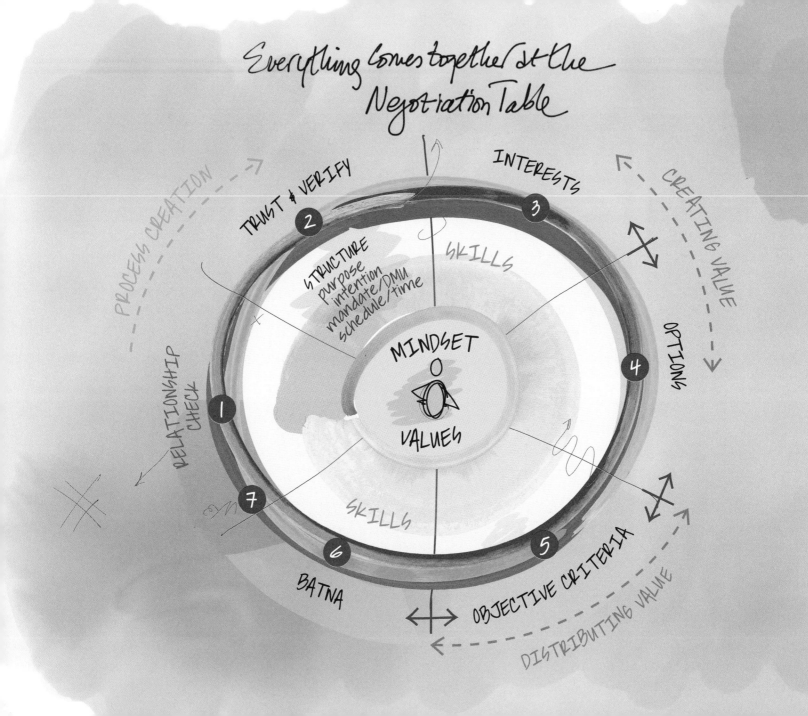

Everything comes together at the
Negotiation Table

PROCESS CREATION

TRUST & VERIFY 2

INTERESTS 3

CREATING VALUE

STRUCTURE
purpose
intention
mandate/DMU
schedule/time

SKILLS

MINDSET

OPTIONS 4

RELATIONSHIP CHECK 1

VALUES

SKILLS

7

6 BATNA

OBJECTIVE CRITERIA 5

DISTRIBUTING VALUE

EVERYTHING COMES TOGETHER AT THE NEGOTIATING TABLE

The guides will help you in the preparations. If you put them in a specific order, they form a guideline that will also give you something to hold on to during the negotiation. The process can be visualised as a circle. A negotiating table – preferably one without sharp corners and edges – that you will be sitting at, together with others. A round table, as a symbol for togetherness, at which you're all on the same side (the one and only side!) even if it doesn't always feel that way. The circular shape also represents the fact that the end of one discussion is often the starting point for the next.

The guides as discussed so far can help steer your preparations. You are aiming to achieve cooperation, decisions or deals that are better than your BATNA. And you have thought about what you want to achieve, what is important for you and for them, who you are going to negotiate with and what the interpersonal relationships are. And about the potential solutions you can already see, where your limits are, what alternatives everyone has, and whether there are specific no-go areas. You have considered whether there are relational aspects that you want to pay attention to specifically. Are there sensitive issues for you or for them that you want to address before the talking starts? This helps you get a picture of exactly what's on the table and who you are dealing with. Does this trigger any particular emotions in you that

THE NEGOTIATION TABLE

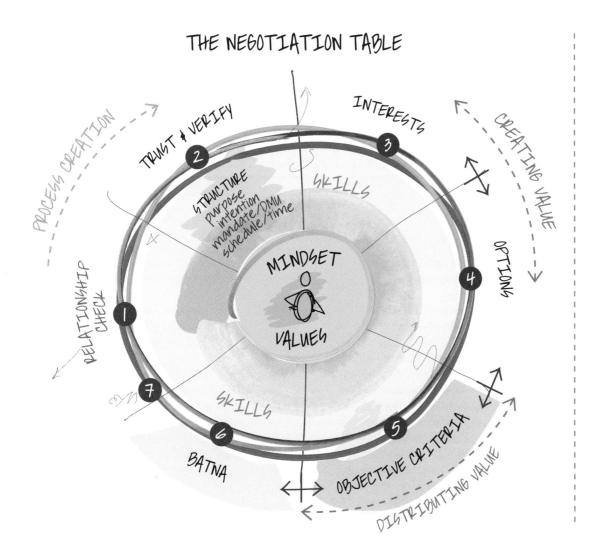

you want to do anything about? Are there people you can't see at the table who should be there? And what do you do if so? Will it be a process with multiple steps? What step will you take first? How are you going to tackle it and what are you working towards? Everything is now going to come together, and the strategy and tactics and process will be important.

You should pay attention to Guides 1 and 2 throughout the entire process. You need to be focused on the substantive content, as well as keeping an eye on the relationship dynamics. At the start of the process, though, you want to consider these two guides *explicitly* because they are also the first steps of the process at the table itself. You use Guides 3, 4 and 5 in order to create good solutions and take the right decisions; the outcome can be checked against your BATNA. Depending on the interests and the complexity of the process, you can run through it in one fell swoop or go round the circle a number of times.

$$E = Q \times A$$

Getting people to go along with you is extremely important if you're trying to manage a process. The formula E = Q x A can help you interpret your actions: the *Effectiveness* of your influence is the product of the *Quality* of the solution you think up multiplied by the level of *Acceptance* you get for it. Being right doesn't mean that everyone will agree with you. You want to go on a joint journey, maintain the bond with the others and get them to buy into the steps you are going to be taking. That's how you keep making progress. Good negotiators can look at things using two different filters: one that highlights the solutions they are attempting to create, and another that picks out the process for gaining acceptance for those solutions. That affects every step you take. You build up trust and commitment step by step. We can now take up our places at the negotiation table.

BUILDING THE RIGHT ATMOSPHERE AND RELATIONSHIP

You like to set a pleasant tone at the start of the discussions. If you don't know each other yet, you make each other's acquaintance and you may perhaps want to pay attention to the relationship. People are often weighing each other up during the initial contacts, looking for a quick answer to the question of whether the other side can be trusted. The familiar ice-breakers and small talk can help you create a sociable atmosphere. Extra bonding can be generated if you focus on the other party and discuss subjects that particularly interest them but are outside the scope of the

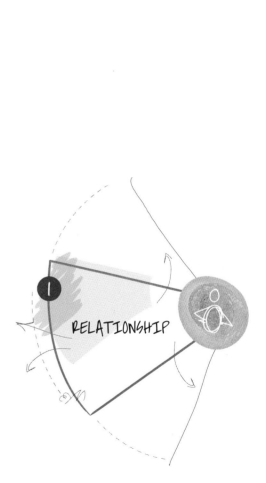

RELATIONSHIP

discussion. It gives you a kind of personal added value. Some discussion partners won't appreciate you going through the motions like that, as they see it, and will want to get straight down to brass tacks. There's nothing wrong with that and the adage remains the same: match pace and lead them forward.

This initial step in the process, in which you want to pay attention to the relationship, can vary in terms of how long it lasts and how intense it is, depending on prior history, subject matter, personalities and cultural aspects. In some cultures you may need several meetings to get to know each other before anyone will talk turkey. Sometimes there will be a brief effort to build the relationship while you enjoy a drink or snack, and then you'll quickly get down to business. If you spend time looking at the people and their preferred styles and culture, you will quickly find clues to how to approach this first phase of the process. A clear view of the metaprogrammes (see page 120) and cultural aspects (see page 159) can also help.

STRUCTURED STEPS AT THE START

After the relationship phase, you'll often notice that the right moment to move on occurs naturally in the discussion. The subject that you are really here about comes to the fore. Why have you met up, what are you going to do, and how are you going to tackle it? Whether it's just a meeting to get to know each other, a preliminary orientation, trouble-shooting, an evaluation or a kick-off meeting, you need to manage expectations properly and make sure you're on the same track. If there's no structure, you won't have an overview and your influence will be less. There are differences between informal discussions and a more formal approach. When important matters are at stake, you want to think in advance about the structural steps in the talks and you should discuss those steps beforehand with those involved. Getting them to buy into the objective and the agenda becomes crucial. During the meeting, you check if the commitment is there and whether anything needs to be expanded upon or adjusted.

Every discussion has a **purpose,** an **agenda** (step-by-step plan) and the **time** factor also plays a part. Depending on the

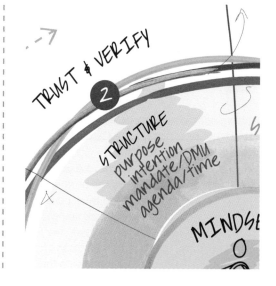

type of discussion, your **intention** (how you want the meeting to go) and the **mandates** (authority to make decisions, both yours and theirs) can be important.

A meeting always has an opening, no matter whether it's the first or second contact or a follow-up. There's what is behind you, the current situation being discussed, and where you want to be headed. Guide 1 was given an explicit task at the start. In your preparations, you check the relationship and you see if that throws up any items that need to be discussed first because they may otherwise inhibit the progress. If the relationship check doesn't come up with anything specific, you can still work on it!

Purpose of the discussion
You should preferably formulate this in rather abstract terms at first, leaving room for manoeuvre in the discussion. You should check that everyone is buying into the objectives of the discussion:

- "It's great that we can talk to each other today. As was stated earlier, the idea is that we want to spend today looking at what we may be able to do for you. Is that also how you see it?"

- "We've met up today to explore as many options as possible that will help us decide what form our cooperation is going to take. Are we on the same track here?"
- "We're at the table today to find a solution for problem X. Is that also what you're expecting from this meeting?"
- "I'm glad that we're able to talk about the new pricing agreements today."
- "There are still quite a lot of loose ends and we've convened today in order to see if we can tie them up. I think we'll need two hours for this meeting and I wonder whether this is still feasible for you?"

Intention
It may be sensible to state how you intend to proceed, the way in which you want to negotiate. You may for instance want the discussions to be open, constructive or productive. "As for me, I'm going to do my best to see if we can resolve this together. Same goes for you?" Or "I'm aware that this is going to need us to be pretty creative, but I'm more than ready to give it a shot. What about you?" Some people are more willing to state their intentions if it's

going to be a tough discussion. It creates a bit of breathing space and sets the tone. Making your intended approach clear also lets you see what the other's attitude is, giving you a sense of whether they're with you or against you. If there isn't much progress, it may be relevant to return to the intentions during the process itself to check up on them: "Mr Scott, I can feel that coming up with a solution together is going to be tricky and I'm wondering whether your side actually wants to continue." Depending on the cultural context, you may need to be somewhat less direct. For more details, please refer to 'Dealing with different cultures' (page 159) and 'Process interventions' (page 106).

Agenda
The agenda is the step-by-step plan for the meeting. Depending on the type of discussion, things will always progress in some specific order. "Gentlemen, we've spoken to each other on the phone and agreed that we'd take a look today to see what we can do for one another. What I'd propose would be to start by taking a look at what the key topics are that we should be focusing on [Guide 2 – often already agreed by this stage]. Then I'd like to discuss what is important for both of us in

that regard, and what preconditions there are [Guide 3], and take a look at how that might be done in practice [Guide 4] and under what conditions [Guide 5]. Is that okay for you?" Variants on Guides 3, 4 and 5 guides can also often provide input for your process agenda.

The advantage of having an agenda set out is that the structure is clear from the start for everyone. Then you are able to intervene in the process if people are long-winded or tend to get side-tracked, or if you're both getting a bit disoriented. "An interesting point. But just to make certain we'll have addressed everything by five o'clock, I'd like to ask whether we could get back to our agenda. We can perhaps come back to your comment later if that's okay with you."
Discussions to determine the agenda can be complex and can take a lot of time in their own right –this is sometimes a negotiation in itself.
The person responsible for the process or project often is also in the lead for the agenda setting. If that's the case and your items are not being covered, you have to get them included.

Time
How long do you think it's going to take? Before the meeting starts, you may want to check the time available and the time needed for the meeting. At the start of the meeting, you may want to check it again. It's possible that less time may be available than is needed and you'll have to act: change the agenda, or perhaps reschedule.

Mandate
Are the people present at the table today able to take decisions, or are others needed too? Who plays a role in the decision-making and how do these actors reach their decisions? This authority to take decisions is often referred to as a 'mandate'. If the discussions are to progress efficiently, it is important to know whether the meeting is able to take decisions about the objectives. You often only discover at the end of a discussion that the right people aren't present, or that the discussions will have to be repeated later with others. That's not helpful for the process and neither is it tactically astute. You may already have made commitments because you thought that you *were* able to make the decisions together. In this context, you also need to think carefully about your

own mandate. Your internal negotiations to determine the limits you are operating within and agree how far you are allowed to go are important aspects. In short, you need to have discussed your own mandate internally before you get to the negotiating table. Think about your tactics and strategy, and always ask as early as possible in a discussion who needs to be involved in the decision-making process so that you can adjust your strategy and tactics accordingly. At the table you would like to check whether the players needed are there. If not so, you could change plans. For more information, please refer to 'Multi-level and multi-party aspects' (page 91).

EXTRA ATTENTION TO THE RELATIONSHIP

It is important to be aware of the quality of your relationships whenever you are working with others (and therefore negotiating in some way). If the quality of your relationship is perceived to be good, the substantive aspects will go more smoothly too. You are then building up a bit of credit that will allow the relationship to take the occasional knock. If you get to know 'them' better and there is an open, respectful understanding in which topics can be discussed – even if things are complicated – then you're on the right track. Conversely, if the relationship is tense and there are conflicts, then you should pay special attention to the relationship.

Building and maintaining relationships

What do you think of the quality of the relationships that you have with the people you work with? Do you know each other superficially or is it more than that? What do you know about each other? When you get to know different facets of each other, under different circumstances, your relationship becomes stronger. It often doesn't take much effort and the rewards can be substantial.

There seems to be a tendency these days to neglect mutual relationships. It is also apparently an awkward subject, because the idea has arisen in many cultures that relationships that are too close are in fact not good for business contacts. It can prevent you from being as sharp and tough as you could, which in turn could affect the commercial results. Business relationships that are too cosy could encourage dishonest practices.

Quite aside from these situations in which the boundaries become blurred, there is less and less time in normal human interactions for keeping up relationships, or at any rate you don't allow yourself enough time. Sometimes others will keep you at a distance, because they don't value a close relationship much. On other occasions, there may be an explicit underlying tactic and someone may remain remote as part of a game. Asses the internal and external relationships with the key actors around you. Are they concerned about the relationship with you? If so, what do they value? Are you able to estimate the quality of your relationship and assess whether you want to reinforce it? You could in fact discuss this with your key contacts as a way of assessing the quality of these relationships. A good question to ask is what they think of how the relationship could be built up further and what could be done better or differently. How can we make sure that the good understanding we have with one another is maintained and what do we need to do to keep it that way? Make agreements with each other about what you want to do to strengthen the relationship and how often you want to meet up. Working on the relationship means that both sides are investing in trust and confidence.

Tensions in relationships

If you have a serious difference of opinion, or even a conflict, it may be important to consider the dynamic of the relationship first before tackling the situation. Conflicts often arise because you have built up differing expectations and perceptions of each other and the situation, triggering emotional reactions in both directions. In order to find the starting point for working towards a solution, it may be a good idea to bring that 'undercurrent' out into the open – very carefully and with due attention to cultural differences. Might discussing the relationship help (expectations, perceptions, emotions)? Is it normal in the culture you are dealing with to be open and direct about such things or not? Will it be constructive in terms of progress? Sometimes you may think this isn't the right time for it. If you value the harmony, you may find it tricky to talk about tensions in a relationship. You may have a tendency to avoid such discussions. Whether or not to bring such things out into the open can be quite a dilemma, because tensions in relationships don't just disappear and there'll be no fertile ground for the substantive talks if the air isn't cleared.

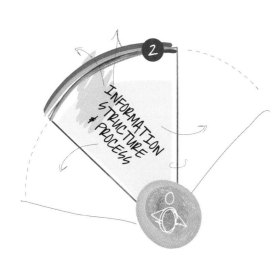

Once people have got that off their chest, assuming there is still any will to proceed, you can move step by step towards a solution in which you then proceed through process stages 3, 4 and 5. After tackling these highly charged items, you can then work further on a solution and make decisions. It may also help – particularly in cultures where such items cannot be discussed explicitly – to take a time-out and let the great healer Father Time do his work. Sometimes it can in fact be wise to skirt around sensitive areas and look to see if there are other ways of making progress constructively. Bringing things into the open for discussion is not an objective *per se* – it's merely a tool, when appropriate. The issues may sometimes be too painful or too sensitive and you will then in fact achieve progress by respectfully circumventing complicated and emotionally charged issues.

EXTRA ATTENTION TO THE STRUCTURE AND PROCESS

Before you tackle more complex processes, explicitly paying attention to the process itself before continuing is a smart move. The preparation for a negotiation process can be quite complex. Subjects to think about and discuss then are:

- The **objective**: what are the aims? What do we want to achieve and when?
- What **information** will we use? Do we all have the same information and do we have the same picture of the information? Or do we want to make agreements about how we are jointly going to get the right information and the same understanding of that information?
- **Intentions**: what are the parties' attitudes? Are the actors ready to proceed and is there a will to invest the time that will be needed? Do the parties also perceive their own responsibility in the process?
- **People and parties involved**: who will be taking part? Are there people or parties we've forgotten?
- What about the **mandates**? Who is involved in the decision-making? How are we going to make decisions and what criteria will we use?
- **Location**: where are the meetings taking place?
- **Time**: what is the timeline? How often will the meetings be held? When do we want to be finished?
- **Process**: how do the various parties want to tackle it? What steps are we going to

take and with whom? Who should lead (or be asked to lead) the process? How will we handle the planning? How do we know if it was a success and how can we measure that? How will we deal with disruptions of the process, such as disputes, schedule overruns or unforeseen circumstances?
- **Communications**: how will we communicate? When, how often, where and with whom?

When negotiations involve multiple parties and people this phase can be a negotiation in its own right.

THE CORE OF THE NEGOTIATION

By paying attention to the relationship and putting a suitable structure in place, you are attempting to maximise the likelihood of **trust and progress** in the discussion itself. After all, commitment was created at the start of the discussion for the path that you are going to be taking together. The heart of the negotiation is provided by Guides 3, 4 and 5. And there is a sequence to this as well. No matter whether you're holding early talks in the process or have

already progressed further, you want to keep an eye on this sequence. It can of course be the case that the other side don't want to follow you, or that they want to turn the discussions into a distribution issue straight away. You may then have to go with the flow. Sometimes you take a step or two forwards, sometimes you go into reverse. But you can only start come up with the plays to make the difficult yards if you know where you are heading.

The whole cycle may be traversed in a single discussion. There's every chance that you'll end up doing laps of various circuits with different people. It may also be a good idea to hold specific discussions that are explicitly focused on adding depth or deepening the conversation. They could for instance be about the interests at stake, in order to learn more about the context and content. After all, you want to get a clear picture of as many of the interests of the various players as possible. That creates scope for solutions later on and you may be able to make the deal sweeter.

Sometimes you may have a separate discussion about exploring possible options and whether you can find a win-win solution. You may also hold separate

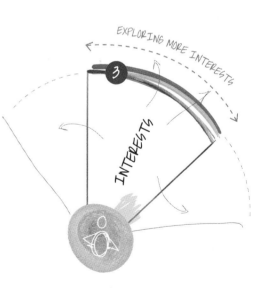

discussions about the distribution of the costs and benefits. That focuses attention on the consequences of the various options: who takes what and who gets what? Who does what and when? You may need several rounds of talks for that as well.

These individual discussions each have their own opening and agenda steps as described earlier. I've already explained what guides 3, 4 and 5 are about, but being able to utilise them in the process is a pig with a different snout altogether. I'm paying extra attention to those steps here, and we'll be progressing to the master stage in 'Next level up' (page 101).

Exploring the interests

Is there enough openness to talk about the interests? Do you want to be open about your own interests and do you know just how far you dare go? Is it clear to you what's negotiable and what isn't? Everyone sitting at the table will be asking these questions. And everyone is entitled to have their own hidden agendas. Sometimes you keep you cards close to your chest because you don't want to have everything out in the open, or aren't in a position to do so. At any rate, you need a certain degree of openness if you're to find solutions together. You may find that openness won't be there spontaneously and you have to accumulate trust step by step in order to get it.

If you focus on the other party's interests first, greater openness may result. Pausing to reflect on this lets you discover what shared interests there may be, what the party-specific elements are and where you can see conflicting interests. Perceiving the shared interests can generate so much commitment and involvement that it's particularly important to consider them. If you can discover what you've got in common, you'll find it easier to move forward together and the share-out later will be easier too.

If the interests are not made explicit, they will often not become part of a solution; you could therefore say that keeping your cards too close to your chest is shooting yourself in the foot. It's surely fine to let the other side know that you want to do business? You should be happy to get aspects that are important for you out into the open so that they can be included in the search for a solution. Then you can tackle the ways in which the cooperation can be implemented and the conditions met. You also weigh up whether the final result will have served your interests sufficiently well.

Not making clear what your own interests are can also have other consequences. You may end up with a deal that is not right for you. When the pressure is on, you may say yes to a solution or decision that twenty-twenty hindsight reveals harmed your interests. Naturally, the openness that you ought to be trying for is sometimes restricted by your own boundaries, or there may be issues of trust, or there may be obstacles in the form of procedures or cultural customs. Don't go looking for something that will never appear or cannot be given. In such cases, try to think 'around' the issue and invent a way of coping with it.

What skills do you need for getting the most out of this step in the process?
Asking questions: this is a way of exploring the value zone and finding out what the business interests are (and perhaps even the personal ones). You will also be able to separate out the short-term and long-term interests and you'll get a feel as well for the context in which those interests apply. If you listen carefully, ask questions and keep zooming in, you will create a positive atmosphere, deepen the relationship and you'll get as many of the interests as possible out into the open. There are several questions you should always be

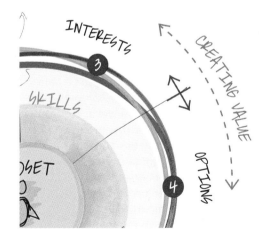

ready to ask the other party. What matters to them? What do they want to achieve here? What preconditions are important for them? What objectives are they aiming to achieve? If you are to find a solution, what are the preconditions you've got to take on board? What's essential for them, in the shorter and longer term?

If you hear them mentioning personal interests, you're getting to the heart of the matter. These are sometimes also called the **core interests**. You can get to those core interests by asking questions that require a personal touch in the answer. "I understand that it's important for us to find a solution together. What would it mean to you if we succeed?" You create extra bonding and uncover information that may be important later when coming up with the solutions. "I can see that it's essential for you that we pay attention to X. Why is that so important for you?" Or "Suppose that we're able to find a solution for this. What would that achieve for you?" In practice you need to have earned the right to ask questions like that. If the trust is there, you can become more personal and ask a lot more. Sometimes you will notice from the response – verbal or otherwise – that you're overdoing it and the connec-

tion has gone. Cultural aspects also play a role in determining whether these kinds of questions are acceptable.

Linking the interests: discuss the shared interests and add your own to the list. "I understand that A, B and C are important to you. I'm pleased to see that we both value C. At the same time, my side think that paying attention to D is also relevant." This lets you create the feeling that you're in it together and you are also asking for attention to be paid to your own interests. The key thing is that as many interests as possible are laid out on the table and become connected so you can work on a 'we're in this together' joint option exploring later on.

Setting priorities: "If I understand you correctly, it comes down to A, B and C for you. Which of those three is most critical for you, and why?" You want to know which interest weighs most heavily. Interests have an intrinsic hierarchy and priorities will therefore play a part. Sometimes another essential interest pops up.

Listening: you can listen actively if you have a mix of skills under your belt such as empathising, encouraging the other party, asking questions, summarising and probing more deeply. Being able to listen without preconceptions is an art and a skill. Listening to what people are saying and how they are communicating can yield a great deal, in terms of both the content and the relationship. Listening properly lets you understand the other party's context and situation better, and they may in turn feel that you understand them. People taking my courses often say that they would like to learn to listen better. It's an interesting question, because anyone (without a hearing impairment) is capable of listening. Why are there times that you don't listen properly? What is preventing you? Have you already thought up an answer or the solution, so that you're no longer paying attention to the other party? Are you in a hurry, or doesn't it interest you, or are you too busy with other things? Are you primarily just hearing what you want to hear, or are you able to listen to the other without preconceptions, even if you have different opinions? Please refer also to your 'Inner game' (page 187) and 'Biases' (page 150).

Zooming in: where necessary or desirable, you can ask further questions. There may be elements that are unclear, where you have misunderstood each other. Keep on asking for specific details if you believe it is necessary and add legitimacy to your questions by explaining why they're being asked, for instance by saying, "I'd like to ask a couple more questions to get a better picture of your situation, so we can be of more help for you later on. Is that all right?" That lets you avoid it turning into a cross-examination.

Empathising: understanding, responding to the other personally and making a bond with them is an essential skill – not only tuning in to *what* someone is saying but also with the *way* it's being said. Extra attention is paid to this in 'Pacing and leading' (page 146) and 'Metaprogrammes' (page 120). If you are interested in the other party and pay them attention, matching pace with them like this will occur almost spontaneously. Without that connection, the personal and underlying interests will remain hidden, and without the bonding there is also less trust. Don't go too quickly: feel what they want and work on the relationship. This creates a certain kind of intimacy and the other will feel safe and comfortable talking to you.

Summarising: "That's interesting. I can see that A, B and C are major precondi-tions for you." It shows that you've understood the other side; that's one function of the summary. You're checking that you understand one another. At the same time, summarising also has a function within the process. Summaries let you manage the process by taking small steps in the process. After summarising, you can check if these were all the interests and whether anything has been overlooked or needs to be added. "Are there other conditions as well as A, B and C that we ought to be including?" It's a way of creating legitimacy for what's been achieved so far.

Exploring options together
The purpose of this stage is primarily an 'enrichment process' based on the interests that have now become clear. The aim is to explore as many options as possible that could result in win-win solutions. Those are always worth investigating. Compare it to that pie again: a variety of ingredients are needed to make a tasty pie. Together, you may also be able to make the pie bigger before getting down to how it will be sliced up, creating added value together on top of what you thought at first.
A useful tool in this context is the **creative question**, one that triggers the creative process. Questions like these are par-

ticularly effective if you are able to link party-specific interests. At first sight, these interests sometimes seem contradictory, but when examined at a higher level of abstraction the apparent contradictions turn out to be party-specific interests. Examples are situations where someone is putting pressure on your rates because they want to reduce their own overall costs, while you do not want to lower them because it would endanger your margin (and thereby also your continuity and level of service). That might seem to be an incompatibility if the discussion is only about rates, but moving the topics up to a higher level of abstraction can create room for manoeuvre. Ask questions such as, "What could we consider that might reduce your costs without hurting our margin?"

This type of question encourages you to look at the other side's interests in greater depth. It creates an atmosphere of shared responsibility for the negotiation issues and their solutions, and it presents an intriguing challenge. The question encourages the enrichment process. The creative process that this engenders will enhance the enthusiasm, commitment and mutual trust. It would naturally be nice if you were

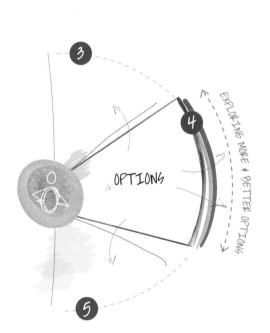

OPTIONS

EXPLORING MORE & BETTER OPTIONS

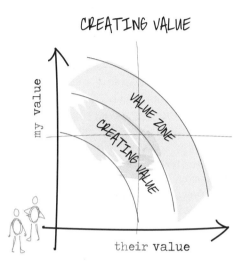

CREATING VALUE

my value

their value

VALUE ZONE

CREATING VALUE

able to add value that goes beyond the obvious solutions. You want to enlarge the value zone.

- **You can do this by thinking up options, assessing them and then deciding together which of the options serve the interests best.** There is a sequence to it. Don't take decisions right away, because the dice are then cast and there's no scope any more. It is possible that not everything that you think up together will be feasible, so you have to keep making careful evaluations of what you will and will not take any further. First think up an option, then weigh it up and assess it, then use the overall picture to decide what conditions you want to attach to it. And that is the next step in the process, because that's where the share-out comes in.

- **You can help each other even more** if you can think up options that cost you little or nothing but yield a great deal for them, or vice versa. This may let you create more attractive options than expected and more wide-ranging solutions than originally estimated. If you do something for them that can be valuable for them, it can draw the sting nicely. A sign of goodwill. A lot can often be thought up that costs relatively little for one side but is valuable for the other. Helping think things through, assisting them a little bit more, bringing them into contact with a third party who may be interesting for them. It can improve the bond and encourage the sense of togetherness. Take a moment to consider the possibilities for extending the deal and making it that bit sweeter. If you want to create added value, you will have to go looking for it.

Sometimes you may lose track for a moment. "I'm aware that X is important for you. But I've lost the thread a bit – how does solution Y fit in with that?" You're looking for congruence between steps 3 and 4, and if you can't find it, you're perfectly entitled to say so. You are then working to link the interests and the options. It may sometimes not be possible to generate options together, for example because you have to submit a proposal or because specific procedures have been agreed. There's no scope at that particular point, but the discussion will undoubtedly resurface. In some situations the other party may not want to cooperate in thinking up options together. They may then expect that to come from you: "You're the specialist here." In any event, you can then look to see if it will help if you point out where looking for options together will yield more than doing so alone. But there may also be other possibilities for winkling someone out of that kind of position. For more on this, please refer to 'Process interventions' (page 106) and 'Coping when games are being played' (page 163).

Distribution issues and the endgame

Determining the conditions under which you can reach an overall agreement is a major challenge. The costs and benefits must be shared out. I described the essence of Guide 5 earlier. One of the keywords is fairness – a nebulous concept yet nevertheless one that people cannot circumvent easily. A word with impact, because nobody wants to be unfair or unreasonable. People still try it on all the same, of course, and all kinds of games are often played during the share-out, principally to gain a better share of the benefits and pass the burdens on to the other side.

In more complex deals, all kinds of items may need to be shared out, and you will see that you first need the right information (Guide 2) before apportioning the goodies (Guide 5).

- Who does what exactly and when? John or Pauline? Who can we entrust with the job and how can we make that decision? Based on suitability, time, commitment or motivation? You are often not aware of it, but you are also looking for criteria here that you can use to underpin your choice. And if things are going as they should, you interests will play a major part. What exactly is at stake here? Because you naturally want to prioritise the things that matter most.

- People will be putting a lot of time into getting the job done. Will we accept an estimate of a thousand hours, or only eight hundred? What is that estimate based on? Is there any previous experience that can give verifiable information to let us assess the situation properly? What assumptions are our baseline for making the decision?
- A rate has to be agreed. You're expecting it to be between one hundred and a hundred and fifty euros an hour. What will it be? What is fair here? Are you going to check that it is in line with the market? Have similar services been purchased before and what were the rates then? What will we get for our hundred or hundred and fifty euros? Are the situations similar or are we comparing apples with oranges? Do we want the very best for the lowest rate? What criteria are we now going to use for making a decision? Is someone going to make a power play, or can a solution be found by working from a fair baseline?
- Risks have to be taken. But what risks, exactly? What price tag can be put on

them? Who'll be taking them, and what criteria will be used for sharing them out?
- There may be additional revenues. What might they be? How will we calculate them? How will they be apportioned – who gets what and why?

During a discussion, you will progress through stages 3, 4 and 5. The distribution stage is a derivative of the earlier steps. Sometimes you take a step or two forwards, sometimes it's backwards. If you know what you're doing, it's not too difficult to make the connections between the various steps. "I heard you saying that you think it's important that X gets done. We're the only ones who can do it for you that way. So as far as I'm concerned, it's not fair to expect us to make that effort and undercut Y's rate as well."
If somebody seems to want to have their cake and eat it, that's a good occasion for the following remark: "If you want us to take these costs on board, then we can only do so if we can implement the solution we suggested. Otherwise it simply doesn't work for us." You're pointing out that they can't have everything without paying fairly. If there's something you find important, there will be solutions that are

appropriate and others that don't work for you. In the endgame, it is important that you are able to refer back within the process to the interests and the options again. And indeed, the alternatives that the two sides have available may make or break it. They affect whether or not it is fair that you sometimes have to say yes to a deal that isn't as good for you as you would have liked.

After going through the third, fourth and fifth steps in the process, you may have an agreement or a deal. The conditions for implementing that cooperation or deal are satisfactory. You record the agreements, check that the parties can both accept the conditions as worded, and you then make verifiable agreements about the follow-on steps. Sometimes the party is not over yet...

The BATNA as the endgame approaches

The endgame often involves making concessions that you do not actually feel are fair. You're pleased that you've reached the finishing line and you're almost there. Maybe you feel you've done enough talking, or you don't want to be the party-pooper, so you agree. Perhaps you've been

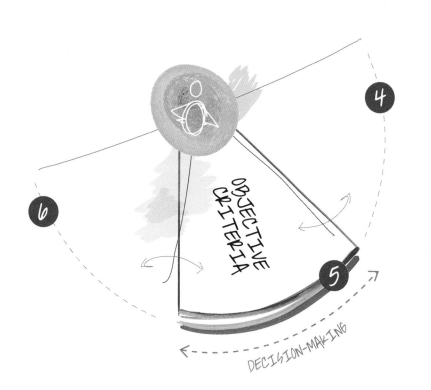

put under additional pressure. The other party may (once again) be looking to test your limits and see whether you'll resist, evade or give ground. I often hear afterwards that too much is then given away at the end: discounts (money), attention (time), extras (higher quality, for example). You can often think up good reasons why this was the right way to do it. That's how many deals are justified: "It was better for the friendship, the continuity of the relationship and the good atmosphere." "You have to let the others make some gains too." Or a favourite: "I see it as an investment that's bound to be repaid later." Stay alert about the principle of fairness and weigh things up against both BATNAs.

I'd like to use the following example to explain about the endgame, the final phase of a discussion. You'll have various options then, which I'll go through step by step. First of all, you have to summarise the ingredients of the potential agreement, using Guides 3, 4 and 5: "If we just hold on and tread water for a moment, I'll list all the points once again. We discussed that it's important for you to reach A and B. B is important for us as well, and we also value C and D. So far, we've agreed to do 1, 2 and 3 [the implementation]. We've agreed on that and we're all enthusiastic about it. As for the conditions: we're thinking the same way on a number of elements, but there's one point that's still open for discussion. We've agreed that we'll spend two hundred hours on it, at a rate of a hundred euros, which will be fine for letting us achieve 1, 2 and 3. We've also agreed that you'll be making an extra investment of Y. What we haven't yet agreed on is the extra investment of Z. You're expecting us to foot the bill for that investment. Have I understood that correctly?"

If you want to be agile and flexible in the endgame, you have a number of possibilities:

- Suppose that you're not satisfied with the deal that's on the table. You feel that you're having to do too much and not getting enough in return. Simply put, you don't think that the costs and benefits are being shared out fairly. Maybe some kind of **swap** is still possible. You may be prepared to accept that investment if they can do something else for you. Maybe you can extend the term of the contract? That might put the deal in the context of a greater whole, making it attractive after all. In the swap, it is important to explore extra opportunities

that don't cost you much but can be very useful for the other side. This cuts both ways: ask for things that could be relevant for you and that cost them little or nothing. If someone is able to introduce you to another contact, that requires very little effort on their part and can be very valuable to you. Sometimes you can make the deal a bit broader and then find possibilities for resolving things together. Think about what you need and what they might need in order to reach an agreement. It is then important that you do so explicitly: "What we need if a deal is to be reached is..." Or the other way round: "What do you need if we're to reach a deal?" Answers that you might get are for instance: "This is unfortunately beyond our budget, but perhaps the investment can be split over two years." "We'll have to think up some extra arguments that will also be acceptable for my manager." Or "We have other priorities at the moment, but if we can get it on the agenda now for the *next* meeting, we'll have a better chance." Keep looking for the scope for a solution, without giving too much away that will cause trouble later.

- Sometimes there's no way round it: you have to **make concessions**. This means

that the deal is too important to let it slip through your fingers, and your BATNA isn't attractive enough. If you have to make concessions, be sure you make clear it's a one-off and that the fact has been noted. "In this specific case, we've accepted Z." You don't want to be setting a precedent for the next time. Otherwise you can expect comments such as, "You agreed to it last time. Why not now?" Concessions are often made because customers state that they really can't pay any more, 'given the current poor market conditions'. Pressure is exerted on the relationship in order to squeeze more out of the deal. You can of course help the other party when times are hard, but at the same time there is the question of whether games are being played. Is the current impasse genuinely the result of poor economic conditions, or is that just an excuse for trying their luck? And if you do decide to play ball, you will want to be able to profit from it in due course when the client does have more financial wiggle room; make clear agreements about this, because what you give them can't be taken back after the event. And be aware of the fact that this kind of concession can affect other relationships in your market if others get to know about what was 'given away' to your customer.

- It is possible that a gap will remain between what is desirable and what seems achievable, creating a **deadlock** at the end of the process with nobody daring or wanting to move. So the big question then is who blinks first. Maybe you don't see a way out either. But have you become trapped because of your own stubbornness? After all, there are undoubtedly all kinds of substantive arguments for your position and you reckon that the other side should make the first move. Don't make it too difficult for yourself. You may be able to think of a way out. Are you prepared to share the pain? Is there a possible trade-off some-where after all? If the interests at stake are substantial, you can ask **someone else** such as a colleague to help you. You can also **escalate** it 'upstairs'. This can ruin your negotiating position, but it may sometimes be necessary. It means you can't resolve it yourself and you've passed it on to the next level up. If you make this suggestion, it often prompts renewed efforts to find a solution together first after all.
- You can also say you'll **'take home'** the proposal for consideration, or call a

'**time-out**'. Give a summary of progress to date and say that you haven't decided and need to think about it. You've almost got your deal, but not entirely. You have agreed that there's a specific part you haven't agreed on yet. Do state why that issue hasn't been resolved yet, or you may leave the table with unjustified expectations. And say that you will come back with a proposal that your side will be able to say yes to. A final, best offer. In principle, this is a positional step in the endgame and no longer open for negotiation.

- At the end of the process, stating your BATNA may be a way of getting things moving again. "We've still got one point of discussion here that we haven't been able to resolve together yet. I can see that neither side has been able to move on this one, and we've both got our rea-sons for that. That leaves us no alterna-tive other than using our resources and our people on a different project." If you state your BATNA, you are hoping this will make the other side keep negotiating with you after all.
- If the interests are significant enough and you can't resolve it yourself, it is possible to consider bringing in an **independent third party** who can be

asked to give a judgement. Mediation in conflicts could be one example. There are cases where **mediation** is desirable, for instance when the relationship is under pressure or has perhaps become severely damaged. The parties will often suggest this themselves, or it may be recommended by the judge if it goes as far as a court case. An independent third party, mediation or the courts: examples of BATNAs that can be deployed as objective criteria that can help shift people from a position with conflicting interests.

There are a lot of games that may be played at the end. A wide range of **process-related tricks** can be pulled out of the hat: the time factor can be deployed, slowing the process down; somebody wants a deal and increases the pressure when you're on the home straight; they ask for more time; they don't respond to your proposal, or they ask for extra concessions at the last minute. There are **content-related tricks** as well, of course: things are requested or put aside and become part of a sophisticated game of exchanges, with-out you realising that you're giving away more than you should. Or the **relationship** itself may become a pawn: "Oh, don't be so awkward – we're almost there. You can surely say yes to that?"

"If you can't agree to this now, we're going to pull the plug."

Or "I'm not going to get any further with you. Where's your boss?"

I'll be listing all these for you and giving some ways of approaching them in the section about the 'Games people play' (on page 163).

MULTI-LEVEL AND MULTI-PARTY ASPECTS

Depending on your role in an organisation or network, you will end up to a greater or lesser extent in negotiations that involve multiple parties and where you have to negotiate within the organisations at different levels. There are often multiple interested parties – stakeholders – and others who are directly involved, for example in cooperation in integrated teams, consortiums, complex projects, networks and co-creation. It is becoming increasingly common to cooperate in fluid groups with changing partners and roles.

When multiple parties and multiple people have roles in the process, it is obviously going to make things more complex. Numerous interests are often involved, there are lots of possible approaches to solutions some of the parties are going to find acceptable, and the distribution issues become more complicated too. There is also a group dynamic to it, as people in a group may end up hindering each other, deliberately or otherwise. Who are you going to sit around the table with, when, and in what groupings? If you want to progress towards a good deal, you'll need to stop and consider what steps will help you on the way most. You may end up playing several games of chess all at the same time. Which makes it particularly sensible to think about how to approach it. Think about your ultimate objective and the route to it. Use the seven guides as a source of inspiration for achieving your goal.

When I'm asked to help with the final evaluation of complex projects, it often turns out that parties and actors have been overlooked who played an important role during the preparations or in the decision-making. As a result, essential interests are often not brought to the fore and processes stagnate, resulting in planning problems, quality issues, irritation, lack of trust and all too often legal problems. That section could be a book in its own right, but in this book I'm going to be content with just a few examples.

Some practical situations

In a bidding process, a contractor received a large order for changing a traffic situation. A tunnel under a railway, new roundabouts, cycle paths, paving, roads and lighting. Everything seemed to be clear and the work was started. As they progressed, it became clear that the interests of a number of stakeholders had been overlooked. Residents who complained about traffic congestion during the roadworks and an environmental group that felt their voice hadn't been heard. Various procedures also seemed to have been neglected. The process became mired down, irritations arose about several aspects and the trust between the two sides was damaged. The project struggled with serious cost overruns and eventually the parties went to court.

In another case, discussions had been going on for months but it only became clear towards the end that someone had been overlooked. A director of a neighbouring department, who had no decision-making power but definitely had an opinion, wanted to be involved in the

MULTI-LEVEL, MULTI-PARTY

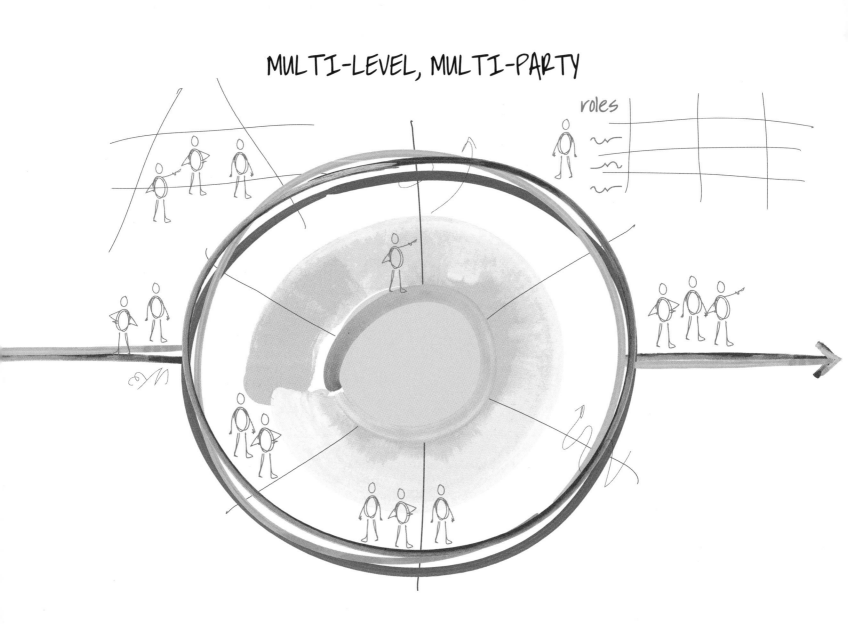

process and threw a spanner in the works. He *did* turn out to have a key position in the decision-making process, in practice. The process stagnated and a lot of extra time and effort was needed to get it back on track. There are many variants on this case. Here, it suddenly became clear that another person had a role. There are occasions when someone is kept out of the process on purpose and then used like an ace up the sleeve to add additional pressure.

A councillor adopted a different agenda around election time, changing his priorities and postponing decisions, which resulted in delays. This was clear enough beforehand, but the issue wasn't spotted. The subcontractor did a lot of work that turned out to be pointless. Other steps could have been taken, but it was too late for that by then. In this case, a simple question at the start had been overlooked: who plays a role in the decision-making process and what steps does that process require?

You can get better results if you're more aware of the context, the playing field and the decision-making process. You often have to negotiate internally and externally at different levels, often with multiple parties involved. There are times when you want to make a proposal but have to deal with multiple parties and stakeholders to reach an agreement. Another time, you may face a situation where you want to make a joint proposal to a client with multiple other parties. And in yet another situation, you may for instance want to set up a partnership to market new ideas together. In short, in complex situations where multiple actors are playing a role, you should stop and think before starting negotiations.

The decision-making process in multi-level and multi-party situations

When negotiating between organisations at different hierarchical levels, it is customary to create horizontal lines of contact between the parties and take the differences in the hierarchies into account, if applicable. Depending on your role, you'll need internal coordination about what lines of contact are needed and who should be in contact with whom. You'll need to coordinate mandates internally and discuss strategy and tactics.

In addition, it's important to have a good overview of the playing field. To help achieve that, you can identify the internal and external decision-making units (DMUs). A DMU is the system comprising the individuals who play a part in the decision-making process. You're more like to serve your own interests and get your ideas considered if you analyse

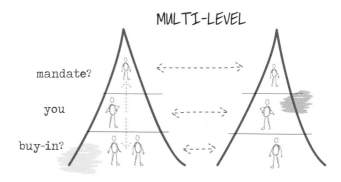

MULTI-LEVEL

mandate?

you

buy-in?

DECISION-MAKING UNIT

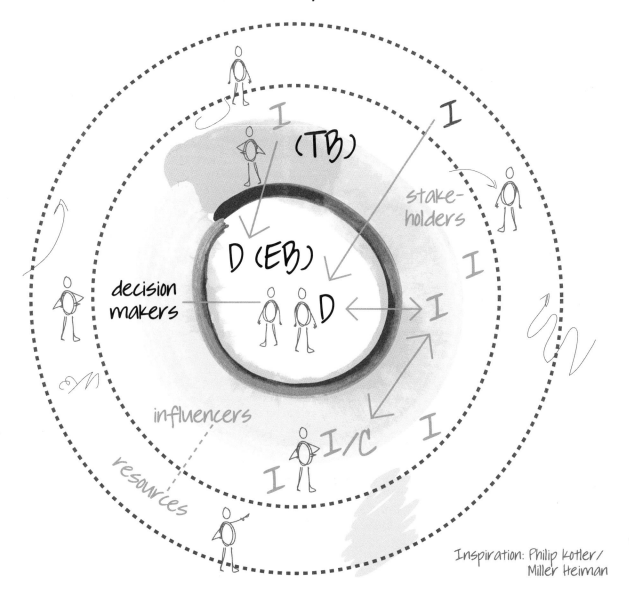

Inspiration: Philip Kotler / Miller Heiman

this system and base your strategy and tactics on the outcome. Taking a moment to reflect on the cultural dynamics is also particularly relevant. Specific customs and cultural aspects can come into play precisely in the way people make decisions. You can read more about that last point under 'Dealing with cultural differences' (page 159).

For identifying the DMU, I use a model based on work by Philip Kotler and Miller Heiman. I've modified the toolset slightly.

A number of roles are defined in the decision-making process:

- the person who primarily monitors the financial interests, such as a buyer or owner or financial director. They are also referred to as the economic buyer (EB)
- the person who is primarily concerned about substantive issues – specifications such as technical quality, reliability, durability and credibility of the solution. This could for instance be a head of innovation, head of technical services or quality manager: this is the technical buyer (TB). The role can also be fulfilled by the consumers of products or services (often listed separately in the analysis).

- the coach (C) is someone who is on your side. Your relationship with them is good and there is mutual trust. You can ask them questions that are awkward to put to others, for instance about the decision-making process.
- the gatekeeper (G) is someone who could keep the door closed.

In addition to the roles described above, these people can also be decision-makers (D) or influencers (I). The roles overlap: an economic buyer can also be a decision-maker or influencer, and could also be your coach at the same time. Stakeholders are important influencers in the process. Based on an analysis like this, you can plan what you want to discuss with whom and in what order.

The ways in which people reach decisions can vary. Cultural differences can come into play too. There may be a consultative form of decision making, with one or more decision-makers consulting others and then making a decision based on the information given. Decisions can also be based on a consensus: the DMU members discuss it until they agree, and a decision can then be taken that everyone supports. Or the process can have a more authoritarian structure, with the leader making

the decision alone and not listening to others. In practice it can all be a lot more nuanced. Everyone draws inspiration from somewhere, so even the last method of decision-making can probably be influenced in some way.

Back to the guides. The seven guides help you prepare; in multi-level and multi-party processes, you will want to pay extra attention to the decision-making process and your tactical steps. You want to identify the decision-making process as early as possible to avoid surprises, so that you can run through the process efficiently and effectively.

You can ask the following questions to gain as much insight in the descision-making unit and process as possible:

- Who is involved in the decision-making?
- What roles do the various actors play in this process (and what are their responsibilities and interests)?
- What steps do they take to reach a decision and how do they come to that decision?
- What criteria (interests) are choices based on?

You can use the circles to assign the various players to their positions in the playing field. You can list the names and roles in them. Think a little bit more about the players in the game. Quite aside from their roles, are they for or against you, do they want to help you and is there any genuine commitment towards you? Are there actors or information you can't see? This gives you a qualitative impression of what the DMU is like. Based on this analysis, see what work needs doing: the information you're missing, how to get it and what will put the actors on your side.

When filling it in, make sure that you:
- include both groupings and individual actors.
- include external actors such as consultants and agents who are negotiating on behalf of others. They also have their own interests.

These are organic systems, so I'd recommend that you regularly revise such analyses. After all, people's positions and roles change, which in turn alters the DMU.

Multi-party aspects

I mentioned above that the approach to multi-level aspects often involves multiple parties. When there are multi-party aspects, it is even more important to identify the actors and their tasks, roles and responsibilities. Again, you can use the seven guides as a starting point:

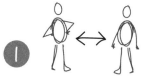

Identify expectations, perceptions and emotions that could come into play between the various groups and individuals. Are there any tensions or major differences in perspectives and expectations? Pay careful attention to cultural differences.

Is there enough trust between the parties to proceed, or do you have to make allowances? Do you want to address this issue before moving forward? Does everyone have the same information?

Identify the interests of the various parties. Which parties have a lot of shared interests, which interests are party-specific and can you see any conflicts? Are there any parties with considerable influence that don't have a role in the core DMU but that ought to be involved? Involve the stakeholders, pay attention to their situations, show an understanding for their interests and make agreements about how you are going to involve them in the overall process.

Depending on the context, consider possible solutions for starting collaboration, for instance, or for reaching an agreement. You may want to take it one step at a time, gradually building the involvement in a process and getting them to buy into the solutions along the way.

MULTI-LEVEL, MULTI-PARTY

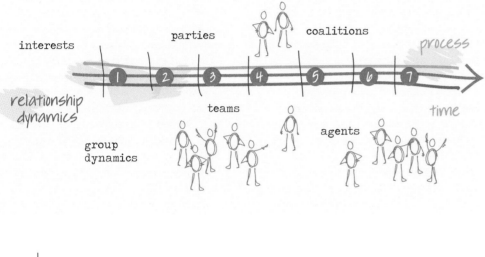

7 ○

This analysis can help you decide on your further strategy and tactics. Who will you sit around the table with first and how will you build up the process, step by step? Be aware that everything can be constrained by time, preconditions and political agendas.

If you want to set up a collaboration between multiple parties, you can also consider clearly identifying your own interests and assessing which of the potential partners for cooperation is the best match. These parties are your BATNAs. If the parties don't seem all that different at first glance, you can repeat the analysis in greater depth. You could also identify the common, party-specific and conflicting interests, providing you with an impression of which parties are the most obvious choice for collaboration, who you would like to include, and where the potential bottlenecks are. If you combine that with the players in the game and link it to a timeline, you have the basis for your strategy and tactics. Bounce your hypothesis off a few colleagues and see if you've overlooked anything. It is complex

5 ⊖

Keep thinking about what possibilities you can see for bridging conflicting interests. What criteria of fairness are there for basing your opinions or decisions on? Is there anyone who can help you if deadlocks are looming on the horizon?

6

What about the various interdependencies with respect to each other (or the lack of them)? Are there parties that are affected by the dominant position of others? What impact does this have on the overall dynamics?

and important enough that you should pay attention to it.

Depending on your responsibilities in the process and your role, you may be in a leading position or just a part of the game. Irrespective of your role, you can think about these issues and the guides can be a guideline. As someone who is often allowed to play a role in such partnerships, I'd like to share a few observations with you.

- "How can we best serve our interests?" This central question is often not answered properly. If you've already taken steps with a party and don't take account of possible alternatives, your chances of the best outcome may already have been compromised. You may have painted yourself into a corner. It's something I see happen quite often, because many people seem to have an inbuilt mechanism for progress: "I've started so I'll finish." That intention is fine as long as you - if appropriate - are able to look at alternatives at the same time. Looking at the broader picture isn't a goal in itself, but it may help you look after your own interests. So

leave a bit of scope for looking at how you can best serve your interests and with whom.

- Expectations about the collaboration get discussed explicitly at too late a stage. Share your expectations as early in the process as possible and clarify them quickly. I've seen processes drag on and eventually break down because people turned out to have different expectations of the collaboration - expectations that were expressed far too late. They were felt but never mentioned.
- State the no-go areas early in the process: issues that can't be negotiated or are non-negotiable in principle. Know which areas you may be able to help each other in. You can spend a long time avoiding the no-go areas and not discussing them, although everyone has interests that are not negotiable. Be aware of this and accept it, because you can't easily change the other's no-go zones. It is especially difficult if the issues are fundamental.
- Distribution issues are often difficult in complex collaborations. Be extra vigilant when sharing out

the costs and benefits. Fairness based on objective criteria remains important here too. If multiple actors have roles in a collaboration, they usually each make specific contributions. For example, one party brings customers or market knowledge, another brings effort and money, and another brings patents and knowledge. Disagreements about the distribution of consequences often appear at the end. Those involved may feel aggrieved, often saying that if there had been constructive discussions about the interests and the principles for the distribution earlier in the process, the collaboration would probably have benefited.

WHEN ARE YOU SATISFIED?

Looking back at the entire process up till now may answer this question. When have you reached a good agreement or made a good decision? I often hear course participants say that they felt afterwards that they could have got more. That it was too easy, that it went so fast that they must have overlooked things. Does that really mean you were on the wrong track? Would the deal still have been feasible and achievable? When I ask managers about their projects, they often have a hard time answering that one. How do you know if your people are heading for a good project result? You apparently don't have a guideline handy for evaluating a deal, project or collaboration. Of course it's true that project results are recorded in various different financial systems and project measurements are performed that may answer the question. However, at the same time I would like to share the seven guides with you to help answer that question. Consider these criteria as something to aim for.

Criteria for a good deal

You have made the right decision or achieved a good result from the deal or negotiation if:

✓ the results are better than your BATNA, unless you can thoroughly justify why you agreed to the deal. I hope that you then made a conscious choice and that the outcome didn't just happen.

✓ both sides acted in as many of their short-term and long-term interests as possible. Your own interests at the very least. The deal is then more resilient, able to take a couple of knocks, making it even more attractive.

✓ you think that the consequences are distributed fairly. This benefits trust and durability.

✓ the relationship has deepened – or in any event not worsened. Even if there are differences of opinion or a conflict.

✓ foreseeable problems and benefit issues have been discussed and resolved, for instance how you deal with extra work or reductions in the work, and how the long-term risks or (additional) revenues will be shared. This improves the level of trust and helps keep the relationship going smoothly in the longer term.

✓ solid agreements about the process were made for unforeseen situations (suppose that… then…). This lets you cover the risks and safeguard the financial situation.

✓ the process has been completed efficiently and effectively. If things take too long, it puts pressure on both the result and the relationship.

A good result can be achieved by consciously using the seven guides when preparing, acting and evaluating (including at interim points). That lets you keep looking at the process and make adjustments where necessary. You don't always manage to, of course. **It's something to aim for though, something that should be thought through at the start, because good negotiators begin with the end result in mind.** They want to move towards a good result and they then consider what they must do to achieve it.

With hindsight, could you have got a better deal? Possibly. You will never know, but if all the elements above have been ticked off, you can be satisfied with the result. It could perhaps have been even tighter, but that's part and parcel of it all. Some people will say, "If I see that the other side had difficulty with it, I know I was doing it right." It's supposed to have hurt them a bit. Well, if you know all the games that are played, that could have been one of them. Do your own thing and keep your interests in mind, because they are key.

NEXT LEVEL UP: MASTERING THE ART

Getting a good deal in a VUCA world is a challenge. It can get even more awkward when multiple parties are involved: the process becomes more complex, games may be played and the pressure increases. I've given you the basic elements. Are you ready to take a step further yourself now? Maybe you're already familiar with what I've said so far and need more. In this section, I want to give you some concepts and tools that can be applied immediately, plus a few aspects to think about carefully. I'll start off with improving and/or speeding up the negotiation process, letting you increase your circle of influence. After that I'll give you some insights and tools to help you stay agile and alert in terms of both the relationships and the content. This will add more substance to the idea of standing firmly and nimbly on your own two feet, with a clear head and a warm heart.

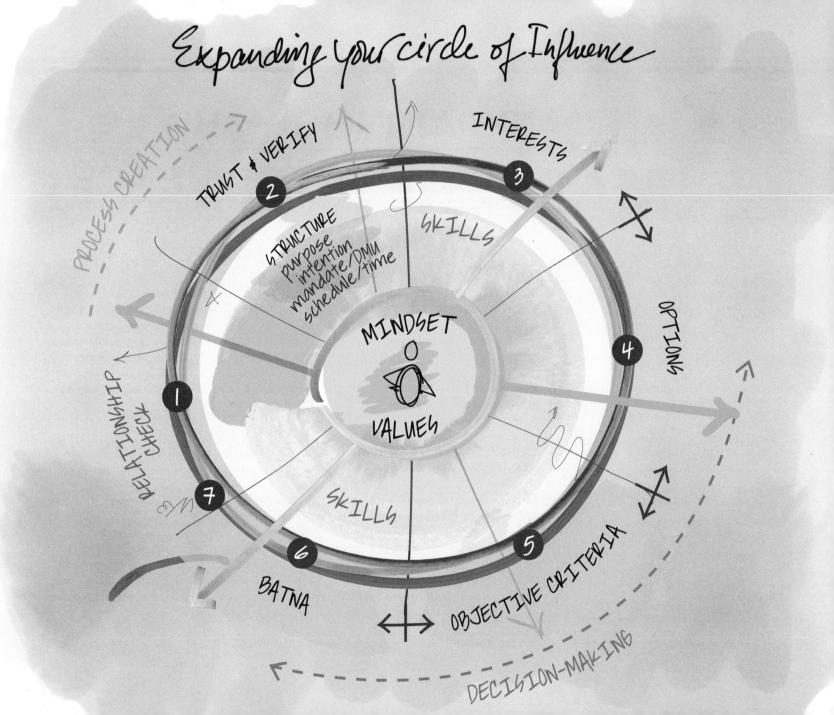

Expanding your circle of Influence

PROCESS CREATION

TRUST & VERIFY 2

INTERESTS 3

STRUCTURE
purpose
intention
mandate/DMU
schedule/time

SKILLS

OPTIONS 4

MINDSET

VALUES

RELATIONSHIP CHECK 1

7

SKILLS

6 BATNA

OBJECTIVE CRITERIA 5

DECISION-MAKING

5

EXPANDING YOUR CIRCLE OF INFLUENCE

Starting the negotiation process and following it through is a challenge, but you want to be able to intervene if you think it should be moving more quickly, more effectively or in another direction. That's why it is important to be able to look and act from an outside perspective, as a neutral observer. I will be introducing ways of intervening in processes, taking time-outs and preventing conflicts. I'll also introduce you to a number of ways of making a deal better and more attractive, focusing on creativity in particular. And I will end by telling you how you can keep learning from negotiation processes and how you can deliberately speed up that learning process in your role as a leader or project manager.

OBSERVING, INTERPRETING AND RESPONDING FROM THE THIRD POSITION

You may get so fired up or tense during a discussion that you don't know what exactly is going on, how far the process has progressed and where you want to go. You can become so caught up in the situation that you get absorbed into it and lose your overview and your influence. The trick is to be able to take a step outside, to dissociate and then look and act from the perspective of an observer. We call this the 'third position'. You and the other negotiator are sitting opposite each other in the first and second positions, and the observer has the third position. If you put yourself in the third position, you may see a whole lot more than from the

clear head

warm heart

strong legs
nimble feet

WHAT'S YOUR OBSERVATION?

THIRD POSITION

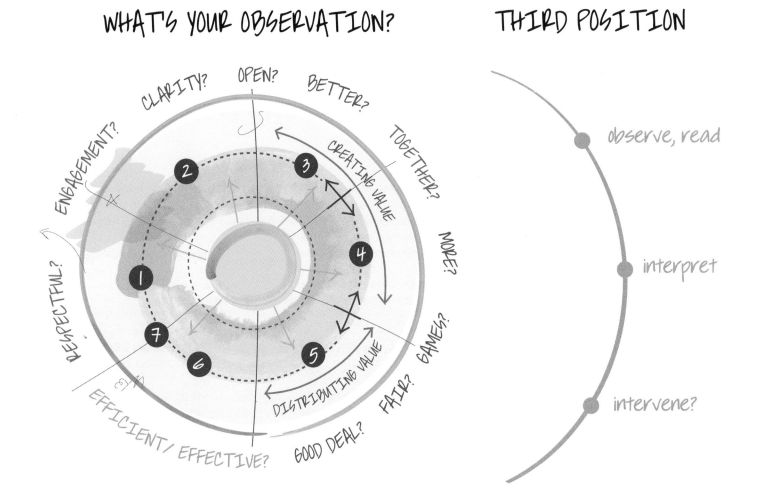

CLARITY?
OPEN?
BETTER?
ENGAGEMENT?
TOGETHER?
CREATING VALUE
MORE?
RESPECTFUL?
DISTRIBUTING VALUE
FAIR?
GAMES?
EFFICIENT/ EFFECTIVE?
GOOD DEAL?

observe, read

interpret

intervene?

first or second position because you have taken a step back.

I'd like to give you a number of tools here for intervening in processes, when necessary. Look beyond your negotiation challenge: step outside the process and take up that third position. Observe and go through the guides, beginning with the end in mind (Guide 7) and then pick it up again from Guide 1:

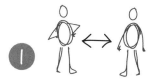

Are you making any progress in the process? Should it be going differently, or better, or more tidily? Are you on the way to a good deal? (See Criteria, page 98.) If you feel it isn't progressing smoothly, does that have to do with the process itself or with something else? Try to find out.

Have a good look at the relationships. Is everyone on board? Are actors or parties missing from the table? Or playing a role in the background? Are there tensions or negative perceptions that are hindering progress? Are the expectations being managed properly? Is there an open atmosphere? What is and isn't being said? Are games being played? (Page 163.)

How much do the two sides trust each other ? Do you both have enough information to continue? Are you being overwhelmed by new information or do you feel there is an information shortfall? Is information being extracted rather than given? Is any of the information biased?

Are the interests out in the open? Is there enough openness? Are the interests being served well enough? Would it be better to get more interests out in the open? If some things are still being kept out of view, that may cause delays. Are there any no-go areas that haven't been mentioned and are making things stagnate?

Are there enough options on the table, or do you need more if you're to become really enthusiastic?

Is the distribution unfair and are there any tensions related to that? Can you see any deadlocks that have occurred or are threatening to?

Are there major differences in how dependent or independent the parties are? Are some actors also working on other alternatives, delaying the process?

A good negotiator feels responsible for the process, and then it will help if you start working from the third position. From there, you can look at the process and manage the process further and see it as a joint challenge in taking the next steps together.

Process managers generally think and talk more about "we" than "I". "Let's have a look at our current progress and decide how to proceed together."

PROCESS INTERVENTIONS

The observations you made from the third position will have given you an impression of the situation and how you are doing. You may now be able to intervene, based on your findings.

A process intervention consists of three components: a **summary of what you see and hear happening** (for clarity), **stating how you feel about it or what your view of the situation is** (for impact) and **stating your expectations**, including a proposal for the process (gives direction).

A summary is often seen as a way of checking if you've understood each other, and it does indeed have that function. At the same time, a summary is an indispensable tool for managing the process. This lets you control the process. If you've lost your way in the process you can regain control by taking a step outside the process for a moment, summarising where

you are so that you can then set the course again and continue.

"We've had several discussions now and I can see that it's important to both of us to achieve ABC, but unfortunately we haven't been able to find a good solution." This is how you summarise where you are in the process and how you feel about it. Summarising the status creates space for taking the next step. Summaries also give you time to think and to put yourself in the third position, outside the process. You retain the overview and increase your influence over the process. "Before we continue: as I understand it, ABC is very important to you. I've been wondering if we have everything we need before we can take the next step? Is this it, or is there anything else we ought to keep in mind?"

After summarising, you can go in various directions. You could switch the process to a different track: "We've had a number of sessions now and I can see that it's important for both of us to achieve ABC, but unfortunately we haven't been able to find a good solution. Who might be able help us resolve the impasse?"

You could change gear and tackle the steps in greater depth, or shuttle back and forth between the various phases (3–4–5)

- Summarise the interests and check if there are any more; this may yield more ingredients for new options.
- Summarise the interests and propose a step towards the options.
- Summarise the options and check if there are more options available, or better ones.
- Summarise the options and see which of them could be worked out in greater detail.
- Ask yourself if the options available are the best way of serving everyone's interests.
- Summarise the objective criteria and chose which ones you will use as a basis for distributing the costs and benefits.
- Summarise the share-out and then take a step back to check whether that distribution is realistic, given the solutions and interests.

Could it be better, faster, fairer or different? The answer to this will be easier to find if you know where you are in the process.

PROCESS INTERVENTION

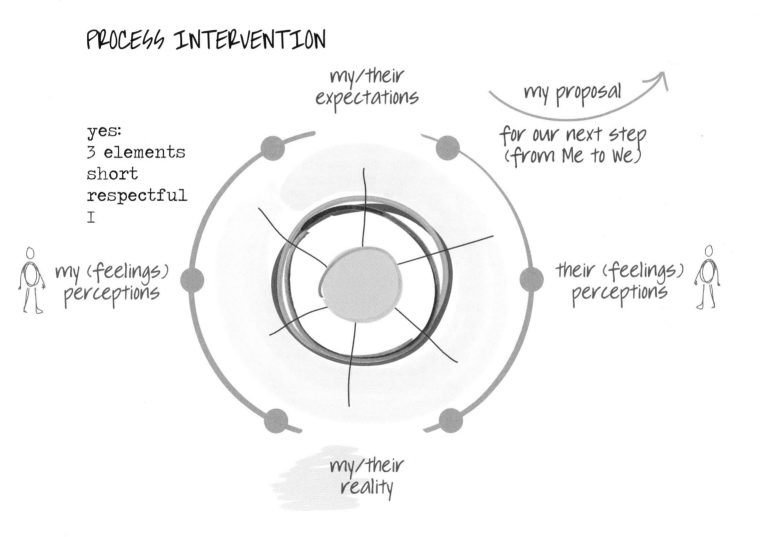

my/their
expectations

my proposal

for our next step
(from Me to We)

yes:
3 elements
short
respectful
I

my (feelings)
perceptions

their (feelings)
perceptions

my/their
reality

Examples

- "I've realised that we don't have enough information to go any further. That information is important for us. I'd propose sharing information about ABC now, so that we can produce a proposal. What do you reckon?"
- "Unless I'm mistaken, the key thing for you is to move forward quickly and start the project before 1 July. If we're to take steps now, I think it's crucial to be clear about who has what role in the decision-making. I've noted you seem somewhat reluctant to share that information, but it's input that we need before we can progress further. What are we going to do about it?"
- "Looking at what we've shared so far, I think there are a few issues that haven't been discussed yet that could make this collaboration much more attractive. I'd propose taking another look at our interests, because I think we've missed something."
- "I do understand that a solution with a lower cost base is important for you. We don't mind discussing that as long as it doesn't hurt our margins. Otherwise it'll be impossible for us to offer any continuity. Let's we look for a solution together that will let you proceed with lower costs while we maintain our margins."
- "Let's tread water for a moment and see if what we've got so far is genuinely interesting for both of us. We've come up with A, B and C as potential solutions for this problem. What other possibilities can we think of for fleshing out the agreement in a way that we can really be enthusiastic about?"
- "I hear what you're saying: you think it is important to come up with a joint solution. In that case, I'll need more information about your assumptions and expectations in order to make a viable proposal. That's information that hasn't been shared so far. How can we get that information on the table?"
- "John, I understand that you're expecting a proposal from us. At the same time, it seems advisable to me to explore a few possibilities together now, so that we can work them out carefully."
- Or "To prevent us from going back and forth later with lots of different proposals, I suggest we take some time now to explore a few possibilities. That'll save us both a lot of time. What do you think?"

There may also be reluctance because your relationship isn't good enough:

- "I notice that our discussions aren't going as well as I'd like, which is a pity. I've been wonder what's wrong and I'd like to focus on that before we go any further. What's your feeling about this?"
- "I can see that we have very different expectations of this collaboration. Perhaps we should discuss our expectations again and see if we can take another step in the process after that."
- "I feel that it still bothers you that our last meeting didn't go smoothly. I think we're getting ahead of ourselves, talking about further collaboration, while something is clearly not right. I'd suggest we focus on this first and then see how we can proceed. What do you think?"

Or disagreements can arise, perhaps even creating an impasse:

- "Continuing talking like this seems pointless to me. We keep repeating ourselves without finding an answer together. I suggest that we both cool off for a day or two and continue talking next Wednesday based on a proposal that I'll send to you. What do you think?"
- "I've noticed that we seem to have fundamentally different opinions about what would be the right solution for the problem. I'm wondering how we can move forward with this. Would it be an idea to start thinking about who can help us out?"

It becomes more difficult if the other side are playing games and the tension mounts (see page 163).

The importance of a pause: the time-out

A time-out in a process can be very useful, but I rarely see this tool being used. We know it exists, but it seems as if many people see pausing as a sign of incompetence. It's often regarded as an admission of weakness. If things aren't progressing, it's always there as an emergency brake. (Or emergency break!) Consider a time-out for:

- creating a little distance, so that you can take a fresh look at the situation from a different perspective. Even if things are going well! Is there room for improvement? Are things perhaps going too smoothly? Have we identified the risks properly? Are we forgetting important information in our enthusiasm?
- a 'breather'. In stressful situations it can be useful to take a step back, cool down for a while and then resume.
- consulting or getting feedback from the people you are representing or other stakeholders who are not at the table (for example colleagues, supervisors or partners from other organisations) about mandates, new insights that emerged as new information was put on the table, or about deadlocks that seem to be on the horizon.

Sometimes you get so immersed in the negotiations that it's good to step outside of them for a while. You can take a step back by making a process summary: that's essentially introducing a mini time-out without leaving the table. You're taking a moment to think. There are many ways

TIME OUT

anytime

to breathe fresh life into a process if you notice that it needs new energy: a coffee break, a short walk, stretching your legs, opening a window, changing your sitting positions, changing seats. Some negotiators do it by disrupting the flow for a while, for example by making a joke or comment that can put things into perspective. This can be massively refreshing. During a recent awkward meeting, for instance, I heard an American apologising for his English. Everyone had a good laugh about it, the tension evaporated and the ice was broken.

CREATIVITY IN THE PROCESS

One specific way of increasing your influence in the process is to think how you could be more creative in finding better options and solutions. Everyone is always looking for new possibilities, 'break-the-mould' innovations, pioneering solutions, quick improvements and new collaborations; creativity is an essential skill for all this. Creativity plays a key role throughout the whole process, and at the same time it has a specific place in the process when you are looking for win-win options together.

Going through the process as indicated at the negotiation table means you are fulfilling the conditions step by step for finding truly creative solutions. At the start of a conversation you focus on the relationship in order to create a bond. Your aim is to reach a common view of the scope of the discussion, and you can set a positive tone by stating your intentions. If the people at the table with you are skilled and you're capable of getting the interests out into the open, you will have gathered all the ingredients you need for an exploration of the options. This is how you create the conditions for open and committed efforts towards a creative process.

Can creativity be learned?

I often hear people say that they aren't creative. But if you don't paint or have some other creative hobby, it doesn't necessarily mean you aren't creative. Maybe we've just forgotten how. As a child you weren't bound by all sorts of limiting expectations and patterns. You gradually learn to conform to them.

We often feel stuck in complex conversations, perhaps because they *are* complex conversations, thanks to their specific context or to expectations of the outcome.

Or we restrict ourselves to a self-imposed timetable and don't give ourselves and other party the time and attention to look at a situation from different angles. The manoeuvring room letting us explore solutions often isn't used because we have already chosen a solution in our minds. This often also applies for the other players at the table too. We all have our pet subjects, our fixed ideas for a solution and we restrict both ourselves and the other side.

Some people may undoubtedly be more creative than others, but we can all achieve a creative process if a number of steps are taken. If you want to find different ways to serve the interests or if you want to find unusual options, you can take a process-oriented approach, helping yourself get into that 'creative space'. There is a specific place in the overall process where brainstorming – a creative process *pur sang* – has a role and you can apply Guide 4: go looking together for options that are interesting to both parties and which are preferably better than what you had thought of before. I've talked about this earlier on page 84. And now I'd like to tell you about a way of paying extra attention to the creative process. You'll probably recognise some of the rules, which also

CREATIVITY IN THE PROCESS

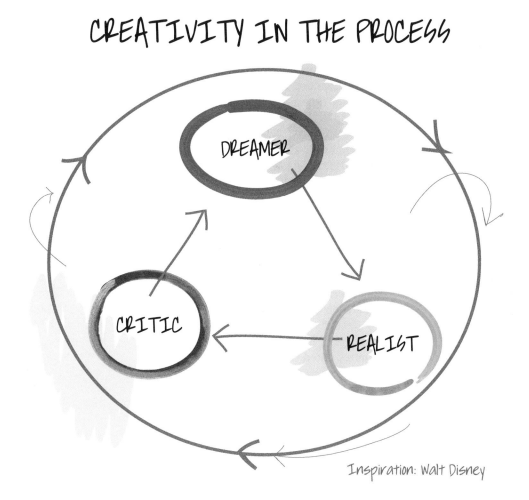

Inspiration: Walt Disney

apply to brainstorming. I'll limit it to just a few suggestions.

The Disney method

If you want to use a session for thinking up as many options as possible that can also be turned into concrete actions, consider using the Disney method. Robert Dilts modelled Walt Disney's way of thinking and acting. Disney was famous for being able to turn ideas and fantasies into attainable and successful solutions.

It works as follows. Set up three physical positions: three tables, three rooms or three chairs that are some distance apart. These three positions symbolise three different roles (the dreamer, the realist and the critic). A number of variations are possible:

- You can do this alone. You then take turns working from each position.
- It can be more effective to do it with other people. There are variations here too. You can assign the positions randomly or based on people's competencies. Although again, this is not necessary.
- You can rotate. First you all take a specific role and then swap them around later.

Suppose that a number of parties in a partnership want to reduce the joint costs of their activities by ten per cent, while at the same time increasing their market share by five per cent. Seems like a tough challenge. Depending on how the question is framed, you may already be leaning in a certain direction. Another question in a more internal situation could be that a project has been taken on at below cost price. What can we do to ensure that we remain cost-effective while delivering the quality we agreed on? Also a challenging question. Once the question is clear, you start looking at the challenge from the perspectives of the three different roles. This lets you come up with solutions that are enriched yet at the same time feasible. Here is the process from the perspective of each of the three roles:

Phase 1: the dreamer

The dreamer position lets you diverge. Any flight of fancy is possible. You collect ideas without looking at the limitations and you disregard risks and feasibility. What kinds of options can you think of? You identify the possibilities and the opportunities.

Phase 2: the realist

Now you quite literally move to a different

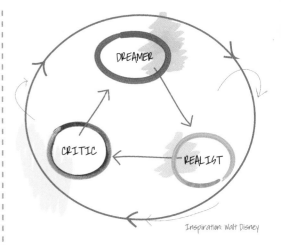

Inspiration: Walt Disney

position. A different room, chair or table. You drop your previous role and now aim to think about how – with the challenge in mind – you could implement the options that were dreamed up in phase 1. What is needed in terms of people, time, money, resources, etc.? What do you need to make it achievable and feasible, and what would it cost? You don't think about risks or limitations in this phase. You just work out the ideas and identify the consequences.

Phase 3: the critic
Again, this is literally another position. You consider issues such as: What could go wrong? What is missing? What problems and obstacles might come your way when setting up or implementing the idea? What or who can stop it? With that information in mind, is the idea still interesting enough to go through with it? Are the various interests served properly? Do the advantages outweigh the disadvantages? And would it serve both short-term and long-term interests?

You can then restart the process. With the input from phase 3, you can continue dreaming of what it will look like, think about what would be needed to make it work and see what's missing and how you

can make the goal achievable. At some point you will have a number of viable options that are all interesting enough to choose.

Creativity is a hot topic. There are many different perceptions of the subject, and about which conditions may or may not stimulate the process. About whether or not it helps to do this together, or if putting pressure on the process encourages creativity or not. My experience is that the flow outlined above can at least help you bring some structure into your approach; it always yields something. Try experimenting with it.

LEARNING ACCELERATORS

It's interesting to learn from substantive input or the ideas of colleagues or teammates during ongoing negotiations. Learning from an approach and/or the process during or after a negotiation can also be relevant.

Quickly enhance your understanding of a practical case study: the Socratic method
I've noticed that people can learn a lot

quickly from each other's negotiation challenges if they use what is known as the Socratic method. This approach provides surprising insights in just a short time for both the person who introduced the case and the others. It's perfect to use in your own team, for example. It strengthens the bonding and the learning effect at the same time, and it only takes about forty-five minutes. Here's a short description of the approach:

Jacob, the case owner, introduces his case and the question that is bothering him. He first shares some context and then he poses his central question. For example, how can we speed up the negotiation process in project X? Any question may be asked to clarify the context and situation, and an explanation can be given in a few minutes.

- Group members write down questions that they think might be useful for Jacob on Post-its. These are meant to be questions designed to make him think and that could immediately provide insights for him. The number of questions permitted per participant depends on the size of the group and the available time. I'd

"A GREAT MAN: WHEN HE MAKES A MISTAKE, HE REALISES IT. HAVING REALISED IT, HE ADMITS IT. HAVING ADMITTED IT, HE CORRECTS IT. HE CONSIDERS THOSE WHO POINT OUT HIS FAULTS AS HIS MOST BENEVOLENT TEACHERS." LAOZI

suggest a maximum of twenty questions for the entire group. Duration: ten minutes.

- The questions are collated and given to Jacob, who reads them one by one and sorts them by their 'emotional value'. For example, he draws three columns on a flipchart and divides them into 'I don't care/useless to me', 'neutral' and 'I like this/great question'. Duration: ten minutes.
- Jacob answers the questions one by one, in a sequence chosen by him. The participants don't say anything, but they listen and observe. Duration: ten to fifteen minutes.
- Jacob then stands a little distance away from the group, though close enough to still hear them. The group discuss their impressions, list possible new questions and suggestions, give advice, etc. Duration: fifteen to twenty minutes.
- He is invited back to give his response. What was it like being on the sidelines, listening in? Did it trigger anything? What insights and questions did he take away from it?

This lets you collect numerous insights easily and quickly that can help you do the right things more rapidly and more efficiently during your negotiation process. Another way to accelerate your learning is to be more aware of the evaluation moments and learn from them.

Mistakes are often repeated, the cost of failure is high. Are we learning enough?

I'm regularly allowed to sit in on interim and final evaluations of complex projects and partnerships that have faced all sorts of negotiation challenges. I often notice that certain logical fallacies and limitations that appeared at the preliminary stage can raise their heads again when the same people look back and evaluate. It's possible to involve an internal colleague in the evaluation, but evaluations do need to be done by someone independent. It's wise to think about who could assist you to get the real learnings on the table.

Business expert Chris Argyris, a great inspiration in the 'conscious learning' field, refers to 'single-loop and double-loop learning'. In the former, you are satisfied with a short analysis – often too short. The evaluations flip quickly through a case, for example, and quick fixes are found for preventing mistakes from being made.

Those directly involved often blame the failure on causes other than themselves. A sort of protective wall is erected and their own contribution is overlooked. "Next time we should do X earlier, or we should do Y better, or handle Z differently." Other people are regularly blamed: "You should have prepared differently, you could have asked different questions and said no sooner." Or the organisation: "We aren't equipped to deal with this and we aren't ready for that. We can't handle that kind of complexity." Often a pattern at the root of the problem is not being addressed and people's own contributions to the development of the problem are overlooked. That's where you need a double-loop learning approach, taking more time to look at the patterns, the causes and the solutions. People are often reluctant to wash their dirty linen in public – be it because of modesty, reticence, shame and fear, or indeed stubbornness and defence mechanisms – and don't look closely enough at their own actions. Outsiders may see it, but they might not be prepared to address it. They beat around the bush, time keeps ticking by and we go back to the order of the day. We can fool ourselves and not learn enough from the (foreseeable) mistakes we make in all kinds of negotiation situations. A double-loop requires more effort, a different perspective and an inviting attitude. Respect, openness and a safe environment help.

There can be all sorts of reasons why someone doesn't say what needs to be said. It's difficult to learn effectively, because such a system can be self-perpetuating. It requires knowledge, skill, attention and courage to get the real learning points out onto the table and it's up to management to create a safe environment in which this is possible. We must be open to learning. Argyris worded the challenge he sees here nicely in *Teaching Smart People how to Learn*: "Because many professionals are almost always successful at what they do, they rarely experience failure. And because they have rarely failed, they have never learned how to learn from failure. So they become defensive, screen out criticism, and put the blame on anyone and everyone but themselves. In short, their ability to learn shuts down precisely at the moment they need it the most."

I regularly hear people say,

- "We can't influence that." Using the 'we' form shows immediately when someone doesn't feel as if they're responsible, and often it turns out that things could have been handled differently but nobody realised. The blame is placed outside their own circle of influence and responsibility is denied.
- "Even knowing what I know now, I'd make the same choices again." Even though the situation was misjudged, perhaps because they were too cautious or else too optimistic. Or they continued stubbornly on the chosen path and now they are seeing the current situation through rose-tinted spectacles. See also 'Biases' (page 150).
- "Based on the facts we had, we did the right thing." Whereas simply asking more probing questions could have revealed other information relevant to the case, which would have led to a different assessment.
- "Business is about taking risks." Despite the fact that various people weren't alert when assessing the facts, interests and risks.

I've presented it as a black-and-white issue here; it's often more subtle than that, but you should keep a sharp eye on the content when evaluating negotiation situations. Create a safe situation in which you can learn consciously, using the seven guides as the ground rules. You can go through the guides, both at interim points and at the end, to see where you want to make adjustments. Afterwards you can check if you achieved the criteria for a good deal and see if there are any learning points. You'll want to go into a little more depth than a single loop and ask yourself and your team questions such as:

- "Looking back now, how would you rate this deal/project/collaboration?" You'll get answers such as 'good', 'moderate' or 'fair'; it's a closed question, after all.
- "Why do you rate the outcome as XYZ?" You are looking for the background and criteria for the assessments.
- Go back to the criteria for a good deal: have as many interests as possible been served (the goals met and the interests served)? Were the burdens distributed fairly? Did the relationship improve? Have the future pros and cons been estimated and resolved and have procedural arrangements been made for unforeseen costs and benefits? Was the process efficient and effective?

THE LEARNING CYCLE

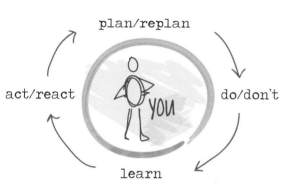

plan/replan

act/react

you

do/don't

learn

You can use that as the basis for taking a look at:

- what everyone could have done differently (or more of or less of) to achieve or improve the 'good deal'.
- why you did what you did. This may expose beliefs that got in the way; together, you can see how the problem could be approached differently next time.
- what we could have done differently (or more of or less of) as a team. You may see patterns in the method of cooperation, communication or leadership that you can discuss.
- what everyone can take from this. Will they do it differently or not at all next time? Identify these points together. This makes the learning process worthwhile and ensures that there is some obligation to act.
- how we can safeguard this knowledge and make it accessible to others.

As a supervisor, team manager or project leader, you can use this to look back on complex situations. Don't stop at just giving tips and exchanging obvious learning moments. Negotiations are inextricably linked to being able to show leadership. And vice versa: being a manager means you have to negotiate, every day.

Learning from each other and with each other lets you put the seven guides into practice, making them come alive and setting a good example. For managers, it also helps make the learning process more transparent. If you can create an open atmosphere in which learning is encouraged, you'll improve your results and your relationships. It will reflect on everyone. Sometimes you'll have to pay your dues in the learning process and that's okay, because you want to show that you're working together to prevent mistakes from happening again. Learn from both good and bad practices.

You can learn a lot quickly because you're confronted with all sorts of negotiation dynamics on a daily basis. You can learn how to improve the learning process in various ways: by consciously experimenting, reading, following current events and websites, watching YouTube videos and sharing cases. Talk to colleagues, share your experiences, and ask for and give feedback.

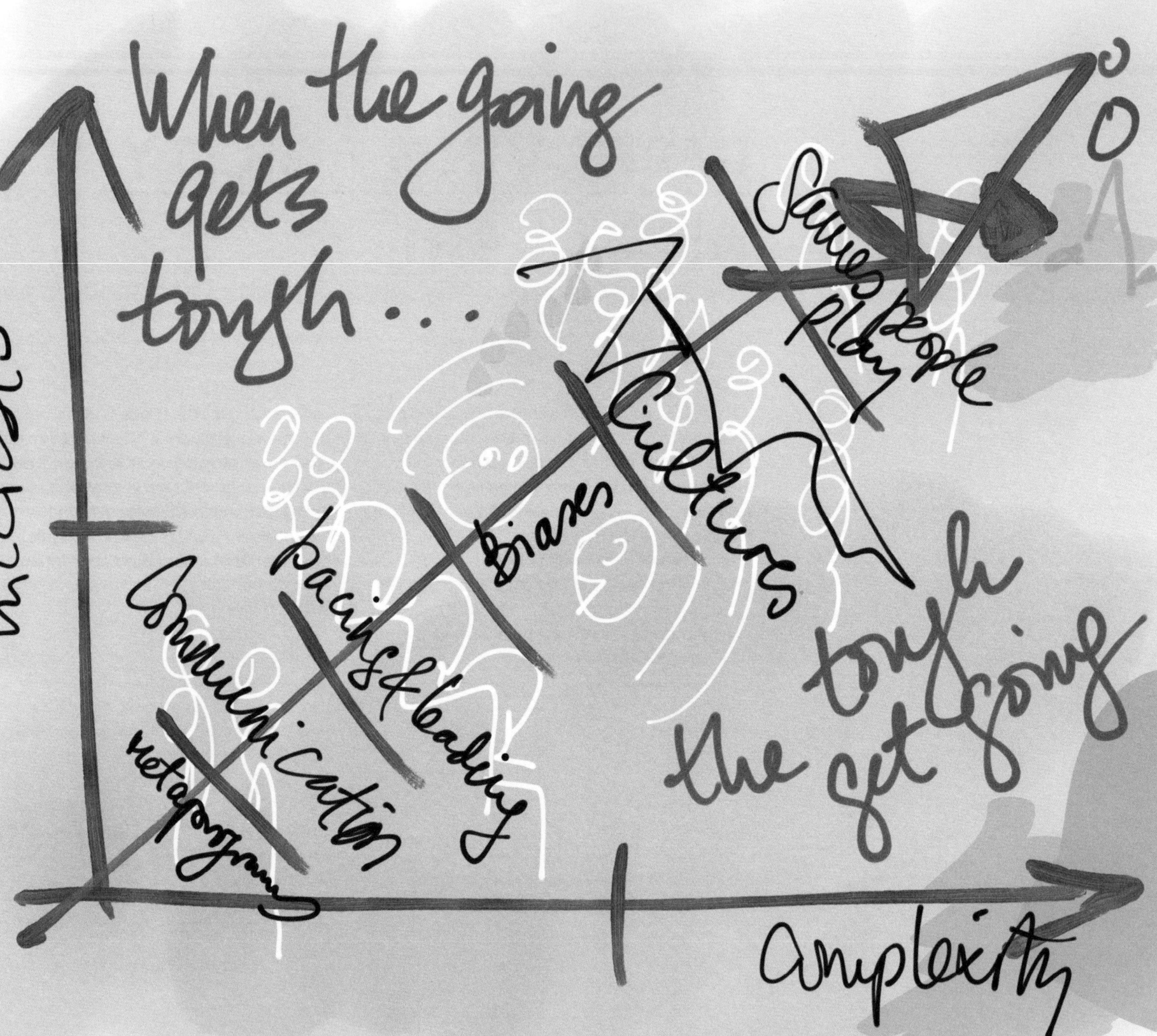

When the going gets tough...
interests
complexity
metaprograms
communication
pacing & leading
Biases
Cultures
Games people play
the tough get going

6

IMPROVING AGILITY AND CLARITY

We have paid attention to helping you increase your influence over the process; your next step could be to deepen and improve the quality of your communication skills. This should make it easier for you to manage the relationship dynamics. I also want to give you the insights and the tools for staying as sharp as you need to be in terms of the content. Communication insights will help you approach the aspect of a 'clear mind, warm heart and nimble legs' from the relational and content-related sides. The complexity is gradually increasing and insights are starting to pile up, so you will hopefully be increasingly capable of responding appropriately to what you come up against when the going gets tougher.

The following subjects will be addressed:

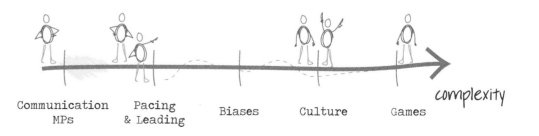

clear head

warm heart

strong legs
nimble feet

- Metaprogrammes (MPs) as a way of reading your own behaviour and that of others, letting you communicate more flexibly.
- Pacing and leading as a way of becoming more connected with others and keeping the momentum going.
- How unconscious biases in the information can influence the decision-making process and how to handle this problem.
- Cultural differences: recognising behaviour at the group level (the culture) will hopefully make you more capable of consciously handling cultural differences. I will share some insights.
- How do you recognise the games that may be played and how do you deal with them?

GETTING BETTER AT READING YOURSELF AND OTHERS

The bond is broken. Some practical situations

- You make an impassioned speech in which you explain the details of your plan. The meeting isn't going well; there is confusion and a few of your colleagues seem to have lost the drift. Your response is rather short and spiky. Is that what you did your best for? Your manager points to the clock and says he has to leave for his next meeting and that he thinks you should plan a follow-up meeting. Everybody leaves and you sit there, full of doubts and thoroughly irritated. What went wrong?
- Your report, which you worked on late into the night, is finally finished. Just in time, and you proudly show the latest version to the senior partner, who is closely involved in the project. He leafs through the report calmly and you can see him thinking. He frowns and says, "I don't see an overview of X on page 2, I'd change the layout, and you should have used our standard template." You get annoyed and snap back, "Why don't you ever have anything constructive to say?" The partner looks shocked and an uncomfortable silence stretches out between the two of you.
- You're in an important meeting to choose a coalition partner with whom you'll be working to win a large order. There's a lot of money involved. There isn't much time because of another meeting that overran, so the discussion is cutting a few corners. The project director, who is also your manager, takes charge: "Based on the information we have, I think we should go for party A." You think they're making the decision too hastily and add, "Peter, I don't agree with that. Looking at the performance of the different parties up till now and our experience with party A, I really believe we should choose party B." More opinions are shared and repeated. Time is ticking. "Guys, we have to make a decision. What do you reckon?" A last round of questions is wrapped up quickly and the findings collated. "Okay, we'll choose A. Thank you all!" You're not happy and think the wrong decision was made. You play the meeting back in your mind and wonder if you could have tackled it differently.

As a negotiator, you want to create progress and serve your own interests. You want to make the correct decision, based on the right information plus the interests at stake and the possibilities for serving them. It's obvious that good communication is essential here, but how can you communicate more consciously and be more effective?

Reading behaviour

There are all sorts of ways of categorising behaviour. We attempt to serve our own interests through the ways we behave, and if we are better able to recognise such behaviour and respond to it, we can then also negotiate better and reach better decisions together. Regardless of the type of system, I want to focus in particular on reading, recognising and interpreting behaviour. Earlier, I briefly mentioned DUTCH as a way of identifying your preferred style in the event of conflicts – a short introduction to the instrument. If you want to read more about it, you can find additional information in the literature list. For a more detailed look at behaviour, I use the concept of metaprogrammes (MPs). Metaprogrammes describe behaviour. It has been shown that people tend to use the same language patterns in similar situations. Styles of working and thinking have been described based on this linguistic

research, yielding a practical, recognisable way of describing behaviour. Not labelling it right or wrong. In that context, I learned a lot from Anneke Durlinger and Guus Hustinx. I have also drawn on their knowledge when it comes to describing MPs. (See the literature list for the reference.)

In some contexts you may need certain behaviour if you're to be effective or successful, and different behaviour may stand in your way. If you listen carefully not only to what people are saying but also to how they say it while observing their non-verbal behaviour, you'll get an idea of how people think, categorise information and go about their work. You'll get a feel for the MPs that are being used. MPs can be identified by the language used. If you can recognise preferred styles in yourself and others and you're aware of the qualities and drawbacks of the behaviour being displayed, you'll recognise why some conversations go well and others don't. Opposing MPs can cause irritation, confusion or simply a lack of understanding. Some of the 'pitfalls' or drawbacks are particularly prominent in certain situations and can present a major risk. When someone overdoes the 'matching' behaviour in uncertain situations, looking mainly at the possibilities and opportu-

nities, that approach may lead to the wrong decisions being taken. The information at hand is seen through rose-tinted spectacles and becomes tinted and tainted. They don't look at the whole picture (pros and cons), but only a selective part of it.

Sometimes you'll notice that people with opposing styles don't understand each other and that may even trigger major irritation:

- If one side largely behaves proactively (act first, think later) and starts acting on their ideas, while the other behaves mainly reactively (think first, then act), they may have a hard time working out what each other is doing because of the differences in style. They may become irritated because they simply don't understand each other. The bond could break, jeopardising the progress.
- If one side is very purposeful ('Towards'), knows what they want to achieve and states it clearly as well as showing it in their body language, while the other mainly sees risks and obstacles on the road ahead, misunderstandings and irritation may occur. One side wants to move forward, but the other seems to want to go backwards.

If you're unaware of these differences in style, you'll often not realise why communication isn't going smoothly even though you have a lot of common ground. The bond can break, despite both sides having numerous shared interests. Differences in style can create an unintended distance between two parties.

In reality you can't constantly focus on trying to recognise MPs. If you're interested and study the topic, you'll start recognising patterns and combinations of MPs, making you more alert. You'll possibly also be able to increase personal and team effectiveness, because understanding MPs teaches you how the behaviour patterns of team members can conflict. The trick with communication is to know your own preferences, recognise the behaviour of the other person, give it a place and use it to help rather than hinder both you and the other. An essential negotiating skill. At the same time, consciously reading people's behaviour provides tools for handling biases more flexibly and you'll deal with cultural differences in a different and more conscious way.

I'll go through a selection of MPs. I'll be focusing on the key features, identifying characteristics, strengths and weaknesses.

I'll describe the MPs as if they are people, which may rather give the impression that particular behaviours are 'good' or 'bad'; however, that value judgement is not my intention. I hope you'll be able to make the mental link with your own discussions and collaborations by examining how you'd feel in that situation, giving you an impression of your preferences. You'll then see what the consequences of those preferences are in your discussions.

METAPROGRAMMES (PMs)

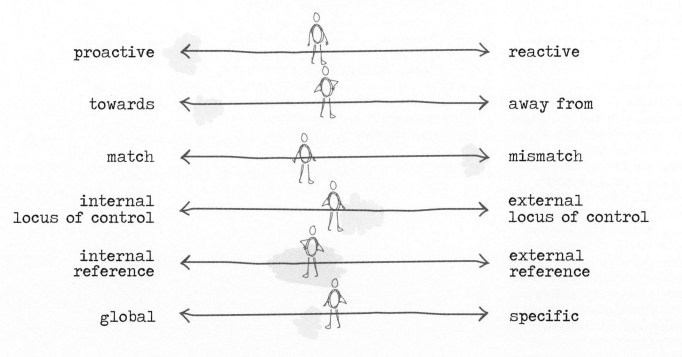

proactive	reactive
towards	away from
match	mismatch
internal locus of control	external locus of control
internal reference	external reference
global	specific

Inspiration: Dilts, Durlinger, Hustinx

METAPROGRAMMES (PMS)

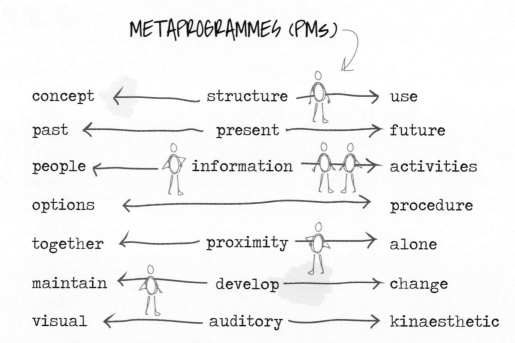

concept ← structure → use

past ← present → future

people ← information → activities

options ← → procedure

together ← proximity → alone

maintain ← develop → change

visual ← auditory → kinaesthetic

Inspiration: Dilts, Durlinger, Hustinx

Metaprogrammes

PROACTIVE

• Take initiative, act • Do, go • Make sure things happen • Active (don't think first) • If taken to extremes, that becomes 'doing without thinking'

CAN BE RECOGNISED BY

• Clear, powerful, short sentences • Straightforward use of language • Active verbs • Act • Now, at once • Action • I take action, do, set in motion

STRENGTHS

• Initiative, action • Roll up their sleeves and get to work • Get to work immediately

PITFALLS

• Hasty • Miss information • Miss the bond with others • Run ahead of the pack • Decide on solutions too quickly • Too quick to start actions that haven't been thought through

REACTIVE

• Think, reflect (without acting) • Wait • Take the time to understand and prepare • Wait for things to happen when others act • If taken to extremes, that becomes 'thinking but not acting'

CAN BE RECOGNISED BY

• Talks about analysing, understanding, waiting, nuancing • Uses indefinite language (sometimes) • I could • Perhaps • Possibly • Reconsider and have another look

STRENGTHS

• Think • Analyse, wanting to understand • Systematic preparation

PITFALLS

• Procrastinate • Still thinking things through • Make no move, or do not move enough • Miss the connection – the other party might be progressing already

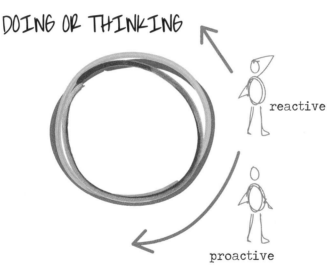

DOING OR THINKING

reactive

proactive

you?   proactive ←———————|———————→ reactive

125

TOWARDS

• Focused on the objectives • Want to achieve
• Set priorities • Want to include something (to
be able to progress towards the objective) • Have
trouble recognising problems

CAN BE RECOGNISED BY

• Use positive language • Achieve • What I (do)
want • Objective, wishes • Including • Results
• Receiving • Having

STRENGTHS

• Effective • Can map out the desired situation
• Can turn problems into objectives

PITFALLS

• Don't see problems • Don't see where something
can go wrong, what the risks are • Get annoyed
with people who point out problems; feel like
you're getting dragged along. You may perceive
this as people preventing you from achieving
your objectives, whereas the input may be highly
relevant • Trivialising the input of the 'away from'
thinker • Denying problems

AWAY FROM

• Focused on the problems • Want to avoid
mistakes/problems • Have an overview of what
could misfire or has already gone wrong • Want to
exclude things • Not so focused on the objective
• Have trouble setting priorities

CAN BE RECOGNISED BY

• Use negative language: impossible, unclear
• Avoiding • What I don't want • Preventing
• Avoiding problems, difficulties • Not including
• Liberating

STRENGTHS

• Map out the threats • See obstacles on the road
ahead

PITFALLS

• Not effective • Keep seeing risks and obstacles
on the road ahead • Being seen as the bringer
of problems, which can create a perception of
someone who doesn't want to be constructive.
Reputations may get damaged

ARE YOU GOING

away from

towards

you? towards away from

INTERNAL REFERENCE

• Focus on own criteria • Self-motivating • Decide what and how themselves • Open to information, decide whether or not to use it themselves
• Evaluate quality against their own findings • Have trouble accepting the opinions and directions chosen by others

CAN BE RECOGNISED BY

• I decide • I determine • I think, in my opinion
• Going by my criteria • "Interesting information"

STRENGTHS

• Motivated by their own internal standard
• Convinced of own vision • Own way
• Independent

PITFALLS

• Clash with others when different preferences
• Headstrong • Lose the connection with others who think differently

EXTERNAL REFERENCE

• Focus on the criteria (and interests) of others
• Need others to give direction • Open to other people's opinions • Trust other people's findings
• Seek confirmation • Interpret information as a direction or decision • Have difficulty making decisions

CAN BE RECOGNISED BY

• Is this okay? • What do you think? • You tell me
• The results show... • With reference to... • Others decide the guidelines • I don't know

STRENGTHS

• Focus on other people's interests • Listening
• Customer-oriented • Work well under supervision

PITFALLS

• Dependence • Lose direction if there's no feedback • Indecisiveness • Unaware of their own best interests or do not use them to contribute

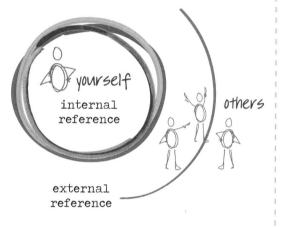

IS YOUR FOCUS ON

yourself
internal reference

others

external reference

you?   internal reference ⟵⎯⎯⎯⎯⎯⎯|⎯⎯⎯⎯⎯⎯⟶ external reference

OPTIONS

• Always sees alternative possibilities, goals, methods, roads, opportunities • Motivated to develop alternatives • The focus is on why – the reason for the choice • Good at developing and tweaking procedures • Can tackle several things at once • Have trouble following procedures and finishing tasks

CAN BE RECOGNISED BY

• Possibilities, alternatives • See options • We can do it like this, or like this • What we can also do • Another possibility is • What's important • Hard to choose

STRENGTHS

• See opportunities and possibilities • See alternatives • Have choices • Creative

PITFALLS

• Not finishing • Continue to explore possibilities • Have trouble following procedures • Castles in the sky

PROCEDURE

• Focused on the procedure as something that should be followed • Don't spontaneously see better options • Motivated to follow the procedure and are good at that • Finish what they started • Tackle one task at a time • The focus is on how – a step-by-step plan, sequentiality • Give chronological overviews of activities • Have difficulty improvising and developing procedures

CAN BE RECOGNISED BY

• First..., then..., and then... • And then..., and then... • The only way • Step by step • The way I do it • See only one way

STRENGTHS

• A set order: first this, then that • Follow procedures • Finishing

PITFALLS

• Want to follow fixed procedural steps, don't see other possibilities • Rigid • Have difficulty improvising • Not open to other ideas that interfere with the fixed order

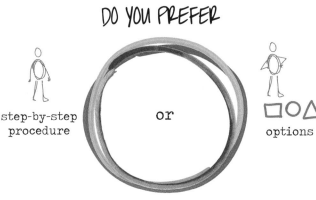

DO YOU PREFER

step-by-step procedure

or

options

you?

options ⟵⎯⎯⎯⎯⎯⎯⎯⎯⎯⎯⟶ procedure

MATCH

• Look for ways to find a fit • Wonder what would fit and how • Focus on what is right, what is correct, what is there • Attention to shared interests • The same, equal

CAN BE RECOGNISED BY

• What is good • Our common points are • What we have in common • What connects us • What is right • What is present again

STRENGTHS

• See what's there, what's correct • What's right • Glass is half full • Good understanding, connection

PITFALLS

• Everything is okay • Too little critical capacity • Overconfident coupled with a strong internal locus of control • Harmony at the expense of clarity • Lose sight of the big picture • Go with the flow

MISMATCH

• Notice what is missing • What does not fit, what is different • What is missing • Differences • What is wrong • What is different, where it differs from their perception

CAN BE RECOGNISED BY

• That's not right, I'm missing something • Wrong • I don't see it like that • Yes, but • You can't... • Where it won't work... • What hasn't been tackled • This contradicts...

STRENGTHS

Eye for what's missing • Glass is half empty • (Capable of being) critical • Can improve • Broaden the mindset of the other

PITFALLS

• Always finding fault • Never good • No longer see what is going well • Connection breaks down because the contribution is seen as resistance or criticism

DOES IT MEET YOUR CRITERIA OR NOT?

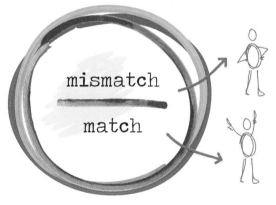

mismatch

match

you? ← match ——————— mismatch →

INTERNAL LOCUS OF CONTROL

• Focus on own responsibility • Internal focus when looking for causes • Assume things can be controlled • Make things happen • Recognise their own contribution

CAN BE RECOGNISED BY

• I make it happen • I'll arrange it, leave it to me • This is what I did in order to... • If I could just... then I'll also... • I let it happen • I am responsible • I'll make sure that they... • My share • Within my power

STRENGTHS

• Recognise own contribution • Assume personal control over achieving the goals • Make things happen • Autonomous

PITFALLS

• Overestimate their own contribution, leading to wrong decisions being made • Lacking the backing, overlooking people • Taking credit for things you didn't do

EXTERNAL LOCUS OF CONTROL

• External focus when looking for causes • Assume things cannot be controlled • Things happen, couldn't do anything about it • Refers more to chance or coincidence

CAN BE RECOGNISED BY

• It happens to me • It's being done to me • The system, the others • The organisation • They • It's out of my hands • Why is it always me? • I'm always the victim • That's beyond my power

STRENGTHS

• Eye for context • Attention to circumstances that complicate achieving the goals

PITFALLS

• Dependent on others • Underdog • It happens to me • Couldn't do anything about it • Don't take responsibility • Minimise their own role

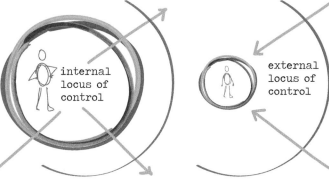

YOUR CIRCLE OF INFLUENCE

internal locus of control

external locus of control

you?   internal locus of control ←——————————|——————————→ external locus of control

GLOBAL

• Focused on the big picture • High-level abstraction, long term • Understand information in chunks • Broad focus • Have difficulty with lots of details

CAN BE RECOGNISED BY

• Talk about subjects in random order • High level of abstraction • Broad lines • Overview • Overall picture • My vision • The process • The people

STRENGTHS

• Broad lines • See problems in context • Discover patterns • Develop vision and see the general direction

PITFALLS

• Have difficulty communicating with specific thinkers • Castles in the sky • Lose attention when there are too many details • Others may have a hard time following them

SPECIFIC

• Focus on details • Focus on small pieces of information • Ask for specific instructions, low level of abstraction • Good at tasks that are specific in nature • Have difficulty getting an overview

CAN BE RECOGNISED BY

• Talk about subjects sequentially • Low level of abstraction • Point out details (additions) • Exact • Specific • That large, brown, hardwood table in the back right-hand corner isn't quite straight

STRENGTHS

• Details, precision • Dotting the i's and crossing the t's

PITFALLS

• Don't have the overview, don't see the common theme • Get lost in the details • Dwell on everything (if this behaviour is seen in combination with 'mismatch')

YOU THINK, OBSERVE

global
big picture

specific
details

you?　global ⟵⎯⎯⎯⎯⎯⎯⎯⎯⟶ specific

MAINTENANCE

• Don't want their own world to change • Focused on maintaining the situation • Prefer change occurring over decades or generations • Great resistance to change • Stability is the keyword

CAN BE RECOGNISED BY

• Remain unchanged • It's always been this way • Keeping things stable • Stay the same • Just like this • Seen this before • Follow its own course

STRENGTHS

• Able to do the same task for a long time • Balance, stability

PITFALLS

• Have a hard time adapting to changes • Boycott changes • Changes cause stress

DEVELOPMENT

• Want their own world to develop • Can handle change as long as it's seen as development • Prefer changes in the five to seven year timescale • Have difficulty with sudden changes • Development is the keyword

CAN BE RECOGNISED BY

• Step by step • Develop • Take it further • Improve

STRENGTHS

• Aiming for lasting improvement

PITFALLS

• Resistance to change • Major changes cause stress

you?   maintain ⬅——————————————— develop ══

... IS IMPORTANT FOR YOU

maintenance of
the status quo

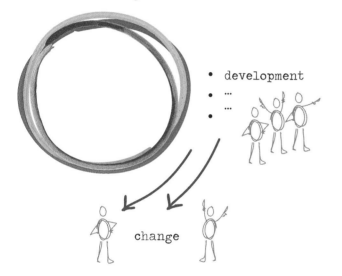

- development
- ...
- ...

change

CHANGE

• Want their own world to be characterised by change • Like big changes • Like changes in the one or two year timeframe • Tend to force changes in favour of development • Resistance to routine • Diversity is the keyword

CAN BE RECOGNISED BY

• Other • New • Dynamic • Change • Revolution • It's different from

STRENGTHS

• Dynamism; create a dynamic environment • A lot happens

PITFALLS

• Resistance to or demotivated by routine • Push changes through (even if stability is needed)

change

PEOPLE

• Focused on people and relationships. Note: preserve harmony and avoid conflicts • See the people as the task • Describe situations in terms of the people • Not much of an eye for activities and information

CAN BE RECOGNISED BY

• People • Relationships • Use first names and surnames • Use personal pronouns

STRENGTHS

• Match pace with others easily • Relationship-oriented • Harmony

PITFALLS

• Too dependent on relationship/mutual dependency • Not much of an eye for information and activities

INFORMATION

• Focused on information and knowledge • See the information as the task • Describe situations in terms of the information • Not much of an eye for relationships and activities

CAN BE RECOGNISED BY

• Knowledge • Reporting • Information • The numbers • The data • Analysing data • Research shows that...

STRENGTHS

• Collecting knowledge • Task analysis

PITFALLS

• Not much of an eye for people and activities • Not enough of an eye for personal connections • If taken to extremes: a bookworm

you?   people ⟵————————————— information

YOU FOCUS ON ...
PAY ATTENTION TO

people

information

activities

ACTIVITIES

• Focused on activities • See activities as the task • Describe situations in terms of the activities • Not much of an eye for relationships and information

CAN BE RECOGNISED BY

• Controlling • Act • Organising • Process • Task • Undertaking

STRENGTHS

• Taking action • Finishing/doing things

PITFALLS

• Tend to lose track of people and information • Too much doing and action, missing out on relationships and backing

activities

CONCEPT

• Principles and essentials • Focus on the 'why' question • The concept is the focal point for the thinking • Where are you going?

CAN BE RECOGNISED BY

• The essence • The principle • To the core of the matter • What it's all about • Why • The underlying concept

STRENGTHS

• The why, the essence, wanting to understand the principles • Theoretical explanation

PITFALLS

• Can get stuck if the concept isn't clear • Lose track of the practical application What can you do with it? • No bonding with other thinkers, who will lose interest. This is particularly true if your descriptions are too conceptual and too abstract.

STRUCTURE

• Cohesion, elements and relationships • 'What' and 'where' questions • Order in chaos • The cohesion is the focal point for the thinking

CAN BE RECOGNISED BY

• The cohesion • The mutual relationships • What we need • Which elements • Structuring • What and where

STRENGTHS

• Creating order from chaos

PITFALLS

• You have to know all the elements before progress can be made • You pin yourself down

you?   concept ⬅━━━━━━━━━━━━━━━━━━━━━━ structure ▬▬▬

THINKING 'PREFERENCE'?

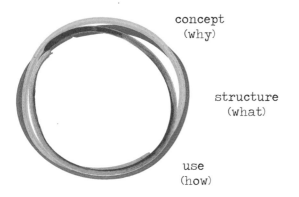

concept
(why)

structure
(what)

use
(how)

USE

• Application and use • The 'how' question • The action is the focal point for the thinking

CAN BE RECOGNISED BY

• The approach • Usefulness • The solution • The use • How we use it • What I can do with it

STRENGTHS

• Solving problems on the fly • Seeing practical applications

PITFALLS

• Get stuck because various items are missing • What was it all about, actually? Things you haven't spotted • Doing things that turn out not to have been useful because they didn't fit in the greater whole or the context or the reason why

 use

TOGETHER

• Want to work together • Want to share responsibility • Team player
• Difficulty working independently and making decisions

CAN BE RECOGNISED BY

• Together • Team • We • Contribute to • Our work • Our responsibility
• Our decision • Our result

STRENGTHS

• 'Need' others • Team player, cooperation

PITFALLS

• Not independent • Don't take own responsibility • Get stressed when given sole responsibility

PROXIMITY

• Want a clearly defined territory • Want their own responsibility • Like having others around them • Have difficulty sharing responsibility and authority

CAN BE RECOGNISED BY

• My territory • My responsibility • My contribution • Independent
• Distinctive • My share

STRENGTHS

• The 'centre forward' who wants to excel • Fit in well with our corporate culture

PITFALLS

• Difficulty sharing responsibility • Difficulty promoting themselves

you?   together ⬅========================= proximity ===

YOU LIKE TO BE/WORK ...

together

close by

alone

ALONE

• Like working alone • Want sole responsibility • Can concentrate for long periods • Tendency not to communicate (except where necessary for the task) • Difficulty working with others

CAN BE RECOGNISED BY

• Independent • Uninterrupted • Alone • Self • Total concentration • Without a break • By myself • Don't need anyone

STRENGTHS

• Independent • Own responsibility • Solo sailor

PITFALLS

• Cooperating • Sharing • Go their own way • Lose the bond

alone

PAST

• Focus on the past • What was • Look at the present from the perspective of the past • No contact with the future • Sit on their laurels

CAN BE RECOGNISED BY

• Back then • In the old days • At first • There always was • I remember well • Always when... • What we did then • What worked at the time was...

STRENGTHS

• What used to be, back then, looking from the perspective of the past
• Able to learn from experience

PITFALLS

• Trapped in the past • Involving past experiences in current actions, thereby getting things confused • Not enjoying the here and now

PRESENT

• Focus on the present • What is • Busy with the here and now • Little contact with past or future • Enjoy the moment

CAN BE RECOGNISED BY

• Now • Here • Current • At this moment • What we're doing now • What we want now • What's important currently

STRENGTHS

• Attention and presence in the now • Presence

PITFALLS

• Difficulty learning from the past • Difficulty envisioning the future

you?   past ⟵————————————   present ═══

YOUR TIME FOCUS

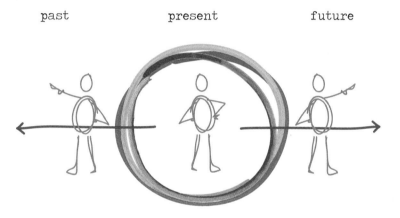

past   present   future

FUTURE

• Focus on the future • What will be • The future determines current actions • Difficulty getting a picture of the past and present • Look forward to what is to come

CAN BE RECOGNISED BY

• Later • In the future • Soon • Aims • Long-term objectives • Will be • What we'll do after that...

STRENGTHS

• Looking forward to the future • Can develop visions

PITFALLS

• Not enough focus on the current challenge • Making too much allowance for the future now, resulting in incorrect decisions being taken • Preoccupied with what will happen soon, or later on, and consequently failing to pay attention to the present • Forget to enjoy the moment • Impatient with people whose focus is on the past

future

VISUAL

• Think in pictures • Learn primarily from visual information • Able to dissociate well • Talk quickly

CAN BE RECOGNISED BY

• Seeing • Looking • Clear • Suppose • Imagine • I can see it in front of me • Think in pictures • Show me

STRENGTHS

• Able to 'see' images, pictures and even words • Visual imagination • Good at both associative and dissociative behaviour

PITFALLS

• Difficulty absorbing spoken information

AUDITORY

• Think in sounds • Learn primarily from the spoken word and from stories • Can be both dissociative and associative • Talk slowly, rhythmically, sequentially

CAN BE RECOGNISED BY

• Sounds like • In tune with • Listen to this • Music to my ears • The story • Verbal • Tell me • Tuned in

STRENGTHS

• Learn easily from the spoken word and from melodies

PITFALLS

• Difficulty absorbing visual information

you?   visual ⟵━━━━━━━━━━   auditory ━━━━

PERCEPTUAL CHANNELS

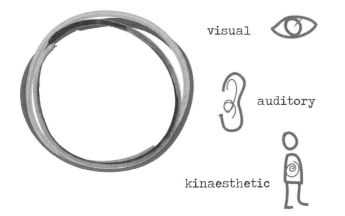

visual

auditory

kinaesthetic

KINAESTHETIC

• Think in emotions and movements • Learn primarily by doing, moving, how it feels, the experience • Are primarily associative; have difficulty dissociating • Talk slowly

CAN BE RECOGNISED BY

• I feel • Resonance • Getting a grip on • In motion • Physically Experiencing • Tearing their hair out • Feeling

STRENGTHS

• Feeling, intuition • Muscle memory

PITFALLS

• Difficulty dissociating ('taking a step back') • Difficulty with visual and auditory information processing

 Kinaesthetic

Developing agility

If you are aware of your strengths and weaknesses, you will also be able to see when you are communicating well and when it is more awkward, with people whose behaviour modes are different. As stated earlier, MPs can reinforce or oppose one another. It may work well for you if your behaviour modes are Proactive, Towards, Global and Matching – but there are also a number of risks. When decisions have to be taken, it may be worthwhile for you to ponder on whether relevant details have been overlooked and the decision taken too quickly. You are after all someone who focuses on the broad lines, seeing above all where things are going well and actively pursuing your goal. If you exhibit Critical and Away From behaviour modes at the negotiating table, there may be no progress made. If there is too much of the Maintain, Past and Mismatch modes, it may be difficult to get the wheels of change in motion. If a team does not have a good balance of thinking and working styles, there are a number of pitfalls waiting to trap you.

If you are aiming to make things progress together and reach decisions, it can help if you deliberately bring a number of essential MPs on board. Deliberate communication with the aim of serving your best interests is a challenge. As an illustration, here is a lengthier example, of the opening to a meeting. It is intended more as an example of a number of MPs being deployed than as a realistic opening. Can you recognise the MPs? "Today we are working towards a decision about about ABC, which is an important one for us. I suggest that we should take a structured look at the information that's already on the table, and then compare it against our own interests to see where the pluses and minuses are. I hope that we'll be able to weigh things up carefully together and reach a decision we can all support. If it turns out that there's information we're missing, we can look to see what the quickest way is of getting it out into the open. I'm asking you to be critical here, because we mustn't overlook anything. It's much too important for that. Nevertheless, I want us to make progress and so I'm counting on your cooperation." Communicating more deliberately and more carefully increases the chance of you all remaining on the same track.

Being able to stay relaxed and observe, interpret what's going on and progress from there together are major challenges for a negotiator. The trick is not only in listening to the content of the message, but also in observing the form that the message is packaged in. Insights and further practice can help you to discover the patterns and get better at empathising and making progress together. It's not either one or the other: it's both. "At the same time" is a key concept.

Examples

Behaving proactively yet at the same time leaving room for reactive thinking. Being inclusive rather than exclusive. "I understand that you want to get things moving quickly. But there are a couple of points I need more details for. Can we take a quick look at those?" Or "I understand that it's important to get it up and running. To keep the wheels rolling, I think it would be smart to discuss a couple of items thoroughly now, otherwise there'll be delays later." Or "I can see you frowning. Am I going too fast? I'll be perfectly happy to take a moment to look at more of the details. What do you need?"

It is possible to focus on the objectives while still seeing the obstacles that are in the way, or having someone else make a list of them. The trick is to do both at once, so that you are limiting the risks while still following the process efficiently. "If we're to achieve our goals as quickly as possible, I'm aware it'd be smart to take a look at the risks we might come across along the way.Tell me David, what do you think might be tricky?" If David is the type of person who sees bogeymen behind every tree, this question is a thoroughly appropriate one, because you're fitting in with what he's good at. If John's thought patterns are largely in the Towards category, he'll have difficulty answering the question or immediately turn potential risks into objectives. Another example of careful communication: "I can see a few items that worry me. I think it would be a good idea to discuss them together and see what the consequences might be for further progress." Or "So that we can achieve the objective as soon as possible."

You can really end up leading yourself and the other party up the garden path. Having too much Global thinking, too little critical capacity and too much of a focus on the targets in the same team means that something will undoubtedly get started, but a lot of mistakes will probably be made and things will be missed. Whether this

behaviour pattern is appropriate or not depends on the context and your goals or interests.

The trick is to do one thing without forgetting the flip side. Retaining the one while developing the other. Seeing the sunny side while still remaining open to the opposite. If you are entrepreneurial by nature, you may perhaps think that business is all about going for it, action, taking risks... Sure, but at the same time those risks should also be calculated. If you want to go quickly, go alone; if you want to go far, go together. After assessing the risks, you can make progress and you'll get further travelling together.

A few more useful things to know

- If your thinking is Global, ask for input about relevant details that you shouldn't forget.
- If your thinking is Match (see the opportunities and possibilities), bring Mismatch thinking on board so that you have enough critical capacity. Please refer also to preventing 'Overconfidence bias' (page 158).
- Explore the options, using a structured process. Realise that you can keep exploring options, but they do have to lead somewhere. You want to serve the

interests, and the options do therefore have to be feasible. Use the Disney method for an organised approach to the issue.
- If you want to get people who don't really want a change to go along with you nonetheless, you can align your thinking with theirs by saying what will remain the same and what you want to develop, one step at a time. Words such as *change*, *hard-hitting* and *transition* can be counter-productive.
- If you and the other party both have a high degree of internal reference, there will be clashes. Invite the other to share the way they perceive things and compare it to your view. That'll make it easier to see what the best choice may be, given the interests. Opinions often stagnate and positions become more entrenched because of stubbornness (on both sides). Who's going to blink first? The atmosphere will be more relaxed if you're more flexible. "Well, I've certainly got my own opinion about that and I'd be happy to share it with you. But I realise you've been thinking about it too. Might it be an idea to take a look first at exactly what we're here to do and then see how our thoughts match up with that?" It's one way of preventing

possible deadlocks. To create a bit of breathing space, you can also present your opinion as an option: "I certainly do have an idea about how we could resolve this, but I suspect there may be several possibilities. Fancy taking a look at them together...?" Engage with the other party, rather than pushing them away.

- During presentations, you should take account of the various styles of thinking that are always present in your audience. Structure your presentation and take things one step at a time. Pay attention to both the concept and the usage, for instance. If you have described things in rather abstract outlines, ask explicitly if more detail is needed. Give people something to experience. Show images and pay attention to the content of your narrative. Anticipate people who are going to see potential problems everywhere and cover the risks too. You may even want to invite people who like Mismatching and being critical to do just that. If there is scope for criticism at the right time, people will be less likely to harp on at other moments. Criticism is often an expression of genuine concern rather than mere unwillingness. If attention is paid to it, the criticism softens (and if that doesn't happen, you

can always intervene in the process). If it's part and parcel of someone playing games, please refer to the section on how to deal with that (page 163).

PACING AND LEADING

In earlier examples of responses, I've mentioned pacing and leading – making a connection with the other party by matching pace, after which you can lead them to take the next step together. I've already given a few examples and I'd now like to give you a little more background to it. If two good friends go out for a pint in the pub together, you'll quickly see that they're 'tuned in' to each other. They may adopt the same pose, or stand by the bar like two mirror images, talking at the same volume. They fit together vocally (timbre, intonation, energy) and non-verbally (body language) and they will seem to understand each other verbally too (the content of what they're saying). When that bonding is there, you're often not aware of it – you're simply enjoying the moment. If the connection breaks, you may notice that there now seems to be a distance, remoteness. In a business environment, the discussions are often a little more standoffish and formal

and you'll perceive the bond less quickly. The question is how you can create a good connection so that people feel understood and are prepared to share information with you and take their lead from you.
I'll limit the discussion here to four verbal levels of communication. Insights into these levels will help you fit in more consciously with others, allowing you to be more agile and flexible, capable of keeping progressing together. It is a way of explicitly applying Guide 1, separating the relational side from the content.

If you analyse what is going on in terms of the communication during a discussion, you may see that people are:

- noticing: absorbing information
- interpreting: assigning meaning to the information (biased or otherwise)
- responding: exhibiting behaviour as a reaction to the information received

Not reacting is impossible: you always respond in some way to what you see, hear or experience. Non-verbally, at least. If you want to increase the impact you have in the negotiation process, it is worth being able to give an effective verbal response to what is being said implicitly or explicitly. I've already covered the observational side

4 LEVELS OF COMMUNICATION

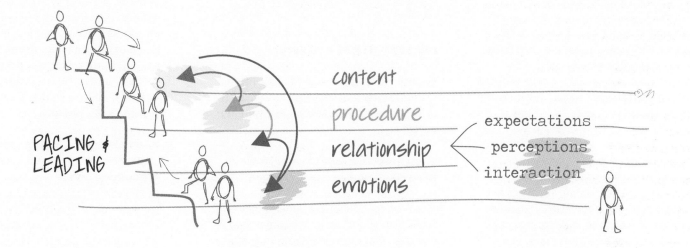

– reading people – in the section on the metaprogrammes. You can use that filter for observing behaviour and describing it.

If you respond verbally to what happens or what is said, there are four levels at which you can react. You can give:

- A **substantive response** to the information content.

- A **procedural response** that explicitly addresses the order items are to be discussed in. First this, then that.
- An **interaction/relationship comment** concerning how you interact with each other, the expectations, perceptions and the way in which you communicate.
- An **emotional response** in which you literally state the emotions.

An example: you are discussing a planning issue with one of the parties you are cooperating with. At a given moment, their project leader says, "John, I'm sorry but I have to point out that this is now the second time that you've failed to meet your deadline." Depending on the atmosphere that has been prevailing in that discussion so far, there are four possible responses:

Content: "We'll do what we can to catch up the backlog as quickly as possible and prevent these issues in future." This is a response to the substance of the message that was just given.

Procedure: "I'd first like to give you a bit of background to the delays and then discuss with you what problems it's causing for you and how we can tackle them. Is that all right?" A response such as this is procedural, because a sequence of actions is described.

Relationship: "I can tell from the way you're saying it that you've got the impression you've joined forces with a bunch of amateurs." Or "I understand that you expected a response from us a lot earlier." Remarks such as these are about the interactions or the relationship, referring to what is going on between the two sides. In any negotiation, you may have to address the way in which the other party regards you and the perceptions you have of each other. If you observe that the way you interact with each other (negative perceptions, expectations, communication) are inhibiting the negotiation process, it is important to respond at the interaction / relationship level.

Emotions: "I can see that this is still a pretty sore point." Or "I'm genuinely distressed that we've caused problems for you." Or "I'm aware that this affects you a lot." This type of comment is emotionally based, referring directly to what you or the other party feel about each other. A response at the emotional level should be given if you think emotions are involved and getting in the way of progress. If emotions are stated explicitly, that may be evident. But you also want to pay attention to implicitly expressed emotions if you think they are getting entangled with the content.

Which response is the most effective in any given situation depends hugely on the context. If you want to influence the progress of the meeting, the general guideline is that you should try to fit in with the level that the other party is **actually** communicating on. What I mean by the 'actual' level is the message that is being given implicitly, the underlying message that the other side is trying to communicate but not necessarily saying. That lets you create bonding and trust because the other party feels that they are being understood.

In everyday practice, it is particularly relevant that you learn to operate at the interaction / relationship level. That you are consciously aware of how you are responding in situations where expectations are unclear and not explicitly stated, where perceptions are in the way of progress and where the way you are interacting is not effective. Insights into the metaprogrammes can help you find the language for categorising the behaviour you are seeing. This describes the interactions and the relationship between the actors sitting around the table, so that 'Pacing and leading' becomes possible.

Examples of switching between the interaction / relationship level and the procedural level

- "I feel as if you're going very fast now [proactive]. Can we go back a step for a moment [procedure], because I'd like to think about that a little [reactive]."

- "I reckon we both want to get things moving now [proactive] and make a decision [towards]. Nevertheless, there are still a few risks we need to talk about [away from] and I suggest that we ought to take the opportunity now to do just that [procedure]." You are describing the interaction, the behaviour (proactive, towards, away from) and making a procedural suggestion.

- "I think you're taking a number of steps very quickly here [proactive, towards]. A bit too quickly, I reckon. I think it'd be a good idea if we go back to point A again, because I'd like to discuss that a little more [procedure]. Tell me."
- "David, I can tell that it's important for you to retain a number of aspects [maintain], and I fully understand that. Even so, I think it's important that a couple of things are modified [develop]. Why don't we take a look together at what we can keep as it is for you, while at the same time taking a step towards…?"

The way in which you talk explicitly about emotions is highly dependent on the cultural context. In some cultures it may not be appropriate, because they communicate very indirectly. In other cultures, however, it may be the norm. As far as I am concerned, it is crucial above all that you are aware of the response levels, so that you can assess – in any given situation – which level you want to (and can) communicate on explicitly. Emotions are an expression of a higher level; they are often the result of negative perceptions and/or expectations that are not being met.

People may feel that they are not being seen, that their contribution is not being acknowledged, or they may be surprised by your actions or feel that you are not giving them credit where it's due. You don't have to talk about the emotions themselves then, but you may be able to speak about the underlying causes of those emotions. Being able to switch between the first three levels is already enough to make you much more effective.

When people express emotions or are angry, disappointed or annoyed, you should pay attention to that. You want to empathise with those emotions, to be able to connect to them. And once you think they've received enough attention, you can continue. The other party will often indicate implicitly when they're ready for you to move on. In those situations, you can use a segue such as, "Jacob, I'm glad we took a moment to discuss X. Do you mind if we take a look at how we can move forward now?" The other party determines the pace. People sometimes make a distinction here between sympathising and empathising. Showing sympathy is in fact not much more than stating that you realise something is difficult for the other side. If you empathise, you take a moment to consider their emotions; you want to help

them and fit in with that emotion. Then you can look to see if you can progress together. If you find something difficult, you also need to ask whether this is affecting the progress. "Annette, I'm unhappy with what's happened. We'd agreed that we would receive information about X and I can see that that hasn't happened yet. And now we can't go any further." Moving between the communication levels creates options for moving forward together.

Examples of empathising at a lower communication level than the actual content:

- "I can see that you're disappointed about how our cooperation is going. I'm very sorry to hear that. What's bothering you?"
- "It seems that you're not happy with how our partnership is working out. I can tell that you think we've dropped the ball a couple of times, and that's a real shame. Please tell me more."
- "I see that we've got different expectations about our cooperation. Why not start by discussing that, before we go any further?"
- "If I put myself in your shoes, and given the information you have, it's logical that you see it like that.

We're apparently got different views about the data that's on the table. Let's compare viewpoints compare our perceptions and see how we want to move ahead?"

- "It's clear to me that the way this meeting is proceeding isn't going to help us get anywhere. Our assessments of the situation are simply too far apart. Do you see it that way too?"
- "I don't think we're singing from the same hymn sheet yet - we've got different ideas about the outcome of this project. Hadn't we better take a look at that together first?"

Moving up and down between the levels lets you respond more effectively. If things are unclear or the way in which you communicate is different, or if negative perceptions or emotions play are role, you will be more capable of continuing together without breaking the bond. It may be quite tricky to apply at first and it will not feel natural. After a little while, it will become more a part of you and you'll be able to use it unconsciously and spontaneously. This will let you switch between the content and the relationship components, and apply Guide 1 more deliberately.

We use aikido principles as a metaphor for the movement in 'Pacing and leading'. We have been working on this for many years with Aalt Aalten. He has helped us and the course participants to see how you can use your strengths and make connections with the other party. Aikido is a Japanese martial art and one of its meanings is 'the path to harmonising your strength with yourself and others'. How you can bring the other in, instead of disabling them as quickly as possible. How you can create and retain the bond. As a metaphor for creating the connection with yourself and with the other party, so that you can progress together as fellow travellers on the same road, rather than as opponents. Aalt helps you become aware of where your focus is and of how to harmonise that focus and connect it to yourself and others. That makes you aware of your inner strength and energy. 'Pacing and leading' become a metaphor for a joint negotiation action in which you include people to keep them on the path with you, shoulder to shoulder, rather than excluding them.

HOW TO DEAL WITH BIASES

Listening and understanding each other really well and reaching decisions together is a challenge. People filter information as they process it during this communication, because it is not possible to absorb all the information. They filter things unintentionally, or distort or generalise or leave information out.   If you know what's happening and you can detect what's left out, distorted or generalised, then you'll be able to see how people – intentionally or otherwise – can interpret information differently to the actual situation. If you listen properly to what someone is saying and keep asking questions about the background to opinions or decisions, then you can verify whether the facts are correct (Guide 2) and get a sharp picture of the content. If people's view of a complicated problem is too rosy, they may lose sight of the reality. If people overestimate their influence, they may take decisions that don't have the backing of others. Don't forget the MPs. You will see that this section has some overlap with a few MPs that have already been introduced. I think this should help increase your awareness of the topic, which is why I decided not to merge the two sections.

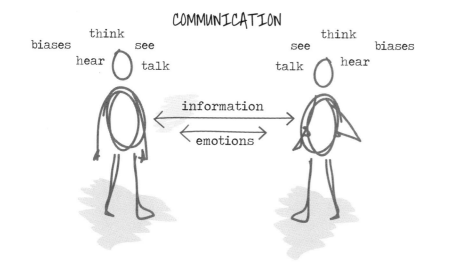

COMMUNICATION

We weigh up options – alone or with others – and take decisions every day. Are we going to continue a project or not, what will we and won't we do to support a project, and which business partner are we going to choose? Go, no-go, make or buy, whether or not to invest, whether or not to say yes to a deal. In contexts that get more and more complex, and where substantial interests are at stake, the right decision-making also becomes more important because of the high risk of failure. Of course you make mistakes: to err is human and it's all part of life's rich tapestry. But I do hope you learn from the errors. Wrong decisions are often taken that hindsight tells you could have been prevented. "In retrospect, it's a nice place to live," I heard someone say only recently, but if you'd thought about it earlier and differently, you wouldn't have fallen into some fairly predictable traps. You can act more appropriately if you are able to stop the process for a moment and evaluate what you hear and see, and what you think of it.

"I was wondering if what he said was correct, but he said it with so much conviction that I believed him." You often understand things better with hindsight, but it is difficult in the heat of the moment. Why are wrong decisions made so often? A few observations:

- Relationship: you have been put under pressure, games were played and you found that difficult to handle (see page 163).
- Content: the right information was not provided, or the fact that information was biased went unnoticed.
- Process: it all went too fast, not enough specifics, with power plays – and too little critical ability or not done carefully enough. Please refer to 'Metaprogrammes' (page 120) and 'Process interventions' (page 106). You may also have thought actors had been missed out.

Emotions may have been used to accelerate processes, and you were pressed for time or tired. Maybe it was not the process but the way that you or the other party looked at the information and how it was processed. Our human brains can fool us and sabotage decision-making processes (unintentionally).

Research into how the brain works when assessing information and making decisions is a relatively new field of science. It is clear that all kinds of subconscious processes are involved and we apparently use them to handle the complexity that you often see when decisions have to be made. A book by Nobel prizewinner Daniel Kahneman about this subject (*Thinking, Fast and Slow*, 2011) was number one for a long time in all kinds of top-ten book lists, and was suddenly in demand again in just the past year. It is a hot topic. Rolf Dobelli's book (*The Art of Thinking Clearly*, 2013) is a bestseller too.

I would like to focus on a number of aspects that will allow you to be more alert about how to manage the content. This knowledge will make it possible for you use Guide 2 ('Trust and verification') in greater depth. If you would like to read more about this, please refer to the literature list. I have been using those same resources here.

Systems I and II
When handling information, we feel the need to reduce the many signals and incentives into 'bite-sized chunks' that you can recognise and use as the basis for taking action. The question, however, is whether these are the right actions. Kahneman refers to two systems that we use to process all information.
System I is the intuitive, automatic system. Subconsciously and without thinking, you perform actions and make decisions. This 'ancient' system requires little effort, works very quickly and is often very convenient. You do not have to think how you brush your teeth, for instance; if you did, you'd be thrown off that automatic flow of actions. System II is the conscious, more rational and reflective system, which requires more attention and time. You categorise the information and you have to explore and consider it. When you need to learn something, it takes a while before it can be done automatically. When learning to drive or mastering any other new skill, practice makes perfect. Only then will you acquire and internalise it.

Both systems are continuously switched on and active. System II is largely monitoring. It gets switched on consciously when the interests and risks start getting more substantial. System I is active in day-to-day, routine actions in particular. In practice you will encounter all kinds of decisions that were made 'too fast and automatically'. System I was running, but System II should have been enabled too. We should stop to think and reflect more, using up-to-date and correct information. The same thing happens when decisions are made in complex negotiation situations.

An example frequently used to illustrate the two systems is the subconscious patterns we develop when driving that help us to estimate distances. If we see a car clearly, we assume that car will be closer than one that we see more hazily. We handle the two situations differently, and so we should. We 'automatically' make different decisions based on the two sets of perceptions.
The surprising thing about this approach is that our brains can fool us. And regularly try to do so. Our brains can sabotage the clear thinking that lets us make the right decisions. If it is foggy, for instance, we may misjudge a car that we perceive hazily as being far away. It's something experience taught us earlier. Extremely dangerous here, though, because the car might be very close. Our brain was fooling us. We apparently have to be reminded all the time to keep our distance in foggy conditions and adjust our driving behaviour. We have to tell ourselves this consciously and repeatedly, because we apparently fail to

do it automatically. Our own judgement can get in the way and let us down precisely when it is needed most, for making correct decisions in complex situations.

If the interests and the complexity are not so great, you will be not running so many risks. But if you put that example of the car in a different context, the risks can be much greater. Take a Boeing 777 pilot, for example. Decisions that the pilot has to make can in many cases not be left to him alone. Objective instrumentation has been introduced because our subjective perceptions do not offer enough certainty in decision-making processes. Good negotiators should therefore base their decisions on accurate, verifiable information and weigh things up after using objective criteria. In other words, not using biased information and subjective criteria. The complicating aspect is that we're often unaware of patterns that may get in the way when we're trying to make the right decision. We have blind spots and fail to recognise those patterns. It would be good if you could ask yourself more often if you are looking at the information objectively enough, if you are interpreting the data 'correctly' and if you have the right picture of it all. This may help you become

aware of your preferred style in the MPs, which means you'll be more aware of your strengths and weaknesses when making decisions.

From an airline pilot to your own practical situation

In practice, you are involved in the assessments and decisions that are made during negotiation processes every day. You must occasionally have had the feeling that 'something' wasn't right, a little voice somewhere telling you that you are fooling yourself. Can you intervene? If the light is amber, do you stomp on the brakes or the accelerator?

It is extremely important to be consciously aware of decision-making processes. You want information that is correct and objective criteria that can help you share out the pie. The decisions you make must serve the interests, and the solutions must be feasible and practicable. The assessment of those parameters can be biased, though. If you recognise that distortion, you can talk about it and you may jointly arrive at a revised solution. You can revise the situation almost literally by looking at it through different eyes.

To give you a broader idea of the topic, I'm now going to give you an overview of a number of frequently occurring biases that can play important roles in decision-making processes. If you are aware of them, and you can read and interpret the mentioned behaviour, you will also recognise a number of MPs in the descriptions. I will foremost focus on handling these biases 'used' by others, but If you are aware of how influencing processes work, you will see that you can also 'use' some biases yourself to influence others. Then they become a part of playing games.

Some common biases in general situations and in uncertainty

Anchoring
Attaching disproportionate value to the information that was obtained initially. The initial experience is anchored in our brain. That information can bias the way that we look at the situation. One well-known experiment involves asking a group of people two questions. The first question is whether the population of Spain is more than forty million. This question gets answered. Then you ask how many people they think live in Spain. The number that you used in the first question will affect

the answer to the second. You attach too much importance to the initial information. If you substitute a hundred million for forty million in the first question, the answers to the second question will almost always be higher. The initial exchange of information is anchored in the brain. It is then difficult to give an objective and unbiased answer to a second question.

That's why people often say in practice that whoever makes the first proposal is in the lead. The information given in it biases the way that you look at the situation and has become the baseline, as it were. If this keeps being reaffirmed with plenty of conviction and emotion, it will become even more ingrained. You should be aware that this happens and that it affects both the relationships and the content. The same applies when estimates have to be assessed: looking back at trends and earlier data can bias your picture of current and future situations. And it's equally applicable when a business case has to be assessed. The initial information starts to lead a life of its own.

Coping with anchoring
- Don't immediately allow initial information to become leading. Use information that is verifiable and not dependent on trust. Information from the past is no guarantee for the future. To what extent is the information from phase X linked to the current situation? Compare, connect and check that the initial information is not affecting the situation too much. The fact that something worked in a certain way in the past does not mean that it is self-evident that it will work the same way now too. One thing does not necessarily have anything to do with the other.
- You should reflect on a specific proposal first, before taking information from the other side on board. What picture do you have of it? What do you think is fair?
- Always check the fairness based on objective criteria when distribution issues are involved. If you are aware of the above, it is certainly important when sharing out the pie to keep checking that the criteria are not too subjective or biased.
- When desirable, use multiple viewpoints to test your perceptions: this is to make sure you develop a broader perspective on a problem, thereby maximising the

chance of reaching the right decision. Create an overall picture.
- Be careful not to be forced into a decision too quickly if your intuition tells you that it isn't right. It's possible that you've sensed that something isn't quite right, but you haven't been able to put a finger on it yet. Always check your interests and risks, and be aware of your BATNA.
- Be aware that you can play the same game too, that the impact of the initial information can also work to your advantage.

Status quo
This 'brain filter' is a common bias in which you want to maintain the current situation even though there are better alternatives.

Status quo thinking is sometimes compared to a magnet: a lot of lines of thought are drawn towards it. Decisions are often taken in favour of maintaining a stable situation. Change often meets resistance, because people have to take responsibility and take the associated risks, given that you don't know exactly what you will run into and what you'll be getting. You also have to consciously consider options and alternatives, which may demand a great deal of your time and attention. System II will need to be switched on, but that may not have happened (yet). The status quo bias is subconsciously enhanced by looking at information that you have and that you can specifically use to reinforce your situation. Availability bias and confirming evidence bias can play a major role here: to help maintain the status quo, you use whatever you have available and look for information that is convenient for you. In short, you go looking for what you want to find in order to remain in a stable position. I've referred to 'you' in this paragraph, but it can of course be 'them' who want to maintain the status quo.

Handling the status quo

For the record: there may well be nothing wrong with a status quo. If you, the negotiator, want to get things moving and you see that information is being used that in particular is aimed at justifying the stable option, you should make the other side aware of other information to see if you can achieve progress.

- If you come up against people who want to assess the situation from the status quo viewpoint, it's important for you to be aware of whether this is a problem at all. Are your interests being

served? If so, you don't need to pay too much attention to it.

- If you do want to move people towards a different situation, don't go too fast! Don't say too quickly that the change would be for the better, or that your information is better. Change is often justified using all kinds of 'convincing' arguments, but you may see the other side thinking, "Fair enough, but it's not for me." The connection is lost, trust starts fading away and it is difficult for you to draw close again. Instead:

- Be open and respect the considerations of others who want to maintain the status quo. The other side clearly think (perhaps subconsciously) that this has its benefits. In your eyes, this may be difficult to imagine because better alternatives are available. It is apparently in the interest of the other party to maintain the current situation. Investigate the arguments and details, try to understand them and compare them against the other information. Take it one step at a time. Make a link with what will stay the same and show the other side what could be changed without harming their interests. Legitimise each of your steps to make sure you can look at the overall situation together and weigh things up.

Sunk costs

Decisions are based on costs that have already been incurred (time, money, effort) rather than on consideration of the current factual situation.

Continuing along the path already taken is seen as better than stopping, whereas this is in fact not true. Loss of face plays a major role in this, as stopping is an implicit admission that you should have handled something differently. For some people, that is a painful step to take. You don't want to suffer that loss of face, so you continue. For example, you fail to make a decision "because so much cash and effort have already been sunk into it. We'd be wasting all that."

The losses, costs or effort already made are included when weighing the options up. As an example, suppose you have bought a ticket for a concert. You suddenly need to do something important on the day of the concert, so you cannot go. But the costs have already been incurred – you've already bought your ticket – so you decide to go to the concert anyway. Doing so may mean you have made a wrong decision that does not serve your interests. Another example: you're in the middle of a negotiation and have put a lot of time and effort into it. It has also cost money. A couple of months have passed: you have incurred costs and you feel that it would be increasingly diffi cult to break off the negotiations. That would be wasting the effort already made! But you may end up with an agreement that does not work out well for you. I come across this bias regularly in multi-party partnerships. Discussions went on for months and all kinds of ways of cooperating were examined, but there was in fact no progress. From a suitable distance, you can see that there were numerous moments when they should have said enough is enough. So be careful: you cannot keep throwing good money after bad. Don't include the efforts made so far when considering if it is wise to continue. After all, you do fi nally want to achieve a good deal (please refer to page 98).

Coping with sunk costs

- Be honest with yourself and be aware of this pitfall. Do the two aspects have anything to do with each other? Why stick with a situation if it isn't the smart thing to do? It is very disarming to indicate that, all things considered, you're forced to conclude that you really have to stop X. That twenty-twenty hindsight suggests you may have made the wrong decision, and that you would like to look back on events and learn from them. How might you have reached a different decision at the time? Or would you still do the same again?

- Be alert to the fact that sunk costs may be included in the decision-making process that you are involved in, and be ready to intervene in the process. "Dear Peter, I understand that you're leaning towards continuing discussions with party X. I also understand that a lot of effort has already been put in. Nevertheless, I think it's an evaluation that should be based on other grounds. Why don't we first look at whether it's useful for us to continue with party X at all, notwithstanding the investments made so far?" Keep weighing things up using the facts that are relevant for the case.

Confirmation bias

Looking for information that will improve your situation and neglecting other information. I mentioned it earlier. "Is that right? I never heard anything about that." Or "That's not relevant." You selectively pick out the information that you want to hear, or leave things out, in order to support your position and retain the status quo. Or vice versa: to support the change that you're aiming for. The greater the tension, the more people stick to their positions, making it all the more awkward to relinquish them.

Coping with confirmation bias

- If you come up against people in whom you can see this happening, you're going to want to juxtapose your own picture of the situation. "I understand what you're saying. But I've got different data and a different picture of it. Why not overlay the two and take a look at the overall picture together?" Or "I can imagine why you look at it that way, but I'd still like to add something to it to make the picture more complete." You want to get them to look at the same facts in a different way. Depending on how rigidly they're committed to their positions, people may be open enough to consider another way of looking at things. Encourage them to see things from your side too.

- It is of course possible that you won't convince people to see it your way and deadlocks will result simply because the two visions differ. The data is not being seen in the same way. There may be no particular reason for seeing it differently. However, it may be the case that it's important for taking the next step, but the parties aren't yet ready to do so or that more time is needed before they can let go of their current ideas and move forward with you without losing face. Think about how you can work on a process for retaining the bonding with the other party while still taking steps in the right direction together. Can you help them get out of the deadlock and see things from a different angle?

- It is possible that games are being played and information is deliberately being left out in order to strengthen their own case. It is then particularly crucial that the perceptions and data should be compared in order to create an overall picture and allow things to be weighed up correctly. You may have to intervene in the process. See page 106.
- Make sure that you don't sketch out a situation for yourself that is so distorted you can no longer see it clearly. Allow yourself to be challenged and then ask expressly for feedback on whether your assessment is correct, hasn't been studied from one side only, and that no relevant information has been left out. If you let people challenge you, don't ask someone whose thinking pattern scores high for Match: instead, pick someone who will dare to be critical enough.

Framing

Framing is the way in which a particular issue or problem is described, thereby putting it in a specific context. People can leave something out of a narrative, thereby altering its framing. What they're saying may be the truth, but not necessarily the whole truth: only one side of the story is being revealed. A manager who says why it may be good for people to make a change now is not necessarily lying, but may be deliberately leaving a few things out. Or the purchasing department, starting a negotiation by pointing out where the product or service fails to meet the quality requirements: not lying, but carefully not mentioning the positives. Mismatching on the benefits highlights the disadvantages. This framing is deliberate. In short, you can frame a story in a specific way by leaving elements out or failing to emphasise them. Depending on the frame that the speaker has chosen, they will be looking to evoke specific behaviours preferentially.

Coping with framing

- Be aware of the phenomenon of framing. When someone pleads a case in a meeting that deliberately emphasises a side of the story that doesn't suit you, then you should put the other side forward for comparison. "I understand that you think X is missing. But if you take Y into account, and look at the whole picture, it seems to me that Z is the best solution." This lets you re-frame the issue and put it in a different context.
- Choose your own frame carefully if you want people to take your side. If you understand the metaprogrammes, you will find that the way you present an issue will affect whether people shift to seeing it your way or not. Pacing and leading are important here.
- Re-framing information is an important negotiation skill. If you can change the frame, you can change the game. You can offer a different perspective on the same information. You want to choose a frame that serves your interests but is still acceptable for the other side.

And if things are not clear, and uncertainty kicks in?

There is always a degree of uncertainty in complex decision-making processes. It will inevitably be an issue if you are not able to assess a situation very well, because it is open to multiple interpretations or for instance because multiple alternatives need to be weighed up. There are two more specific biases I'd like to mention here that may become manifest when people feel uncertain:

- **Overconfidence bias:** an exaggeratedly rosy view is taken of the issues. For example an estimate, a turnover prognosis, a contribution that is being made, the reasons why the takeover should work, the likelihood of success. Many people have an inbuilt tendency to present their own estimates too positively. Whereas in fact (objectively) the assessment should be quite different. There are also people who are overconfident about their own role and influence. "I'll arrange that, yes I can, I'll do that." Watch out for Matching behaviour here combined with a high degree of internal locus of control. Someone who's going for the result, under pressure, not wanting to see the missing data and looking too much on the bright side, blinded by the need to book a result and prove how successful they are. When the pressure gets ramped up, the risks in the decision-making increase too. Sometimes with serious consequences.

- **Prudence bias/loss aversion bias:** exaggerated caution when you want to make certain estimates. You choose safety, rather than looking at the reality of the situation, and perhaps don't dare move. Too many snares and traps up ahead, so no progress is made. You can no longer see the other side of the coin and take decisions that are overcautious, or perhaps don't dare take a decision at all.

How to deal with these pitfalls

- It is important to check the perceptions and facts, especially when people announce their message emphatically and firmly. Verifiable data in the here and now, not based on subjective distortions. Check and challenge, but do so respectfully. Experiences from the past are no guarantee for the future.
- Take the overall picture and ask yourself questions such as whether relevant items have been left out. Has anything been painted too positively or too negatively? Have both sides of the coin been looked at and evaluated objectively and fairly, using correct data?
- Observe others, and also check your own thoughts when making decisions. It's a small negotiation with yourself. And do reality checks.

In conclusion

If you can describe behaviour patterns, it makes it easier to empathise and progress together (MPs). If you can understand and apply Guides 1 and 2, it will be easier to build bridges and you will have the courage to intervene. If you can sit at the table in dialogues like these, relaxed and on an equal footing, life will be easier. You can focus more on what's being said and how. Insights into the biases can be an additional aid, helping you to stay alert during the decision-making moments.

If you notice that you are not yet able to come to a decision, take some time to reflect and you may come up with small interventions in the process, such as:

- As far as you're concerned, the information needed for making the right decision is not yet complete and you propose XYZ so that you can all weigh things up properly.
- The opinions that have been expressed so far are all personal and subjective, so it would be a good idea to verify the information because you like having data that is as factual as possible. Consequently, you propose…

- Other data suggests that this estimate is too optimistic (or overly cautious) and you would like to compare the information properly once again so that the risks can be estimated correctly. You propose having another look together at…
- You've noticed that the data from the previous meeting has started leading a life of its own and the discussion has now got sidetracked from its main purpose. You'd like to take a step back and then jointly examine… Or halt the meeting for a moment to discuss…
- You observe that a choice has to be made too quickly and based on incomplete data. You wonder where that pressure is coming from. There may be more space, or perhaps you can create more. And if that's not possible, you want to estimate your risks better and you need X amount of time to reach a proper judgement.
- You see that there are emotions associated with this discussion that are making the situation awkward and you propose taking a short time-out so that the other side has an opportunity to look at things from a different viewpoint again.

HANDLING DIFFERENT CULTURES

Borders are becoming less distinct and cooperative partnerships are increasingly international. As a result, negotiating with people from other cultures is an important focal point. A great deal has been written about the topic and you can find various suggestions for further reading at the back of this book. I'm going to go no further here than simply pointing out a few essentials that you can compare against your own experiences. In particular, I have drawn inspiration from practical situations and I have used the seven guides to bind a number of cultural dimensions together. If you have got the hang of the section about metaprogrammes and are able to read people, you will also recognise certain forms of behaviour that are said to be more common in some cultures than in others. The term 'culture' describes the average behaviour of a group, so descriptions of cultures tend often to be stereotypes. That's inevitable, given that the information often consists of generalisations, but as a result it can also be stigmatising. "Westerners are direct and open, people from the Far East are closed and indirect." These are blunt statements and taking them as a reference point can be completely wrong. To stop it being one-way traffic and to help demonstrate the complexity of this subject, I'll give you a couple of observations about the Dutch.

Paul Meerts, who works for Clingendael (the Netherlands Institute of International Relations), gave a description in the December 2012 issue of *International Spectator* of his experiences with Dutch diplomats and civil servants during international negotiations. Freely paraphrased, "There are four main characteristics that let you recognise the Dutch when they're involved in international negotiations: they are direct and inflexible, focused more on the result than the process, focused more on the content than the people, and focused more on cooperation than competition."
The same picture is sketched by Erin Meyer, a lecturer at INSEAD, in her recent book *The Culture Map*, published in 2014: "The Dutch are often seen as being much too direct, having difficulty with authority, wanting to give their opinions about everything, and wanting to be involved in the decision-making." Here too, I'm taking small liberties with elements that you'll also find in parts of her work and in the

MULTICULTURAL ASPECTS

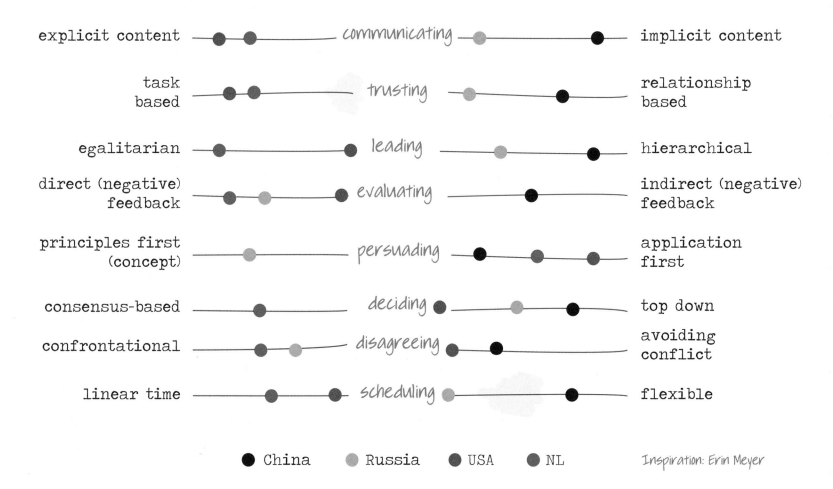

	communicating		
explicit content			implicit content
task based	trusting		relationship based
egalitarian	leading		hierarchical
direct (negative) feedback	evaluating		indirect (negative) feedback
principles first (concept)	persuading		application first
consensus-based	deciding		top down
confrontational	disagreeing		avoiding conflict
linear time	scheduling		flexible

● China   ● Russia   ● USA   ● NL

Inspiration: Erin Meyer

drawing. This drawing is based on her work and an article that was published in the NRC on 3 Februari 2015 by Reinier Kist. 'Caricatures' that I have used are about the Dutch, Americans, Russians and Chinese.

In the *Financieel Dagblad* newspaper in 2014, Wilbur Perlot – who is a specialist in international negotiations at the Clingendael Academy – explained where things often go wrong. "Negotiators who are going to achieve a win-win situation must first have a clear mental picture of their own interests. That may sound obvious, but oddly enough it is not always the case. Entrepreneurs may for example not know exactly what they can expect from a new market. Or whether the expectations within a company are all properly aligned. In addition, you must be able to understand the other party's interests. That boils down to listening and empathising. To do that, you need to know the background of the people you're sitting round the table with." Matthijs Rombouts, a consultant, adds: "In negotiations, many business people use their gut instinct, but that can let you down in a big way in another culture. There are countries where not making eye contact is a sign of respect, but a Dutchman isn't going to interpret it that way." If you study the negotiator's national culture, you will know for instance that the Chinese and Indians like working on the personal relationship first, before talking about business. "But it's more important," say Perlot and Rombouts, "to know the background of the negotiator, the person. An Indian who has lived in London for ten years is going to respond differently to a compatriot who's never been outside the country. It's also crucial to know what position the negotiator has in the organisation. Particularly in countries where the hierarchy is powerful, the final decision is always taken by the CEO. A Dutchman who lays all his cards on the table for a lower-ranked negotiator is creating a poor position for himself, because you can bet your bottom dollar that the boss will pull some additional requirements out of the hat."

If you think only in terms of stereotypes, you will regularly be surprised in practice, because borders and boundaries are becoming less distinct and you will increasingly be dealing with people who have mastered the art of doing business internationally. They may perhaps deliberately make their actions contrast with the obvious behaviour you might expect from them. Cultural differences can play a major role in habits and communication – or sometimes no role whatsoever. In the context of your negotiation, you should therefore observe the actual behaviour of the other party, while being ready for culture-specific customs and habits. When I refer to 'culture', this is generally the cumulative conduct of a group, which may sometimes be expressed quite explicitly and at other times may be quite elusive.

Cultural differences can be expressed in all sorts of ways. At the very least, you may see them in how people:

- communicate with each other to achieve their objectives and to move towards decisions.
- interact with each other, in which specific customs can play a part.
- resolve their differences.

Over the years, the principles we have used in our practice are those of Hofstede and of Trompenaars and Hampden-Turner. Erin Meyer expresses cultural dimensions in a rather different way. I have been using these sources to add depth to the seven guides for when you want to prepare for negotiations with people from cultures you are not familiar with.

It may be good to take a moment first

to consider the value patterns that are embedded in a culture. You may want to be open and respectful in your dealings with the other party and perhaps see fairness as an underlying assumption, but such things may not necessarily be the norm in the other culture. Where you expect reciprocity, it may only be a one-way street. I've included these aspects in the checklist below. If you have to negotiate with people from other cultures, you could run through this checklist for a first impression and then study various aspects in greater depth if necessary.

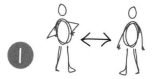

Relationships and content
How do people deal with the dynamic of the relationship, and therefore with communication with each other:
- How important do they think it is to have and to develop a good relationship? Do they build their trust on the tasks that are to be carried out or on the relationship?
- How do they deal with emotions? The further south you go, the more explicitly and more often emotions will

be expressed. Towards the east (Asia), people are less forward with expressing their emotions.
- How direct is the communication, or are there lots of circumlocutions? Is it implicit communication (highly contextual, packed in lots of flowery language) or explicit communication (not so contextual, direct)?
- How do you acquire status in that culture: because of who you are, your background, or what you have done and achieved?

Trust and verification
- How do they deal with information? How open is the communication? Do people keep their cards close to their chest, and is verification even possible?
- To what extent does trust play a specific role in the culture in question? It may take a very long time before you have earned enough trust.
- How strict are they with agreements and planning? Promises are promises? Punctual or flexible?

Interests and positions
- Are the interests discussed openly, or is that a bridge too far?
- Does the way in which the interests are discussed show you what their preferred style is (MPs) and does that tell you anything about how they want to interact with you?

My options and yours
- Are they helping think the options through? Or do they expect all the input to be from you, because you are seen as the expert and they value your judgement?

Sharing and fairness
- How do they deal with disagreements and conflicts? Directly or indirectly? Open or closed?
- What kind of a role does fairness have in their culture? Are they sensitive to a back-and-forth approach with questions

and answers, or is it more authoritarian with instructions being given?

DEAL?
BATNA

My BATNA and theirs
- Do they have alternatives? Do you? This may be difficult to work out. Relationship, reputation and status can play important roles. Sometimes you have proposals that look better on paper than the other party's BATNA, but the work still gets awarded to actors they are familiar with and have had a relationship with for a long time. Better the devil you know...

Structure and process
- Do they prescribe what they want, or can you influence that?
- How do they deal with decision-making? Are there specific agreements about it? What is customary? Do they value procedures and contracts, or is it more a question of 'my word is my bond', a handshake and trusting it will be done? In other words, is the decision-making formal or informal?

- Are communication and decision-making from the top down, or consensus-oriented? What role does seniority take in the decision-making: does the oldest person decide?
- Is there an orientation towards individuals or towards the group, and what does this mean for the decision-making and your approach?
- Are there specific stakeholders who should be more involved in the process and who exert a great deal of influence despite apparently having no role?

Because we have a tendency to see cultural differences through stereotypical imagery, our ability to listen and observe may get blanked out, making us miss important information. If you want to get better insights into the cultural differences between people, the starting point is being prepared to study them in depth. Genuinely being interested in what the other is doing, why they are doing it and what the driving forces are. You will come across all sorts of ways of getting a clearer idea of the cultural aspects during your preparation. When you are sitting at the negotiation table, it is a good idea to remain alert to what you are seeing and hearing:
- What are they saying? And what isn't

being said that they still intend to be communicated?
- What norms or customs could that be an expression of?
- What value patterns and which interests could be underlying it?

WHAT IF THEY'RE PLAYING GAMES?

This is perhaps my most frequently asked question: how do you handle the games people play? Sometimes they're only pinpricks, but even then you're being put under pressure because the other side are trying to get more out of the situation. Tricks are then utilised deliberately and the relationship is made part of the game. Positions are adopted that go somewhat further than a difference of opinion. As far as I'm concerned, this means you're now in the Game Zone (see next page), where it may feel neither pleasant nor safe. You start feeling the relationship becoming more distant and you often start losing track of the content. So how do you handle that?

Projects get larger and more complex and the same happens to the interests and the risks. On occasions, tensions may accumulate without that being the intention. On others it may be deliberate, with people looking to see how far they can push you, where your limits are and where it starts hurting. You are being examined and tested. The other side may have a strong position and be able to ask a lot from you. This is particularly truewhen you could be exchanged for a comparable alternative; it's not unreasonable then for their nego-tiating stance to be tough. The awkward thing is that the pressures can also build up when the other side *is* dependent on you. So how do you handle *that*? How can you stay on your feet, apply opposing pres-sure, yet keep progressing nonetheless? Quite a challenge.

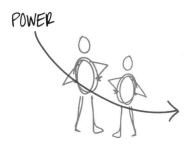

POWER

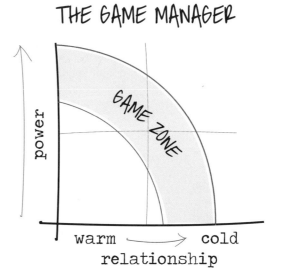

THE GAME MANAGER

power

GAME ZONE

warm ⟶ cold

relationship

To help you cope with the games that are most widely deployed, I've produced a list of most of these tricks. I have grouped them around the seven dilemmas you are facing. This should let you recognise them, and I hope that the guides will give you some angles to let you take on the mantle of game manager. If you recognise the games and can see what the other is trying to do, you can make up your own mind whether to ignore it or respond to it. Then it becomes a choice.

In general, the games all boil down to the same thing: pressure is applied to the rela-tionship, the content or the process in an attempt to squeeze more out of the deal.

The way in which the pressure is exerted can vary. I'm going to describe the games associated with the seven dilemmas. They can be played at all sorts of levels and in a huge range of contexts.

7 DILEMMAS	GAMES PEOPLE PLAY	EXAMPLES
1 **Relationship dynamics**	• Power-play • Going for the emotions and the individual	• "We think that we ought to be able to expect at least A and B from you, given how long we've been working together." • "I'm deeply disappointed with this approach. Unless a substantially better offer appears, we're going to stop all the activities." • "But I told you that this isn't enough. I want you to arrange X and Y for us. You'll have to come up with something way better than this steaming pile! Same thing, every time. I said it before and now I'm going to say it again: you've got to learn to listen." • Acting angry, indignant or disappointed and playing mind games to get more out of you.
	• Marginalising your role, your position and you as an individual	• "You can't do much about that because you haven't got the experience yet. Your predecessor would have tackled it differently." • "You're making a right pig's ear of it. I hadn't expected that of you. How long have you been doing this job? You've still got a lot to learn. Send your boss next time – at least I can do business with him!"
	• Good cop/bad cop	• A familiar move: one goes in hard and the other softens the blow. Muddies the waters and builds up the pressure. • The same person can sometimes combine both roles, so that you feel like you're on a roller coaster.
	• Building up pressure by creating negative perceptions and then exaggerating them	• "Always the same with you lot. You never understand us. Blathering on about customer focus, but I never see it for real. Your predecessor didn't understand it either – what am I going to do with you?" • In larger negotiations: bringing negative perceptions to the fore. Playing to the gallery by putting a spin on negative perceptions. This increases the pressure and you 'have' to do something and make a move, whether fair or not and factually correct or not. Creating a negative perception is a phenomenon in its own right and a powerful way of exerting pressure, particularly in the political domain. See also 'Framing' (page 157).

7 DILEMMAS	GAMES PEOPLE PLAY	EXAMPLES
I **Relationship dynamics**	• I deserve pity, I've got a problem and you've got to help me	• "I'd like to do it, but we simply don't have that much cash. Can't you do it for a lot less than that?" There's one 'pathetic' party, asking for help. If you fall for that one, you're going to help them when there's no need. Not that there's anything wrong with helping others, but the question remains as to whether it's necessary or desirable or fair. • "You think *this* is unfair? Who's got the problem here? Us! Because of you lot, we've now got a major problem with ABC and I expect you to resolve it, pronto!"
	• Trivialisation, bluff	• "Oh, it's not that tricky. Plenty of others can do it, and they're always knocking on our door." • In other words: "You're nothing special and I've got alternatives." A combination of pressure on the relationship and threatening with their BATNA. "I'm not the dependent one; you are."

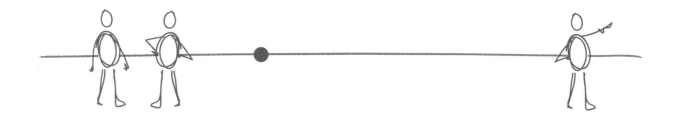

7 DILEMMAS	GAMES PEOPLE PLAY	EXAMPLES
2 **Information / trust**	• Building the pressure up by mixing information with trust • 'Playing' with information and commitment	• "Believe me, that's the way it is. You're ten per cent pricier than the competition and you'll have to do your best. You're offering lower quality and I'm having to pay more for it too." Chalk-and-cheese comparisons that don't hold water anyway. Pretending to be certain. Using personal trust as a pawn in the game to try to get more out of it.
	• Not sticking to verifiable agreements and playing dumb • Muddying the waters and discouraging clarity • Creating a smokescreen • Not making commitments in order to retain manoeuvring room • Being smart, acting stupid	• You make commitments but they won't. A promise is not a promise. Example: agreeing that there will be a financial reward if targets are met, but then claiming the reward and applying it in the rates even though the target wasn't met. That combination of agreements doesn't apply to me and I'm going to do my own thing. • Invoices not paid as agreed. A promise is not a promise. Until you make a complaint. If *you* don't take the initiative, nothing will happen. Sometimes a final payment instalment never gets paid. • "But surely that was in the scope? We're not going to pay more for it now." Even if factually incorrect. • Placing new facts on the table that undermine your statements. Sowing confusion. • Keeping information back. Keeping the scope unclear in order to create the impression that items are within it, waiting to see what happens and then – if you respond – pointing out that you didn't object earlier and that it had therefore been assumed that it was within scope. • Giving woolly, incomplete and incorrect information. "Yes, that's not clear yet here either." Or "We'll have to look at that, but we'll let you know." • "Is that what we agreed? Surely not? Would I do that? No idea? How exactly does that work on our side? Well. This wasn't what we agreed! Did I receive that?"
	• Mixing up the future with the current situation to get more out of it, even if the information is incorrect	• "You have to agree now. We won't be able to sign this next week." • "If you say yes this time, you'll get the rest of our volume too next time." • "No problem – we'll arrange that for you."

7 DILEMMAS	GAMES PEOPLE PLAY	EXAMPLES
3 Hard / positional / open	• Giving little but asking a lot • Merely adopting positions • You versus me – no "us"	• "You know exactly what matters to us. I'd say you should do your best and surprise me. You know us, don't you? Then you ought to know." • "I want…" "I think…" Adopting positions that immediately define boundaries. "That's how it is, that's how I want it, or else…"
	• Trivialising your interests	• "What, you've got to make a penny or two from it as well? That's okay as it is then. Seems more than enough. I'm not asking you to do anything tricky. Just streamline your processes a bit better. There are bound to be costs there that you can cut. Be creative!"
4 Solutions	• Me versus you • You think up solutions, I'll shoot them down	• "Make your proposal and then we'll look at it." And shoot it down. The pattern is then repeated. • "You really ought to be able to do better than this." • Always making it a swap, always wanting something in return. • Asking for impossible options, then withdrawing them and asking for something more valuable in return.
	• Cherry-picking	• Selecting only the elements from a proposal that suit their cause. Other items, which are important to you, are then swept aside.

7 DILEMMAS	GAMES PEOPLE PLAY	EXAMPLES
⑤ Distribution	• There's no such thing as fairness • I'll do what I want	• Insufficient, not going far enough, I want more (more of the benefits, less of the costs) "That'll be at your expense. I decide what's reasonable here, and I don't care what your angle is. Take it or leave it." • "Fair? What's reasonable to *me*."
	• Salami-slicing (piecemeal when you'd never accept the whole)	• You think you have a deal. "Right. And if you do this as well, we're moving in the right direction. Then we're there." • Deals can still be opened up again – even if they've already been signed. "We've checked it again, but if you now do this..." • These examples blend swapping, salami-slicing and positional endgames.
	• Stating unrealistic expectations and asking the impossible, in order to get something else • A known strategy in the endgame	• "You know that A and B are very important to us. If you can sort that out for us, we'll be there." Spending a long time on that one point and getting you to work on it, although the other side know that you can't comply. Exerting pressure on that point and then changing the tactics at the last minute. "That's a real shame, disappointing. But if you can do C and D, we'll accept that." Thereby getting C and D, which are worth more than A and B.
⑥ Position / BATNA	• Threatening (with the BATNA) • Bluffing and looking for your limits	• "If you don't agree, we're dropping you. There are ten more like you. It's not that complex, after all. Anyone can do this." And for less, of course. Various dilemmas get interlinked. • The other party are trying to bludgeon a way to what they want by bluffing and acting tough. "You really have to be able to do better than this, otherwise we're calling it a day." Although there's no position. • "If you don't agree to this, we'll cancel contract X as well." • You're being dunked under water to see if your defences are watertight. If there's a leak, they've found your limits...

7 DILEMMAS	GAMES PEOPLE PLAY	EXAMPLES
⑦ **Process**	• I determine the process	• Setting up the process in a way that puts you at a disadvantage, for instance in terms of the time, the location or the agenda, thinking that it's possible to create an advantage or a head start. • Deciding on a location or room that's convenient for one but not the other. • Changing the location and only notifying the other side at the last minute.
	• Keeping actors away or suddenly introducing them	• Keeping relevant actors who ought to be involved away from the action and then introducing them at an unexpected moment.
	• Creating a lack of clarity about the mandate and the decision-making	• You think you're on the home straight and then they say that further internal discussions are needed. • "I think we're there. Just got to pass it by the purchasing department, though. That's the norm here." Having to tackle the same issue twice.
	• At the very last minute...	• Wait until the last possible moment and then start bluffing and threatening when the time pressure is on. A lot of extras get given away at the very end (if you let that happen).
	• A war of attrition	• Everything can become fluid under pressure. Keep going until deep into the night. Everyone gets tired. The biggest concessions are made at the end. Just think of the classic collective bargaining talks between employers and unions.
	• Agenda manipulation	• Agenda manipulation: removing things from the agenda or suddenly adding them.
	• Hiding behind others	• "By the way, I've just spoken to my boss again and I'm not going to be able to push this through. You'll have to do a lot more if you want to keep doing business with us."

7 DILEMMAS	GAMES PEOPLE PLAY	EXAMPLES
7 Process	• Tactical needling	• Leaving you waiting, not looking you in the eye, not shaking your hand, pouring themselves coffee but not offering you one, remaining remote. Above all, not sounding enthusiastic. • Walking away from the table, passing responsibility for that onto you, and saying so to all and sundry. • The classics: putting you on the side of the table where the sun's in your eyes, sitting you on lower chairs. • Removing people from their assigned positions quickly so that there's no chance for relationships between people to build up.
	• Breaking off the negotiation	• Always being ready to break off a negotiation in the middle, increasing the pressure and pretending it's now the other's problem.

If you recognise the games, you can deal with them much more easily. As long as progress isn't being hindered and your interests aren't being harmed, I hope you will just be able to let them pass you by. Just accept that there will always be negotiators who use emotions, paint negative images and aren't afraid to play dirty. It's their way of serving their own interests as well as possible, by looking for *your* limits, in terms of both the business content and the relationships. When games are played in positional negotiation situations, everything I have discussed so far comes together. Think back once again to your preferred style for dealing with conflicts (see the DUTCH method, page 39). Some will have a tendency to go on the attack, others are more likely to evade the awkward discussion or give ground. When things become awkward, you will need to respond consciously to the dynamics. Or to phrase it more colourfully, "If you can't stand the heat, stay out of the kitchen". I hope that you will soon be able to make it a conscious choice: to leave the kitchen, open a window, turn the thermostat down a notch, or whatever. And occasionally you need to fan the flames too; sometimes you need the clash before you can progress constructively again.

It is important to be aware of:
- where in the process the games are being played. Is pressure being exerted right at the start, or gradually throughout the process? Or is it for instance more of a tactic in the endgame?
- what is being said and who's saying it. Accept that there are certain roles in which specific behaviour patterns are virtually inevitable. The information above is virtually enough to let you write a procurement department's handbook yourself. All in all, what they can scrape together to increase the pressure can add up to quite a large box of tricks.
- whether you want to respond and how. It's not always desirable and often not necessary to respond. You can see that some items are just pinpricks and you can let them pass you by. There are others you may want to respond to in order to apply counteracting pressure and remain sitting at the tables as equals, because there will be consequences for the perceptions being built up and for the content if you fail to react.
- if you do want to respond, look at it from the third-position perspective first. If you can see through what they're up to, it will affect you less and you can maybe intervene in the process and keep progress-

ing. Although it may be difficult, it helps if you remain respectful and constructive when games are being played.

They're often looking to see how far you will go, how far you will let them push you and when your limit is reached. If it is in your interests to remain in discussion, you want to keep looking constructively for possibilities. That can be done in a similar way. The art is to apply a counteracting pressure, to show where your limits are while at the same time keeping looking for ways of serving the various interests. Be ready to break off a discussion and know what you will do in that case. Sometimes you have no alternative, but agreeing to a bad deal is always a bad move. Be aware of your own style and biases. Do you keep going too long because you think it'll work out okay in the end? Or because you think you'll get it fixed? Are you so keen on getting the deal that you're no longer able to see the risks properly and you talk yourself into an awkward situation? At least make sure you have a clear picture of your own interests.

If you are aware of the seven guides, my experience is that they can show you the way – help you find the right words and stand firm during the negotiation. After all, if you have a BATNA as a fallback position and you know what your interests are and you have a clear picture of your arguments for what would be fair, then it's easy to exert an opposing pressure and find solutions for these situations. Managing expectations and telling the other side what you think is fair: now it is all starting to come together.

I am now going to use the games listed above in a number of examples and give you some ways of responding, inspired by the seven guides. Look for your own wording that will suit your own context and situations. It will often be the case that the same sorts of objections are raised and therefore that the same kinds of games keep on being repeated. And you can prepare for that.

The examples may be somewhat exaggerated, in order to make the dynamics clearer.

Ways of responding to games

GUIDES	SUMMARY OF THE KEY GAMES	RESPONSES YOU CAN USE
	"But I told you that this isn't enough. I want you to arrange X and Y for us. You'll have to come up with something way better than this useless effort! Same thing, every time. I've said it before and now I'm going to say it yet again: you lot have still got to learn to listen."	• "I understand that you're expecting something different from us. It seems that we haven't understood each other properly yet. Let's have a look at how we might be able to arrange X and Y for you without it necessarily hurting our margin, shall we?" • Or this rather more bracing intervention: "I'm unhappy that you've got the idea that we're not listening. I believe we've been listening very carefully, but it seems we can't deliver what you're after. It has to remain feasible and fair for us as well; that's surely a given. My proposal would be..." • "Not nice to hear. I think that we've understood each other well enough, but the problem's more that we can't agree. So I'd suggest that we begin by..." • "It's unfortunate that you've got an impression that we're not listening properly, or maybe don't even want to listen. Have I understood that correctly?" First try to empathise and encourage them to share their perceptions, and then move on together: "I'm pleased that you're not bottling that up inside, at any rate, and that you're calling a spade a spade. May I tell you what I think our fundamental problem is?"
	"Always the same with you lot. You never understand us. Blathering on and on about customer focus, but I never see it. Your predecessor didn't understand it either – what am I going to do with you? Always the same old tune."	• "I can see that you're pretty upset. Maybe I haven't understood you correctly. I'd be pretty unhappy if we had to stop now. Shall we discuss your expectations again and see how we can reach a solution?"
	"You're making a right pig's ear of it. I hadn't expected that of you. How long have you been doing this job? You've still got a lot to learn. Send your boss next time – at least I can do business with her!"	• "It looks as if we've got different expectations for the solution. I'm unhappy to see that's how you're looking at it. And I don't believe my boss would actually see it any differently, because we discussed all this thoroughly beforehand and I have a mandate to reach a solution. Why not perhaps take another look at what might work for you?"

GUIDES	SUMMARY OF THE KEY GAMES	RESPONSES YOU CAN USE
1	If the way people are interacting with one another becomes unpleasant, unfair or disrespectful, you can also respond to that.	• "The way in which we're conducting this process isn't what I would call pleasant. I'm wondering whether you want to take the next step at all. If you do, then I'd like to suggest that..." • "You've put your finger on some fairly intense emotions and I'm not immune to them. I feel that it's making it difficult for me to keep looking constructively for the right solution. Much as I would like to. I'd suggest we first clear up these emotions and then see if we can progress further." • You can use your BATNA to help decide what to do. And BATNA or no BATNA, there are limits. Keep them in mind, because you've always got a choice. You too can simply stop.
2	"Believe me, that's the way it is. You're ten per cent pricier than your competitor and I can't sell that internally. You're offering lower quality and I'm having to pay more for it too. It's in the scope, so I'm not going to pay extra for it."	• "You're always entitled to go elsewhere, as you know full well. That would be a real shame, though, and I hope we can work it out together. Let me ask you: exactly what were you comparing our offer against there?" • "Maybe we should take another look at what was agreed? Given that information, I think it will be clear that this is an additional request and that was communicated too. So it looks fair to me that it should be paid for." A combination of Guides 2 and 5. • "Perfectly understandable that you don't want to pay for work that was within the scope. I wouldn't want to either, so you're fully entitled to say so. But that's exactly why it's a good idea in cases like these to have a close look at exactly what was agreed."
	Unconsciously distorted information.	• Be careful of how biases are handled. Sometimes you will think that it's a game, but in fact there have been unconscious misinterpretations of information, and you can discuss that by asking questions and looking for verification.
	There are also limits to what is acceptable in dealing with information.	• If items are being deliberately distorted or kept back, you'll soon stop trusting them. You have a choice.

GUIDES	SUMMARY OF THE KEY GAMES	RESPONSES YOU CAN USE
❸ ❹	"You know exactly what matters to us, so I'd suggest you should do your best and surprise us. You know us, don't you? Then you ought to know."	• "You can expect us to produce a good proposal. At the same time, I understand from the previous discussions that you would like to move forward with us. If we now take a little while together to look at what we each see as preconditions and understand them, then I'm sure we'll be better able to achieve the next step and do so more quickly, rather than getting bogged down in a process in which proposals are flying back and forth." • "I'm sure we can surprise you. I'd propose that we therefore take time to look together at the options that will help serve your interests. Two heads are better than one."
	Lack of openness, not cooperating on constructive solutions, "my way or the highway".	• If you can't change this process, it's time to decide if it's worth the candle. Do you want to keep making proposals unilaterally and ending up with a pattern in which you make a proposal that isn't accepted, and so *ad infinitum*? You also have a choice here. Sometimes it's not much of a choice and you go along with it. Sometimes you can change the process.

GUIDES	SUMMARY OF THE KEY GAMES	RESPONSES YOU CAN USE
⑤ ⑥ DEAL? ――― BATNA	Insufficient, not going far enough, I want more (more of the benefits, less of the costs) "I decide what's fair here, and I don't care what your angle is. Take it or leave it." They may adopt that position even if their BATNA is poor. Looking to test your limits, to your detriment.	A few variations on the theme: • "I understand that you're expecting more from us. If I go back with what we're currently doing for you and look at the investment that'll take, we won't be able to take that step. What we could do though, is look at the content of the proposal together and go through the individual items to see what could be cut or done differently." • "I'm very sorry. If I add up what we're doing for you now and you want another extra from us, then – given A, B and C – I don't think that's fair. We can't agree to that. What might work is if we're able to find a way to..." • "If we now take a look at what we're doing for you, then I reckon that we're playing a key role in your process. As far as I'm concerned, and given the effort we're putting in, I don't think it's fair to be putting the pressure on our conditions like that. I'd suggest that we take a look together at how we can reduce the costs without it compromising our margin further." • "If I now add up what we've put on the table and then put it next to your additional request, then it's not going to work for us. And I can't make it fit with the interests that were discussed either. It seems to me that what we've put on the table serves your interests perfectly well. My proposal would be to..." And then make a proposal that the other can say yes to. • "As far as I'm concerned, we've reached a limit. If we aren't capable of finding a solution together that is still acceptable for use, then I unfortunately have no option other than calling it a day. But before that, I'd like to make one more attempt to see if we can sort this out. What would you think if we..." • "Well, if you've got a better solution then you should naturally consider it – you've always got that option. As I see it, we're in a situation where you want to achieve ABC and we want to achieve XYZ." And indicate your own limits when explaining. Then, "It really would be a waste of all our efforts if we don't make something of this, wouldn't it? Why don't we try one more time?"

GUIDES	SUMMARY OF THE KEY GAMES	RESPONSES YOU CAN USE
5 ⊘ **6** DEAL? / BATNA	"If you don't agree, we're dropping you. There are ten more like you. It's not that complex, after all. Anyone can do this." And for less, of course.	• "I'm unhappy that you're lumping us together with all the other bidders now. It seems I haven't been able to convince you of the added value we offer. Let's take another look at the assumptions and sum up the various possibilities together again. Then we can see whether or not it's in your best interests to dump us." • In positional endgames, you can always draw a line in the sand too – check their intentions and see if you want to continue.
	Be aware of where your limits lie, for the distribution issues in particular.	• Keep your BATNA clearly in mind. If they keep pressing but don't really have a BATNA, you can also break the talks off and see what happens. Who's got the problem then? • What is your BATNA? Saying yes because you don't dare walk away? Don't walk into a trap with your eyes wide open.
7 ◯	All kinds of tricks for undermining the process, from minor pinpricks to major manipulation.	• Don't bother about the small tricks. You can recognise them for what they are and see through them. But are those pinpricks inhibiting progress? • Intervene if a pattern of that type of needling arises. • At the process level you may able to prevent them by making clear agreements right from the start. Roles, responsibilities and mandates need to be clear. Intervention in the process is an option if things happen that can damage your interests.

I often hear people saying that they would like to have said no earlier. What they actually mean is that they'd like to have intervened earlier and ought to have said what their limits were. You felt that it wasn't going smoothly or that they were asking for things that weren't fair, but you were unable to intervene or didn't dare to. Would it be culturally acceptable to intervene directly, or is a more indirect approach required? Experience teaches that people who are prepared to play games against you will be capable of taking a few knocks. But as far as I'm concerned, the hand that is reaching out and inviting them to look at the problem together is more constructive than a clenched fist that is ready to start trading blows. Sure, you sometimes have to be prepared to dish it out as well if you want results. But that can be done verbally, staying resolute and agile while retaining the bonding.

THE JOURNEY'S OVER: TIME FOR THE NEXT ADVENTURE

If you want to become a good negotiator, you need to practice a lot. Fortunately, you have an interesting playground around you every day – a wonderful space where you can play around and practice, acquire experience, feel what success and failure are like, learn from them and continue. You can learn how to negotiate. Not everyone will turn into a top-class negotiator, but you can still develop your skills. The best way to learn is on the job. And also by mastering a particular approach, focusing on a number of guides and perfecting them.

If you have done the exercises based on the DUTCH method, you will know what your preferred style is when you come up against a conflict. A thorough understanding of the seven guides can help you prepare for and conduct negotiations. Insights into the metaprogrammes and the biases will help you take a more dispassionate look at yourself and others in your day-to-day communications, remaining 'agile' in the way you respond to what you see happening at the table. I hope that this will let you see where you're being too hasty at times – or indeed not pushing things along enough – and where you are perhaps making it too easy or being sloppy, or maybe even too stubborn in a decision-making process. Insights into the games can help you recognise the tricks being played and know what to do if you finally do have to intervene.

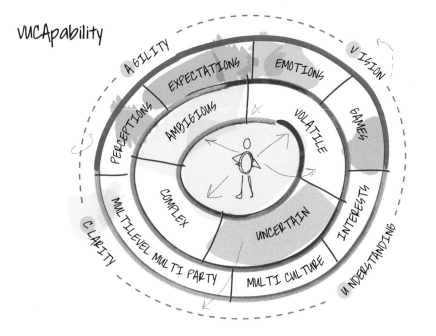

VUCApability

That sounds quite something: progressing to become a 'master negotiator'. It would at least be nice if you now feel that you're able to cope with most negotiations and that you don't have to worry about it and won't be lying awake at night. That you will be able to sit down at the negotiation table in a relaxed frame of mind, despite the differences in perspective and the games that are being played, capable of defending your own interests and coming up with attractive solutions and good deals.

WHERE HAVE YOU GOT TO AND WHAT DO YOU WANT TO DEVELOP FURTHER?

If you want to keep concentrating on your own learning process, I've provided an overview of the three levels of behaviour to give you a little more inspiration. Behaviour that would be expected from a negotiator who's more of a beginner, or what a more advanced negotiator might do, or the things that reveal a master at work. It's always possible to pick holes in this kind of summary, because it's somewhat generalised and by no means complete. Have a look at where you are now, and what you might still need to improve.

I hope you have attained a certain level of VUCA skills and that you have found ways of coping with a VUCA context. That you have developed your own way of looking at negotiation issues and situations. That you're able to read and understand what the others (and you yourself) want, that you have a clear picture of what to focus on in all kinds of areas, and that you have become more agile. That you are ready and able to stand firm when necessary, that you can deliberately step away from a challenge when that's better for the situation as a whole, that you're able to give ground when needed in order to make progress, and that you can collaborate with the other side when desirable. I've been aiming to give negotiators – both beginners and experts – a basic skeleton for day-to-day negotiation situations, fleshing it out with concepts, insights and angles that you can use during the negotiation process.

Three levels of negotiating behaviour

GUIDES FOR...	LEVEL I: BEGINNERS	LEVEL II: GOOD NEGOTIATORS	LEVEL III: MASTERS
	Know that attention has to be paid to the relationship at the start.	Know that allowances need to be made in the negotiation for emotions. Know how to deal with both their own emotions feelings of resistance and those of the other party.	Have an eye on the undercurrents and the surface currents. Know how to manage the dynamics of the relationship: are capable of dealing with tensions and emotions – on both sides of the table – and are able to handle the expectations are able to pace and leadthe other forward people on these issues as and when necessary. Know how to influence the relationship in a positive way and how to deal with people who are exerting pressure and pushing the games to the limits. Know how to manage the pitfalls in their own behaviour and are sensitive to cultural differences.
	Do not prepare extensively for the substance: we'll cross that bridge when we come to it – it'll be fine. Have lots of other things to do.	Have a good business case. Know what they're talking about. Takes time to find out about the other side. Make good agreements, both for now and for later.	Have a clear picture of their case. Know the agreements that have been made and have the contract clear in their mind's eye. Have thought through the consequences of fulfilling the contract... or failing to do so. Know that the facts may be less than objective and so they verify their information, which also helps reveal biases. Find it important for both parties to keep everything verifiable, both now and in future. Can formulate contracts clearly. Will not be thrown if new facts are presented. Move appropriately with the punches.

GUIDES FOR...	LEVEL I: BEGINNERS	LEVEL II: GOOD NEGOTIATORS	LEVEL III: MASTERS
3 ⋀⋁	Know that they have to ask questions. Can listen, summarise and probe deeper. Tend to try and sell their own story and have good arguments up their sleeve if questioned.	Know what they need to ask about: interests and preconditions – not only for those they are speaking with directly, but also for other members of the DMU (decision-making unit). Are prepared to adopt a position when necessary. Know what is negotiable and what isn't.	Realise that they also have to handle the internal negotiations and pay appropriate attention to that aspect. Realise that internal negotiations can sometimes be thornier than the external ones; accept this as part of the game. Know how to ask questions that will make their negotiating partners think about their own situations and interests. Know how to shift people away from positions they have adopted, capable of handling the positional games flexibly. Are not over-hasty, but do keep an eye open for as many interests as possible, including the interests in a broader scope. Can handle complexity. Steer things in the right direction and create room for manoeuvre. Focus on doing things together.
4 □○△	Often have a solution ready for the other party. Are able to make proposals and justify them. If there is resistance, they find explanatory arguments. May not have listened quite enough and not extracted enough key ingredients from the interests phase to be able to come up with attractive options. The deals are suboptimal.	Know how to bring the other party on board and create options together. Not yet really in the 'value zone', though. Are able to make a dialogue of it increasingly often.	Know how to enrich and extend the deal. Explore the value zone, looking for options that may be interesting in both the shorter and the longer term. Win-win, and maybe even win-win-win. Can also see the interests of the greater whole. Will not be satisfied with a suboptimal deal. Realise that being right doesn't mean that everyone will agree with them. Pay attention consciously to generating support as the playing field gets more complex, capable of getting even positional negotiators on board in a joint process.

GUIDES FOR...	LEVEL I: BEGINNERS	LEVEL II: GOOD NEGOTIATORS	LEVEL III: MASTERS
5	Can still easily create stalemates through clashes, or may give way too quickly. Are less ready with arguments about what is fair. More a case of attack and defence than discussions about principles.	Are prepared to push back or apply the brakes. Are sometimes more focused on the negotiation zone. Are a little too happy to be creative with taking costs on board and apportioning them.	Work towards agreements that can withstand the test of 'fairness'. It may not always work, but it's something to aim for. Masters look at both the component parts and the overall picture. Can handle the positional distribution games. Know how to show a positional negotiator that there are 'principles of fairness' and shared interests, that there's often more uniting you than separating you. Prepared to exert opposing pressure when needed and remain relaxed but resolute. Investigate multiple possibilities and don't lock themselves into any one of them too quickly. Realise that decision-making processes are negotiation processes, and act accordingly. Are not afraid to walk away and have prepared for that eventuality.
6 DEAL? BATNA	Do not yet think deliberately and strategically about the alternatives.	Think about their own BATNA. Are capable of estimating the other's BATNA.	Investigate and if necessary develop their own BATNA and understand the other party's BATNA. Are aware of positions and dependencies (or independence). Are ready to discuss the other party's BATNA. Know whether it is desirable to introduce the BATNA. Can play simultaneous chess games when needed. Know when the positional endgame has to be tackled. Are able to accept less if they know that's the best outcome from the hand they were dealt this time – not out of habit or because they are backing down or avoiding confrontation, but when it's the outcome of a process.

GUIDES FOR...	LEVEL I: BEGINNERS	LEVEL II: GOOD NEGOTIATORS	LEVEL III: MASTERS
⑦ ◯	Can structure a discussion or meeting to have an opening, an agenda and a close. See the games as a way of handling resistance, but not yet as part of a greater whole or a pattern.	Can add agenda management. Are capable of steering a process and managing the progress. Can spot the obvious games.	Act as the process architect, director and supervisor all rolled into one. Promote the interests at the strategic and tactical levels, adding value productively. See everything that's going on internally and externally throughout the process and can deal with the issues. Know when time-outs are needed. Are properly prepared but know when to deviate from the script – can create structure, improvising when necessary. Are on top of the situation and feel responsible for the process. Can make interventions and get people on board. Know how to avoid stalemates and how to cope when they occur nevertheless. Switch their viewpoints from the first position to the third and back again. Know how to manage progress and can play simultaneous chess. Realise that they are at the heart of the $E = Q \times A$ process. Can learn consciously from other people's mistakes. Help accelerate the learning process.

If you want to take further steps, the questions are:
- where you are with respect to the various phases,
- where you want to be headed and what you would then like to develop further, and
- how you're going to go about it.

You can work on self-development by not demanding answers immediately, but instead reflecting, demanding feedback, carrying out small experiments and looking to see what happens and what you get from this. Learning has to be planned. I hope that you'll enjoy doing a few small experiments, that there'll be good results even if you're only testing the water, and that you'll continue to learn and be able to help others. And if you want to zoom in a little further, you can also consider your inner game.

YOUR INNER GAME

If you're thinking about your own development, you could consider your skills and behaviour as described above. However, sometimes you may have opinions, perceptions and beliefs that are stopping you from doing what you should, or from doing it the right way.

In 1981, I was given a book called *The Inner Game of Golf* by Timothy Gallwey as a present. The title alone was fascinating enough. He had previously written a similar book about tennis, and would later add *The Inner Game of Work*. Anyway, this one was about inner putting, inner swinging and more. How you can get into the groove, how concentrating in a certain way can make you more aware of your mind and body, allowing you both to relax and to concentrate. Nothing very new, but still relevant. It's something that sportsmen and women are well aware of: if you take things too quickly, you may mess it up. If you want something too much, you won't get what you were after. If you concentrate too much, you'll get stuck in a rut. If you're too tense, you'll stiffen up. Sometimes you may become a hostage at the table. On the other hand, if you can rely on what you've learned and are ready to let go a little, you maximise the chance of getting in the 'flow' state. Preparing and being able to let go, looking for that relaxed concentration.

If you're prepared and you've already been through the negotiation, it's already part of your experience and it's in your system. You are then able to let go of your preparations where appropriate and you can be fully focused – and relaxed – in the here and now. You can improvise if you've practised plenty; you can also perform if you know you've done it before. Good performances are something you can come up with if you are relaxed and you can see clearly: paying attention to the others lets you see what's going on, hear what's being said or left out. If you eat an apple too quickly, you won't taste it. The same applies to the communication in negotiations. If you take things too fast, the bonding won't be there and you probably won't really get round to investigating the interests or finding attractive solutions. Too proactive, too reactive, too eager or too relaxed, overprepared or too off-the-cuff, too uncertain or too cocksure — these extremes often prevent you from being effective. And at the same time, you know that you sometimes have to act quickly and confidently and persevere.

It is wise for a negotiator to take a close look at their own inner game occasionally. What's your angle? What disrupts your concentration and breaks the flow? Are you your own worst enemy? What happens to you when the going gets tough? Sometimes it's a result of your surroundings: your counterparts, your organisation or your colleagues are putting almost tangible pressure on you. And sometimes you do it to yourself. So what is stopping you from remaining relaxed, alert and flexible? To let you ponder this one a little more on a rainy afternoon sometime, I'm going to approach this topic using the levels of learning.

Levels of learning
Albert Einstein once said that you can't solve a problem using the same lines of thought that created it. You need something else. If you see that you are getting bogged down and keep encountering the same challenge time and time again, then looking at it differently may help. One tool for that could be the 'levels of learning' model, also known as the 'logical levels'. It was introduced by the anthropologist Gregory Bateson and later expanded upon by Robert Dilts. The model states that there are six levels at which we function, communicate and learn.

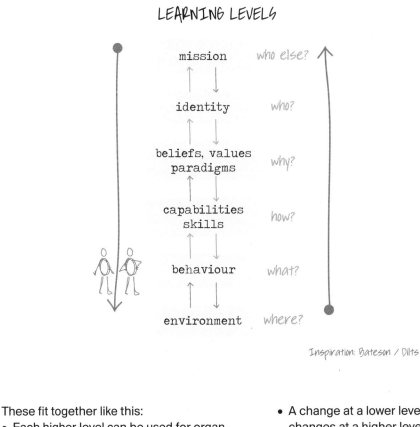

LEARNING LEVELS

mission — who else?
identity — who?
beliefs, values paradigms — why?
capabilities skills — how?
behaviour — what?
environment — where?

Inspiration: Bateson / Dilts

These fit together like this:
- Each higher level can be used for organising the information at an underlying level.
- A change at a higher logical level **will** trigger changes at the lower levels.
- A change at a lower level **may** trigger changes at a higher level.
- The solution to a thorny problem is rarely found in the level at which it is diagnosed; the answer is almost always at a different level, usually higher.

I'm introducing this model because it can help you get a picture of the interrelationship between your beliefs, your skills and your patterns of behaviour. There are occasions when you unconsciously put your foot on the brake to change your behaviour, and the brake is often at the level of your own convictions and beliefs.

Mission/vision
Where do you stand and what are your goals? This level is also associated with spirituality and the philosophy of life: what animates you, what do you feel part of?

Identity
Who are you? How do you perceive yourself? What kind of negotiator do you want to be?

Values and beliefs
What do you believe in? What drives your actions? What do you think is important? What values are important to you and why? Your beliefs can inhibit or help you in letting you deploy your skills.

Capabilities
How will you tackle it? What are you capable of? What skills do you have available? Skills such as empathising, listening, summarising, dissociating (being able to take the third position), asking questions, finding things out, presenting, advising, intervening, completing tasks, etc. We've discussed plenty.

Behaviour
What can you let others see? Observable actions and reactions on your part. Metaprogrammes describe behaviour. Your behaviour has an impact on your surroundings. The question is whether or not your manifest behaviour is in your best interests.

Surroundings
The impact you have on the other party and on the surrounding environment.

Some examples to illustrate this:
- You may note that you actually do not have enough information about the other party to work out a suitable next step. You could ask more questions the next time. If you notice that you often seem not to have enough information, it's possible that there's a pattern: perhaps you regularly fail to ask enough questions. You could then resolve to ask more questions next time and that might help you. This means you are thinking at the skills level. Does this help you? After all, you do know what you have to do and you're capable of it – only it hasn't become a natural or permanent habit. You can also consider it at another level. Suppose you are not asking enough questions because you're afraid of looking stupid? You're in an advisory capacity and being paid for it too, so shouldn't you know everything already? Or are you letting yourself be pressured by a lack of time, so that you don't have any time for asking questions? Or do you already know what the answer will be? Maybe you aren't even interested in what the others have to say. What is stopping you from asking those questions? If you can work out where your bottlenecks are and you are aware of why you do things the way you do and can see that there are alternatives, you may well ask those questions next time after all. This is what I mean when I say that "a change at a higher level **will** trigger changes at a lower level". You start looking at the problem differently, ascribe a different meaning to it, start tackling it differently – and when you see that this approach works, you'll repeat it and keep doing it that way. You have created a breakthrough, all by yourself. That lets you

change your behaviour patterns quickly.

- A variation on the preceding theme: people often want to learn to listen better. Managers may tell their team members that too in their job performance reviews. People often regard listening as one of the key skills in negotiation. It's certainly essential, but is it a skill? Everyone can listen (unless they have a hearing impairment). So it's more a question of *why* they don't listen. Or to phrase it less directly, what's stopping you from listening? The principle that you first want to understand as much as possible about the other party before progressing any further may help you to listen. Then you'll ask questions and keep probing. The challenge is often not so much learning to listen as being prepared to shift the focus onto the other party.

- If you believe that the opinions of people who are higher up the hierarchical or social ladder than you outweigh yours and are worth more, then you might not dare to go against them and you may feel that you ought to give ground or make way. Perhaps you're too sensitive to authority. Conversely, if you believe that you should make a choice in a respectful way but based on correct information, you will feel free to work with

the other side and progress together further. That belief gives you the courage to act as an equal and it will be easier to find the right words: "I understand your viewpoint, but it's not what I've been told and I'd very much like to compare the details."

- If you are uncertain about whether you have a strong position in a negotiation, that may inhibit you. Do they actually need you? Do they have any alternatives? It can leave you feeling uncertain, making you more likely to hurry through various steps. It stops you from making contact, prevents you from having proper in-depth discussions, and so forth. Once you have considered each other's BATNAs, you may discover that you do indeed have a strong position and that the other party depends on you. This is how using Guide 6 can help you let go of a belief that is inhibiting your actions. It lets you do a reality check and stay at the table, relaxed.

- If you know that you're liable to run through the process quickly, proactively and rather idiosyncratically, you know that you may forget steps and not create enough of a bond, and that it may possibly fail to develop into a joint process. If you resolve to follow a proper

agenda and if you decide to stick to this fixed sequence, it will help you take the time for the various steps and it will force you to move forward with greater care. Guides 3, 4 and 5 then essentially become a guideline to help you deal with your own traps and pitfalls.

It can be interesting to take another close look at your own Inner Game, in terms of the beliefs level. Earlier, I referred to the behaviour and skills needed if you are to try to become a master. You can also take a moment to look at the beliefs you have about your own approach and the way in which you want to negotiate. Some of these beliefs can be inhibitors when you want to apply your skills. As far as I am concerned, you can also see the seven guides as beliefs that in fact help you to stay relaxed and on an equal footing at the negotiating table.

I have made a list of beliefs and paradigms that I often come across. This may let you think about yourself in a different way and show you how the guides can help you further.

Examples of beliefs and values that can be counter-productive and how the seven guides can help

WHAT MAY BE STOPPING YOU	HOW IT IS EXPRESSED	THE SEVEN GUIDES CAN HELP YOU REMAIN BOTH CONCENTRATED AND RELAXED
Who am I to be saying anything about that? If *he* says it, it's bound to be right. I'm oversensitive to authority and dominant behaviour.	Uncertainty, acting small, being self-effacing, giving way, evasion.	If I can separate the dynamics of the relationship from the content, I can sit at the table as an equal. We both have the right to be there. If they think they need games in order to exert pressure, bring it on! That's their right. Fighting back a bit does authoritarian figures a favour. I recognise the games and the emotions, I can see where they fit in and they don't bother me. I'll keep my eyes on the prize and focus on the facts and on my own interests. I won't allow power-plays or pressure to lead me by the nose: I'll work from the facts, and when it comes to the distribution issues, I have criteria of fairness that will put my proposal on a solid footing. My BATNA gives me freedom and confidence.
I shouldn't show emotions in a business environment. That's not what's expected of me.	Uncomfortable situations. Everyone can see something's wrong, but nobody mentions it. You feel all sorts of things intuitively, but you don't cover them in the conversation.	Emotions are part and parcel of it and I want them to have an effective role in my negotiations. I also make allowances for cultural differences and I want to treat the other party with respect. At the same time, I will be prepared to point out the undercurrents if they're blocking progress. I do realise that emotions are expressions of perceptions (and sometimes of unfulfilled expectations) and are sometimes used as pawns in the game. I do not have to talk explicitly about emotions when it's not appropriate, but I can then address the triggers for those emotions instead.
I am not sure whether or not I can intervene in this process. I can see that it's not going smoothly, but can I stick an oar in?	Progress is difficult and suboptimal. You've lost the connection with the other, but you're continuing. This can arise in one-on-one situations or in groups.	I want to manage the process and state what needs stating. If progress is being endangered, I will say something about that, respectfully. At the same time, I realise that I have to pick the right moment to do that. I will take cultural differences into account and keep thinking about the timing (tactics and strategy).
I can hear what they're saying, but I'm not sure that it's correct. If they say so, it must be right. Who am I to doubt it?	Incomplete, incorrect information that starts leading a life of its own.	I see verifiability as an attitude and, when asking for verification, I know how to make clear why it's important that I'm asking these questions. I realise that we could well be heading off up the garden path if we have incomplete or false information. Making things clear gives us the best chance of retaining confidence in each other.

WHAT MAY BE STOPPING YOU	HOW IT IS EXPRESSED	THE SEVEN GUIDES CAN HELP YOU REMAIN BOTH CONCENTRATED AND RELAXED
I'm not going to put my cards on the table, because they could misuse the fact. They've got to make the first move...	Closed attitude, feelings of vulnerability. Talking at cross purposes, yielding processes that are below par.	I am ready to state my interests, because that is the most likely way of ensuring that they become part of the solution. I do realise that there is a right time for exploring things, though, and we can put flesh on the bones and share things out later. The sequence of events gives me confidence that I'm going to be part of it, able to weigh up whether the deal is in my own best interests. This lets me be both open and resolute, lets me create space, lets me ask questions and be clear about what are no-go areas for me.
I've got to make this work, because I'm depending on this.	Tension, rigidity, the 'hostage at the table'.	I'm going to take it step by step, realising that I may get more if I don't go too fast. I'll have the best chance of getting somewhere if I pay attention to the person and the process. I realise that it's a game of give and take. And if they only want to take, I can always respond to that. But it's not a requirement. If I 'insist' on less, I may get more. And thinking about my BATNA always helps me create or perceive freedom to move.
I can see the solution in front of me already, and I feel responsible for getting there quickly.	Overlooking possibilities, heading too quickly for a solution that makes it highly likely we won't get the best possible deal.	I focus on the process. Above all, I feel responsible for the process instead of for the solution. And I'll go through all the steps. I believe that I'll then have the best chance of working towards an attractive solution. I'm aware that two heads are better than one and I'm happy to explore things before deciding. If I take a broader look at things, paying attention to the context and the playing field, I can also create solutions that contain the right elements (Q) and will get the right backing (A).
I've noticed that there are loose ends and the pressure is being cranked up. I can see the risks, but I don't want to be the one putting a spanner in the works.	Caution, evasive behaviour although you feel that your interests are losing out.	I am aware of my own personal pitfalls. I keep the criteria for the right deal clear in my mind's eye and evaluate the conditions against those criteria. That will keep me focused on the content, letting me weigh up my risks in terms of my own best interests, the options that are available and whether or not things have been divided fairly. And I won't let myself be put under pressure. Priority where it's due.

If the guides can really come alive for you, you may discover that they can be pillars of support when the going gets tough. These guides can act as principles that will help you feel on an equal footing and act as an equal when necessary. If you come up against obstacles in practical situations that are really blocking your progress, there are plenty of good coaches out there who can help you.

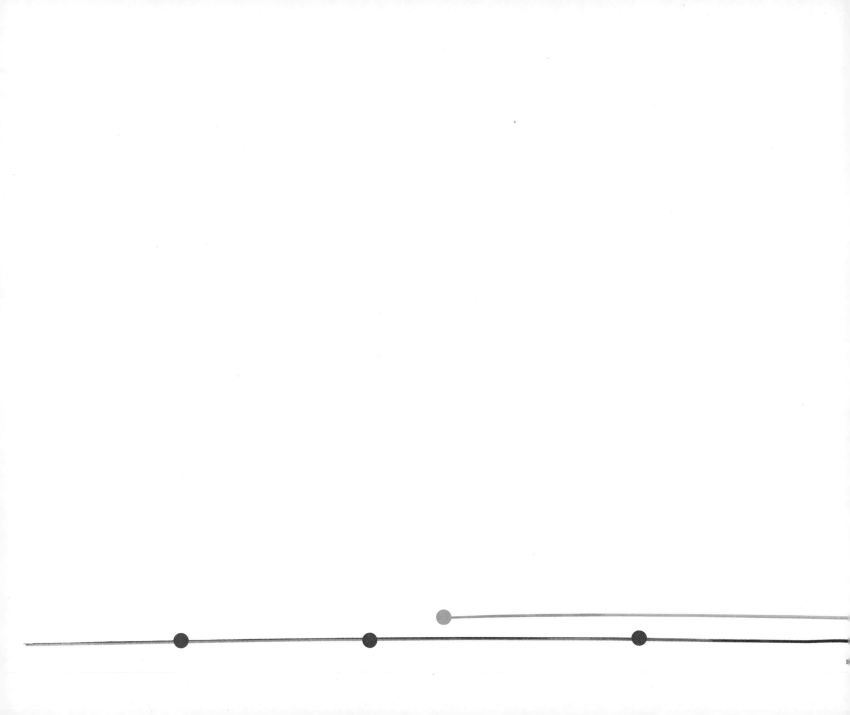

THE ROAD TO MASTERY NEVER ENDS

I hope that a few seeds have been sown, that I've shown you ways of tackling issues and provided some insights. I'm going to close with the final words that Bruce Springsteen spoke at his recent concert in The Hague, which Hugo, Jacob, Merel and myself — and thousands of others — had the pleasure of being at: "Stay hungry, stay foolish, stay alive."
Enjoy the ride...

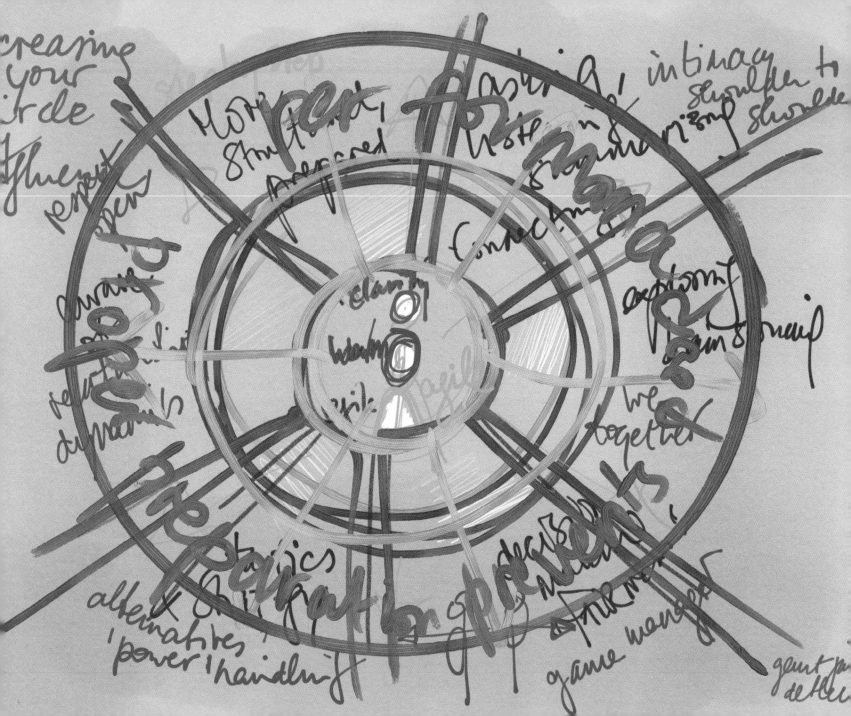

PREPARATION AND CHECKLIST

Preparing properly is half the job – and if the interests are significant and the complexity increases, proper preparation is indispensable. This isn't something that just happens. If you are a proactive and straightforward person, someone who sees the outlines clearly and can find possibilities for a solution even when the going gets tough, you'll be less likely to pause for a moment and think in a structured way about your approach. The trick is often to prepare in such a way that the subsequent process can no longer hold any surprises. That's why negotiation is sometimes compared to playing jazz. It seems as if improvisation takes little or no effort, but the musicians are able to improvise because they've practised the runs and riffs so often. Always in such-and-such a key, using the same chord progressions and variations until they're ingrained in the musicians' system. And if you then start improvising when you find you need to, the improvisation may well comprise linking together various previous exercises and experiments. When I was in New York in 2014, I heard Lou Donaldson play in the Blue Note Jazz Club, an iconic spot for jazz aficionados. Lou Donaldson, then aged eighty-eight, is a musician who has played with all the greats. After a superb solo, he turned to the audience while his fellow musicians were still playing and said, "This is the real music, folks! This ain't the Kenny G stuff, but music you have to practice for." I'm a fan of Kenny G too, and I think that Lou wasn't really doing him justice there, but nevertheless: this is music you have to practice for.

You often don't give yourself the time. You run from one meeting to the next, or respond overly hastily to an e-mail. And if you've prepared anything, it's often focused on what you want and what you're trying to achieve: where the financial boundaries are, rather than what you think is important. If you want to be able to hold a negotiation on relaxed and equal terms and keep things nicely balanced, then preparation (mental too) is crucial.

Pause a moment before setting out

Find a moment when you can plot out the journey you are about to make, in your head. Realise what your personal challenges are too. If you are aware of your own style, your qualities and your weaknesses, then you know what you have to be looking out for. You can include that in your preparation. When you're on the journey with other parties, consider:

- the past. Check the route that you took with the same parties before. What do you take with you to the negotiating table in terms of the substantive items that are expected and/or have been discussed, or in terms of the relationship experiences (are there old wounds or is it harmonious). And what did you think

of the process in the past – efficient and effective?

- the future. Where is the journey going? Where do you want to end up? And what do you need if you are to be satisfied when you get there? Will you then have a good deal? Can you then look back with pride at the outcome, the bond with the people and the process that you followed?

- taking a step back to the present. What does that mean for the structure of your discussions and the process that you want to follow?

Look at the situation from various positions and perspectives

Scan the entire situation – a 360° scan, as it were – from various positions in order to get a clear picture of the whole. You should scan not just the negotiating table, but also the surroundings. The seven guides are a baseline that you can work from, beginning at several different positions.

First position: from your role as a negotiator. How do you see the situation?

Second position: the other party. Put yourself in their shoes. How do they see you, when would they call it a good deal and

what's the prize they want to take home with them?

Third position: the role of an observer, looking at the whole. How will things proceed, what complexity are you going to encounter and what will you then do? How can you have a positive effect on the whole? Go through the script and look at various possible scenarios. You can make a film of your journey in your mind.

The internal negotiation

I often hear that internal negotiations are perceived as being more awkward than external ones. The lack of time, different perceptions, varying expectations, egos and jockeying for position also mean that people adopt different attitudes internally. Despite the fact that you may expect there to be a lot of shared interests, the action/reaction mechanism often seems to make things awkward here too. It is a negotiation in itself: include it in your overall approach.

Allocation of roles and internal agreement

Pay extra attention to achieving **internal agreement** if you are going into negotiations with various colleagues or team members. You often make agreements on substantive points while forgetting to check your perceptions, expectations and interests. How do you allocate the roles? Who is primarily keeping an eye on the content and who is monitoring the process? The latter person will therefore be defining the structure, watching the individual steps, summarising and intervening when necessary. Go through the case together: what will you do if things get more awkward, if differences of opinion come to light or if there is a deadlock? Don't forget that a time-out can be a useful tool.

The power of simulations

Putting yourself in the opposite party's shoes beforehand and thinking what they might do and say is a form of preparation. They may perhaps ask for too much, not want to pay or get things from you that you can't or won't give. Try a simulation, looking at it from the first, second and third positions. It is often extremely interesting to genuinely put yourself in the second position, that of the other party. How do they see you? How do they perceive the discussions? Do they feel they are being treated with respect? What are their interests?

Play the situation out and practice responses. Help each other and repeat the exercise. When there's something you're not looking forward to, it can help a lot if you've already been through it. Then you've already done the experimenting and you will feel more certain of your ground. Think of it as behavioural therapy. If you're dreading something, that is precisely why you should tackle it in a safe environment and keep repeating it until that feeling has gone. You can learn to negotiate and you can improvise, as long as you've practiced enough.

I have summarised most of the items that we discussed so far in a checklist. It's quite extensive; just take what you can use when you need it. When your negotiation is complex, you have to take more time for your preparation.

Checklist

GUIDES	TOPICS	CHECK AND/OR 'TO DO' BEFORE YOU'RE AT THE TABLE...	ACTIONS. CHECK AND/OR 'TO DO' AT THE TABLE AND AFTERWARDS
Themes/subjects	Are you going to negotiate? What are you negotiating about?	Is the business case tight and the context clear? Do you *want* to negotiate or do you *have* to? Check your BATNA. Perhaps you don't have to negotiate because you reckon your BATNA is so good that there's no point wasting time and effort on a new adventure. Is everyone internally toeing the same line? Are people buying into your approach and your mandate? Look for a challenge and stay open!	Check the scope of the negotiation.
Learning	What can you learn from the previous times?	Have you learned anything specific from the last time you negotiated (particularly with the same group)? What are you bringing to the table in this negotiation? Remember your own good qualities and weaknesses.	
	Invest in the relationship.	If there is tension: what can you do before the negotiation to clear the air and sort out any issues? Think about what, when and how. Your timing is important. So are the culture and customs. Make sure to avoid anyone losing face. If there is no tension in the relationship, think about what you can do to affect the relationship positively. You can put people at ease by creating a good atmosphere, receiving them openly and paying them attention. Can you start the Trust building already?	Pay attention to the relationship.Manage expectations and perceptions. Discuss problems in the relationship at the start, if that is culturally appropriate. Invest in the relationship. Build trust and show respect.

GUIDES	TOPICS	CHECK AND/OR 'TO DO' BEFORE YOU'RE AT THE TABLE...	ACTIONS. CHECK AND/OR 'TO DO' AT THE TABLE AND AFTERWARDS
	Parties or players at the table and the perceptions and expectations involved.	Who will you be negotiating with (the parties, actors, roles, positions and styles – see also the process). How do you perceive them and vice versa? Are there items that have to be tackled beforehand? How can you positively affect the perceptions? Be aware of managing the perceptions: is there information that could start leading a life of its own and create negative images in the outside world? What do they expect from us? This can apply to proposals or to the approach or the position. Can you surprise them in a positive sense? Keep an eye on the actors who aren't involved in the game.	Raise perceptions and expectations as an issue if they are hindering progress or if you aren't all seeing things the same way. Intervene, while taking account of cultural differences.
	Games?	What games might be played? You can prepare for them. See page 163.	Games may be played throughout the process. Stay alert.
	Personal state of mind.	How do you feel about it? Be honest with yourself. What are you not looking forward to? Where's the blockage? Pay attention – consciously – to your worries or emotions. Are they just minor wrinkles that are part and parcel of it all, or do they bother you? Go through the seven guides. Looking at the BATNAs may show you that you're less dependent than you thought. Look to see what and who can help you find the right place for your feelings. Talking about it is sure to lessen the burden and you may get a more realistic picture of the situation. Be prepared to ask for help!	Listen to your intuition. Sometimes you may notice insecurity, a lack of trust, incorrect information, double agendas and so forth. Can you do anything with those signals?

GUIDES	TOPICS	CHECK AND/OR 'TO DO' BEFORE YOU'RE AT THE TABLE...	ACTIONS. CHECK AND/OR 'TO DO' AT THE TABLE AND AFTERWARDS
2	Background/context in time.	Fit the themes into a large picture. Are there links with previous negotiations? Can you see a line from the past to the present, and what does it tell you?	Keep an eye on the verification of all the information that is exchanged and when agreements are made.
	Facts.	Do you have all the data and do you understand the facts? Is the information correct? What do you need before the negotiation starts and what more can you do? Do the parties have the same picture of the information? Do you have to go through the content or the facts before the discussion or negotiation starts, so that you can be sure that everyone is negotiating based on the same facts?	Note that you may sometimes have to negotiate first about the assumptions or information that is needed to make sure the negotiation goes well.
	Opinions. Opinions aren't facts.	What is the background to the opinions that were previously expressed and how would you interpret them? Are they factually based?	If you see that information is getting coloured or distorted, be ready for biases. Keep asking, and keep an eye on verification. Do a fact check/reality check.

GUIDES	TOPICS	CHECK AND/OR 'TO DO' BEFORE YOU'RE AT THE TABLE...	ACTIONS. CHECK AND/OR 'TO DO' AT THE TABLE AND AFTERWARDS
3 W	What interests are involved? Shared / party-specific / conflicting.	Make an inventory, think about your interests and those of the others. Consider their interests carefully. What might they find particularly important, which could therefore help them? Put yourself in their shoes (second position). Check publicly available sources such as the Internet, websites, dossiers, colleagues, etc. Keep an eye open for party-specific interests that are suitable for bundling together. What is negotiable for you and what isn't? Where are the boundaries and the no-go areas? Where is there room for manoeuvre and where not? Think about whether there are other stakeholders too, and therefore other interests playing a role in the process.	Ask about interests. Listen, summarise, keep probing and reordering. Go into the breadth and the depth. Put your cards on the table (without being naive). Look for commonality, the shared interests. There's often more connecting you than dividing you. Bundling party-specific interests together creates space for options.Win-win.
	What positions are being adopted?	Examine the positions that are being taken. What might this be an expression of? What interests do those positions conceal? What interests are so important to you that you are adopting a position? Think about how you want to put your position into words by stating the background (your interests). When might they relinquish their positions – what might they need for that and how could you achieve it?	Ask questions and keep probing to find the interests underlying those positions. Pacing and leading.
	See if you can bundle party-specific interests together to create a win-win.	What can we think up together so that you get X and we get Y? Think about it.	Creative question. Start looking for options. Action.

GUIDES	TOPICS	CHECK AND/OR 'TO DO' BEFORE YOU'RE AT THE TABLE...	ACTIONS. CHECK AND/OR 'TO DO' AT THE TABLE AND AFTERWARDS
4 □○△	What options can you see (possibilities, potential solutions)?	What possibilities can you see that will be in your own interests and those of the others? What are you able to give? Are there things you can do for them that would not require much from you but can mean a lot for them? And vice versa: what could you ask them to do that will benefit you a lot without being difficult for them? Are there things that can be swapped? Can you make the deal better for both?	Explore. Look for possibilities. Turn it into a specific step in the process. Don't head for a solution too quickly – examine the options together first. Make it a conscious phase of improvement. See how summaries can be used as pointers towards a better or more attractive solution. Test the options against the interests. Win-win? Take another look at the Disney Method.
5	Map out the consequences. The distribution issues.	Who gets what and who does what? How can you share out the 'conflicting interests' such as returns, risks, timelines, money, hours worked, capacity, human resources, etc.? Prepare yourself for the positions they are going to adopt and consider whether or not that will be reasonable. Prepare your business case thoroughly so that your position is strong. Go beyond a merely subjective approach. Keep an eye on the biases and thought patterns that are used for substantiating what is reasonable (subjectively). What are objective criteria for the distribution issue? Which criteria are favourable for you, and which for them?	Keep questioning about fairness and criteria. Be ready to point out unfairness. Know where your limit is. What could be asked in return? Keep a watch on the individual elements as well as the overall picture. Compare the conditions against your own interests and the options that are available. You do not *have* to accept a deal. Watch out for your own pitfalls and weaknesses here. Be firm, fair and flexible.

GUIDES	TOPICS	CHECK AND/OR 'TO DO' BEFORE YOU'RE AT THE TABLE...	ACTIONS. CHECK AND/OR 'TO DO' AT THE TABLE AND AFTERWARDS
6 DEAL? BATNA	What is your BATNA? What's theirs?	You may need to develop your own BATNA if you are starting from an unfavourable position. It's something that has to be weighed up, because developing a BATNA takes effort. What is their BATNA? They may be playing a game: "There are ten more like you." Or "We have all sorts of better offers." But is it true? Where's your limit, and how far do you think they can go? Plan B. Think why the direction you want to go in for a solution may be different from their possible BATNAs (doing it themselves, doing nothing, going to your competitor). See what makes you stand out and what that means for them. How strong is your business case or proposal?	The deal that you're going to make has to be better than your BATNA, or you must have strong arguments why the deal needs to be signed. Don't delude yourself. Be ready to discuss the other party's BATNA if necessary. Watch out for games.

GUIDES	TOPICS	CHECK AND/OR 'TO DO' BEFORE YOU'RE AT THE TABLE...	ACTIONS. CHECK AND/OR 'TO DO' AT THE TABLE AND AFTERWARDS
⑦ ◯	The general process.	Begin with the end in mind. What do you want to achieve? Considering that, do you need a meeting or a process for it? Look at the situation through a negotiator's eyes and run through the seven guides. Then you know what you need to do in terms of the process to make it a success. You know who can help you. Allow yourself to be challenged! Strategy and tactics are important: make sure the sequence is right if multiple parties and levels are involved. Who do you start with and why?	Take it one step at a time, each element at the appropriate moment. Everything comes together at the negotiating table.
	The actors who are at the table, the DMU and the decision-making process.	Keep an eye on the DMU. Who is involved in making the decisions, what does that process look like and what criteria will be used for making the decisions? Who decides and who has influence (in what specific roles)? To what extent are cultural customs and behaviour affecting it? Pay extra attention to whether the negotiators are acting on somebody's behalf or in their own right. When intermediaries or representatives are involved, there are always other unstated interests, of course! What do your findings mean for your strategy, tactics and process?	As part of the structure within your process, ask who plays a role in the decision-making, what role they have and how they are going to reach a decision (the steps they will be taking).

GUIDES	TOPICS	CHECK AND/OR 'TO DO' BEFORE YOU'RE AT THE TABLE...	ACTIONS. CHECK AND/OR 'TO DO' AT THE TABLE AND AFTERWARDS
7 ⭕	Actors who are not sitting at the table.	Are any parties missing who you would like to have around the the table or who you might want to speak to at some other time? Players behind the scenes who you'd like to have centre stage? Parties you'd like involved to make sure that the solution will have broad support? Take account of the wider context and the surroundings. Who can help check your findings? Do you have a coach? Look for challenges and test your hypotheses.	During a discussion, you should also ask which actors or parties should be included if the decisions are to be accepted. $E = Q \times A$ process.
	Structure.	Take a moment to consider the structure of the meeting and the process: the purpose, intentions, agendas, mandates and timelines. Ensure that people buy into these steps beforehand.	Keep checking during the discussions: purpose (check), intentions, agendas, mandates and timelines. Avoid having to tackle issues twice. Are you able to take a step towards the meeting's objectives or make a decision today?
	Influencing the process.	What can you do to get the process running smoothly? Think of the setting, the place, the room and apparently trivial details such as food and drink, breaks and moments for relaxation. Invest in the process – it's vitally important! Be ready for the games that will be played, any delays and potential deadlocks. Where could they turn up, whose problem would it be, and what are you then going to do?	

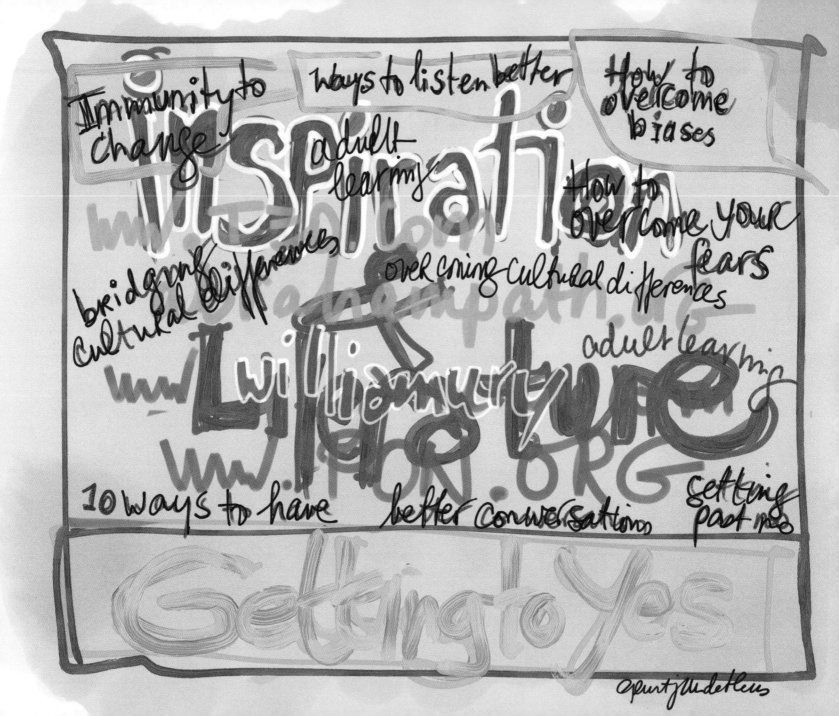

INSPIRATION AND LITERATURE

Over the years, I have drawn inspiration myself from a variety of sources, often from the areas of intersection and overlap between the literature on negotiation, articles about decision-making, communication, psychology, leadership and so forth. There are several points where I referred to specific sources in the book and I'd like to list them here. I'll supplement that with a few books and articles that could be interesting for you. And it should of course be clear that searches on the Internet will yield numerous blogs, articles, clips and websites where you can find lots of information about these various themes. Once you start on that, you'll often start jumping from one article to the next and you'll be able to find all sorts of material. There is an abundance of information and I hope that this will be a way of helping you find it.

Basic books about negotiation:
As I stated earlier, I see William Ury as the founding father who has greatly influenced my thinking. *Getting to Yes* is a compact book that sets out the foundations superbly. I can also strongly recommend other books by him.

- Fisher, Roger, William Ury and Bruce Patton. (1991). *Getting to Yes: Negotiating Agreement Without Giving In*. Penguin Books.
- Ury, William. (1993). *Getting Past No: Negotiating in Difficult Situations*. Bantam Books.
- Ury, William. (2015). *Getting to Yes with Yourself: And Other Worthy Opponents*. Harper One.

There are of course other authors you can also learn a lot from:
- De Dreu, Carsten K.W. (2014). *Bang voor conflict? De psychologie van conflicten in organisaties [Afraid of conflict? The psychology of conflicts in organisations]*. I used this for the DUTCH input. Koninklijke van Gorcum.
- Demarr, Beverly and Suzanne C. De Janasz. (2012). *Negotiation and Dispute Resolution*. Pearson.
- Falcao, Horacio. (2012). *Value Negotiation: How to Finally Get the Win-Win Right*. FT Press.

- Fisher, Roger and Daniel Shapiro. (2006). *Beyond Reason: Using Emotions as You Negotiate*. Penguin Books.
- Lax, David A. and James K. Sebenius. (2006). *3D Negotiation: Powerful Tools to Change the Game in Your Most Important Deals*. Harvard Business Review Press.
- Mnookin, Robert H, Scott R. Peppet and Andrew S. Tulumello. (2004). *Beyond Winning: Negotiating to Create Value in Deals and Disputes*. Belknap Press.
- Schranner, Matthias. (2011). *Costly Mistakes: the 7 Biggest Errors in Negotiations*. Evergreen Review, Inc.
- Susskind, Lawrence. (2004). *What Gets Lost in Translation*. Harvard Business Review Press.
- Susskind, Lawrence. (2014). *Good for You, Great for Me: Finding the Trading Zone and Winning at Win-Win Negotiation*. Public Affairs.
- Watkins, Michael. (2006). *Shaping the Game: The New Leader's Guide to Effective Negotiating*. Harvard Business Review Press.
- Wesselink, Marc and Ronald Paul. (2010). *Handboek Strategisch Omgevings-management [Guide to Strategic Management of your Environment]*. Vakmedianet.

- Wheeler, Michael. (2013). *The Art of Negotiation: How to Improvise Agreement in a Chaotic World*. Simon & Schuster.

About leadership, with links to negotiation, communication, trust and learning:
- Anderson, Robert J. and William A. Adams. (2015). *Mastering Leadership: An Integrated Framework for Breakthrough Performance and Extraordinary Business Results*. Wiley.
- Argyris, Chris. (1990). *Overcoming Organizational Defenses: Facilitating Organizational Learning*. Pearson.
- Argyris, Chris, Donald A. Schon. (1992). *Theory in Practice: Increasing Professional Effectiveness*. Jossey-Bass.
- Argyris, Chris. (2000). *Flawed Advice and the Management Trap: How Managers Can Know When They're Getting Good Advice and When They're Not*. Oxford University Press.
- Argyris, Chris. (2008). *Teaching Smart People How to Learn*. Harvard Business Review Press.
- Covey, Stephen R. (2005). *The 8th Habit: From Effectiveness to Greatness*. Free Press.
- Covey, Stephan R. (2012). *The 3rd*

Alternative: Solving Life's Most Difficult Problems. Free Press.

- Covey, Stephen R. (2013). *The 7 Habits of Highly Effective People: Powerful Lessons in Personal Change*. Simon & Schuster.
- Fox, Erica Ariel. (2013). *Winning from Within: A Breakthrough Method for Leading, Living, and Lasting Change*. HarperBusiness.
- Gallwey, W. Timothy. (2000). *The Inner Game of Work: Overcoming Mental Obstacles for Maximum Performance*. Orion Business.
- Gallwey, W. Timothy. (1981). *The Inner Game of Golf*. A.S. Barnes & Company.
- Kegan, Robert and Lisa Laskow Lahey. (2009). *Immunity to Change: How to Overcome It and Unlock the Potential in Yourself and Your Organization*. Harvard Business Review Press.
- Kohlrieser, George and Joe W. Forehand. (2006). *Hostage at the Table: How Leaders Can Overcome Conflict, Influence Others, and Raise Performance*. Jossey-Bass.
- Kohlrieser, George, Susan Goldsworthy and Duncan Coombe. (2012). *Care to Dare: Unleashing Astonishing Potential Through Secure Base Leadership*. Jossey-Bass.

- Kotter, John P. (2012). *Leading Change*. Harvard Business Review Press.
- Maister, David H., Galford, Robert, Green, Charles. (2002). *The Trusted Advisor*. Simon & Schuster.
- Senge, Peter M. (2006). *The Fifth Discipline: The Art & Practice of The Learning Organization*. Doubleday.
- Senge, Peter M., Bryan Smith, Nina Kruschwitz, Joe Laur and Sara Schley. (2010). *The Necessary Revolution: How Individuals and Organizations Are Working Together to Create a Sustainable World*. Crown Business.

About metaprogrammes and more:

I said that I had found it very useful to interpret behaviour using metaprogrammes. There are of course many other ways of categorising behaviour, but I find that many of the methods soon start to stigmatise. They quickly become stereotypical caricatures, descriptions that try to give a simplified representation of behaviour. It means that you are 'assigned a colour' quickly, or people say they are 'dominant' – whereas I place greater store by being able to see what people are doing than by thinking that's just the way they are. I've noticed that if you can take a more nuanced view of behaviour and are capable of recognising

behaviour patterns and seeing how they fit into the negotiation process, you will find it easier to learn how to communicate and how to serve your interests better. Have a look on the site www.mindsonar.info, where Jaap Hollander of the IEP has developed a nice tool.

- Charvet, Shelle Rose. (1997). *The Words That Change Minds*. Kendall/Hunt Publishing Co.
- Dilts, Robert. (1999). *Sleight of Mouth. The Magic of Conversational Belief Change*. Meta Publications.
- Hustinx, Guus, Anneke Durlinger-Van der Horst. (2006). *Voorbij je eigen wijze: effectief communiceren met meta-programma's in professionele relaties [Beyond your own approach: Effective communication using metaprogrammes in professional relationships]*. Uitgeverij Boom/Nelissen.

About biases and decision-making:

- Ariely, Dan. (2008). *Predictably Irrational: The Hidden forces That Shape Our Decision*. HarperCollins.
- Argyris, Chris. (1966). *Interpersonal Barriers to Decision Making*. Harvard Business Review Press.
- Dobelli, Rolf. (2013). *The Art of Thinking*

Clearly. Harper Paperbacks.
- Finkelstein, Sydney, Jo Whitehead and Andrew Campbell. (2009). *Think Again: Why Good Leaders Make Bad Decisions and How to Keep It from Happening.* Harvard Business Review Press.
- Hammond, John S., Ralph L. Keeney and Howard Raiffa. (1999). *Smart Choices: A Practical Guide to Making Better Decisions*. Harvard Business School Press.
- Kahneman, Daniel. (2011). *Thinking, Fast and Slow*. Farrar, Straus and Giroux.
- Thaler, Richard H. and Cass R. Sunstein. 2009. *Nudge: Improving Decisions About Health, Wealth, and Happiness.* Penguin Books.
- Watts, Duncan J. (2012). *Everything is Obvious: How Common Sense Fails Us.* Crown Business.

About cultures
- Hampden-Turner, Charles and Fons Trompenaars. (1997). *Riding The Waves of Culture: Understanding Diversity in Global Business*. McGraw-Hill.
- Meyer, Erin. (2014). *The Culture Map: Breaking Through the Invisible Boundaries of Global Business.* PublicAffairs. Have a look on www.erinmeyer.com too.
- Molinsky, Andy. (2013). *Global Dexterity: How to Adapt Your Behaviour Across Cultures without Losing Yourself in the Process*. Harvard Business Review Press.
- Salacuse, Jeswald J. (2003). *The Global Negotiator: Making, Managing, and Mending Deals Around the World in the Twenty-First Century*. St. Martin's Press.

Articles
A large amount of literature is available about the subjects covered. I'd like to draw your attention to the *Harvard Business Review*. If you would like a source that always provides inspiration, is easily accessible and rapidly lets you access a broad spectrum of inspirational sources, look at the journal and the website www.hbr.org

The sources I used for the chapters on biases and culture included the following:

- Hammond John S., Ralph L. Keeney and Howard Raiffa. (2006). *The Hidden Traps in Decision Making.* Harvard Business Review Press.
- De Dreu, Beersma, Steinel, van Kleef. *The Psychology of Negotiation*, chapter 26. *Handbook of Basic Principles of Social Psychology.*
- Carsten de Dreu (2014). *Negotiating Deals and Settling Conflict can Create Value of Both Sides. The Behavioral and Brain Sciences.*
- Meyer, Erin. (2015). *Getting to Si, Ja, Oui, Hai and Da. How to Negotiate Across Cultures*. Harvard Business Review Press.
- Morris, Michael W. (2005). *When Culture Counts—and When It Doesn't*. Harvard Business Review Press.
- Quarterly, McKinsey. (2010). *The Case for Behavioral Strategy.*

Websites
I enjoy going to www.pon.org and it's a website I can heartily recommend. The *Program On Negotiation* (PON) is in my opinion a fantastic source for articles, blogs, interviews, training courses, book suggestions and more about negotiation in the broadest sense of the term.
On www.williamury.com, there are many interesting clips by William about various negotiation challenges.
If you are interested in learning more about negotiation in the broadest sense of the term, there's no limit to what you can find. Examples of websites where you will find interesting topics include www.ted.com, www.youtube.com, www.forbes.com, www.inc.com, www.fastcompany.com,

www.nytimes.com, www.hbr.org,
www.sfcg.org and www.abrahampath.org
etc.

All feedback is welcome by e-mail to
deheus@routslaeven.nl, through the
website www.allesisonderhandelen.nl or
via www.routslaeven.nl

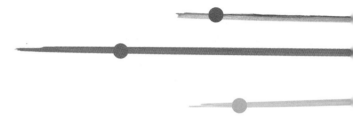

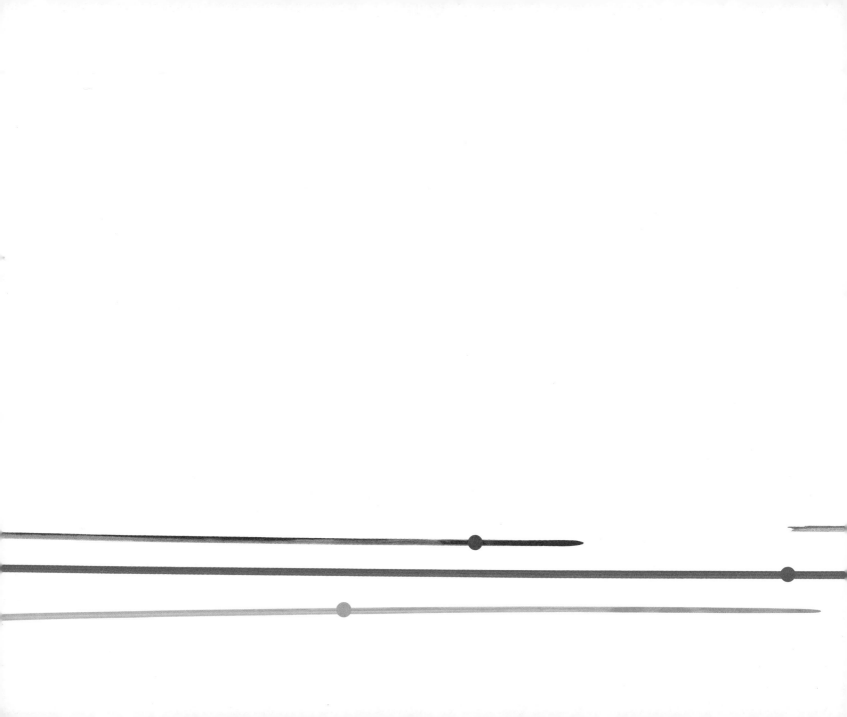

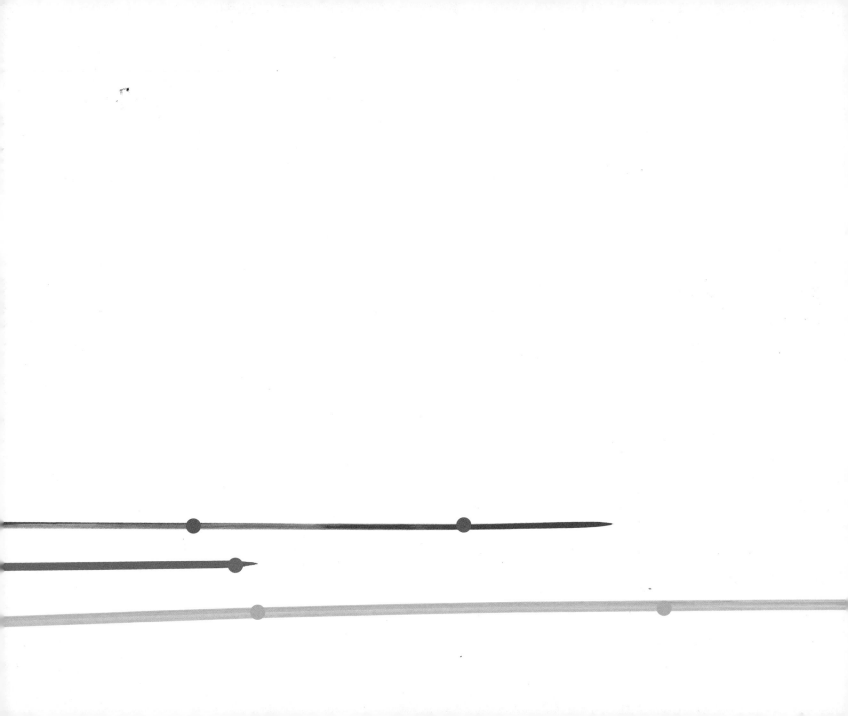